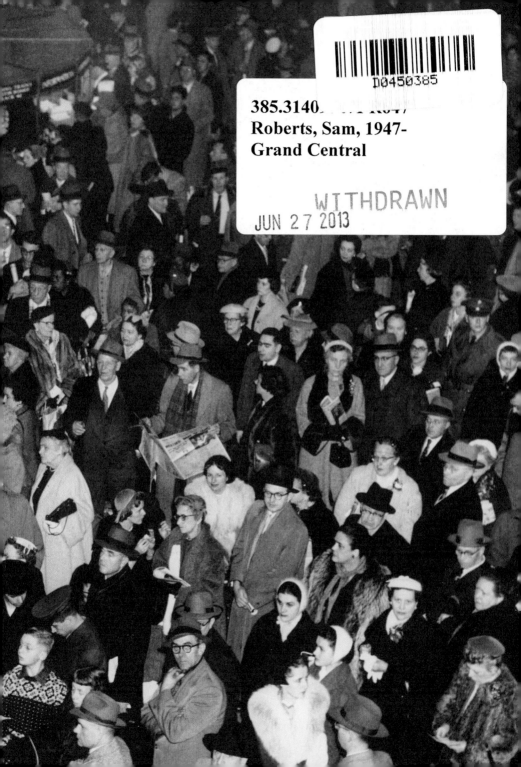

GRAND CENTRAL

GRAND
CENTRAL

HOW A TRAIN STATION
TRANSFORMED AMERICA

SAM ROBERTS

FOREWORD BY
PETE HAMILL

GRAND CENTRAL
PUBLISHING

NEW YORK • BOSTON

Grand Central Publishing
Hachette Book Group
237 Park Avenue
New York, NY 10017
www.HachetteBookGroup.com

Printed in the United States of America
Designed by BTDNYC

Wor

First Edition: January 2013
10 9 8 7 6 5 4 3 2 1

Grand Central Publishing is a division of Hachette Book Group, Inc.
The Grand Central Publishing name and logo is a trademark of
Hachette Book Group, Inc.

The Hachette Speakers Bureau provides a wide range of authors for speaking events.
To find out more, go to www.hachettespeakersbureau.com or call (866) 376-6591.

The publisher is not responsible for websites (or their content) that are not
owned by the publisher.

ISBN: 978-1-4555-2596-6

Library of Congress Control Number: 2012950875

FOR MARIE

CONTENTS

FOREWORD

PETE HAMILL

A WEEK BEFORE CHRISTMAS IN 1945, my mother took me and my brother Tom on a trip from Brooklyn to the place that she once described as Oz: Manhattan. I was ten, my brother two years younger. The war was over, and so was the Depression (although we knew almost nothing about what that word meant). We were going to see Santa Claus. At the place where our father's favorite newspaper, the *Daily News*, was made.

That meant we had to change subways at least twice, crossing platforms, hurrying upstairs and down, and making our way to the Lexington Avenue line, which would take us to 42nd Street. Our final train was packed, the cars hurtling through the tunnels with a kind of squealing ferocity. And then we joined the crowd emptying the car, heading up still more stairs, and out through a last door.

"Wait," my mother said. "I want to show you something."

And she led us into the largest indoor space I had ever seen. There were people moving across shiny marble floors in many directions

THE PERPETUAL URBAN BALLET WITH THE
INFORMATION BOOTH AS ITS CENTERPIECE—
AN ESTHER WILLIAMS—LIKE VIEW. ❖ IX ❖

and a gigantic clock with four sides, and a large board with numbers and the names of cities. A deep voice kept speaking from somewhere, talking about times and tracks, the voice echoing off the gleaming walls. We were in a place called Grand Central Station.

There were soldiers there, too, in heavy military coats, and a few sailors in pea jackets. Late arrivals from the war. They all carried duffle bags, but were not in any military formation. They came upstairs from somewhere, some of them wide-eyed and astonished, and they pushed out into the crowd of the immense building. Looking, turning, squinting. And the immense murmur of the crowd was cut open by screams. Screams of joy. Screams of delight. A woman, always a woman, came bursting forward, almost leaping, some with kids tagging behind them, kids younger than Tommy and I were then. The soldier and the woman, the sailor and the woman, embraced each other. Sobbing. And we saw an older man off on the side, suddenly erect, saluting. And then another. And another. And then a young soldier on crutches was there, hauling his bag behind him. And there was nobody to meet him. He just stood there. Staring around him. Looking lost. The trouser of one leg folded and pinned above his knee.

My mother went to him, to ask him if he needed help. And the three of us led the one-legged soldier to the counter beneath the four-sided clock. A woman behind that counter listened, nodded, pulled a microphone close, and began speaking into it. We could hear the message: "Could the party meeting Corporal Jennings please come to the clock in the center of the terminal?" Years later, I still remembered the name. Jennings. And how, when my mother turned away from him, I saw tears in her eyes.

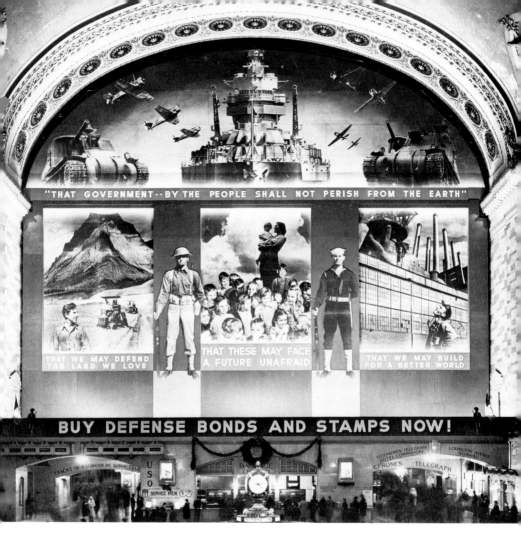

A MONTAGE OF 22 PHOTOGRAPHS 118 FEET WIDE WAS UNVEILED IN DECEMBER 1941 ON THE EAST WALL.

We went on to the old *Daily News* building, with the gigantic globe in the lobby, and there, beyond many hundreds of kids and parents, was Santa Claus on a kind of throne. I don't know anymore what toy he handed to me or my brother. I remember vaguely the

Christmas music playing in that amazing lobby, and I remember that we ate in a glorious automat, full of the sound of nickels rolling into small trays, and the aromas of fresh bread and coffee. But when we returned to Brooklyn, what I remembered most of all was that gigantic, almost golden room, the clock, the constant movement of strangers, and the men home from the war. In particular, the soldier on crutches, because he had only one leg. Just like my father, who had lost his own left leg after a soccer game in 1927, three years after he arrived from Ireland.

In all the years that followed, Grand Central, not Times Square, was for me the center of Midtown Manhattan. It still is. A place full of arrivals and departures, of sad farewells and new beginnings. A place charged with time, in the constant presence of clocks and changing schedules and looming appointments. Three decades after I first

saw it, I was working for the *Daily News*, climbing subway stairs, with the energizing urgency of passing time driven by the imminence of deadlines. But it was also a place of rewards too, when the deadlines were met: the magazine shops, the Oyster Bar, the places full of bread and croissants to carry home.

In this wonderful book, Sam Roberts, another alumnus of the *Daily News*, tells me many things that I did not know until now about the layers of time in Grand Central. Here are the visionaries who imagined it, the pragmatists who made the visions real, the great craftsmen and workers who transformed it into such a huge, majestic, and glorious fact. Not simply a New York fact. A real, surviving part of the country itself. In novels, poems, and movies, it is woven into the American imagination. Sam Roberts reminds us that in Grand

Central the palimpsests have palimpsests. Unveil one buried layer of the story and there is another layer underneath.

He also reminds us of the bad times in Grand Central's century-long narrative. The rise of domestic airlines, with rapid service on jets to cities once reached by rail, was an obvious part of the change in Grand Central. But there were also larger factors involved in what seemed to be a tale of steady, irreversible decay. By the 1960s, the economy of New York was changing too. Factories were closing. The commerce of the port was ebbing away. By the late 1970s, the garment district was shrinking. As the old manufacturing jobs vanished, welfare cases escalated, along with homelessness and heroin addiction. You could see panhandlers in Grand Central, and a general grunginess spreading, along with a certain level of fear. Or generalized anxiety. Too often a passenger on a train could not find room on a bench in the waiting room. The homeless seemed there to stay.

And yet, Grand Central would survive, and flourish anew. The story of its salvation is told in the pages of this book. It was driven by people who wanted to save it from the fate of Penn Station, which had been demolished. They had nothing to gain for themselves. They just wanted this enormous, once-beautiful piece of our lives to continue. One of the most important leaders of this movement was, of course, Jacqueline Kennedy Onassis, who used her prestige and eloquence to get the message to a wide audience. Once again, a combination of visionaries and pragmatists made something glorious. Plans were drawn, and then revised; budgets were cobbled together, and then revised too; work started. But like most good things, it took awhile.

One Friday morning in the mid-1980s, before the last of the work was done, a fierce snowstorm hit the city. My wife was upstate with our car, in our hideout in Ulster County, so when I finished work I headed to Grand Central for the train. I just missed one, but, having no choice, I bought a ticket for the next one.

I wandered around the great main room of the station, looking for a bench where I could sip coffee and read a newspaper. There were no benches. They had all been removed to discourage their use as cots for the homeless. So I bought my coffee and went up the stairs at Vanderbilt Avenue, to watch the falling snow.

I was dressed for the weather, in a ratty ski jacket, equally ratty jeans, and boots and baseball cap. I had finished half the coffee when a woman came through the door from Grand Central, walked toward me at an angle, dropped a quarter into my coffee, and kept moving.

I laughed out loud.

She paused. "Oh," she said, "I'm *so* sorry."

"Forget it," I said. "It was very kind of you."

I poured the coffee out at the curb, retrieved the quarter, went back downstairs to the station, and gave the coin to a homeless guy.

Every time I go to Grand Central now, I think of that moment. And of the day, long before, when my mother led that baffled one-legged veteran to the information counter. Millions of people surely have other memories that are triggered simply by the mention of the name. If they read this book, they will think of many things they did not witness, or know. As I do now. Many of them are as grand as the place itself.

GRAND CENTRAL

PROLOGUE:
THE ACCIDENTAL
TERMINAL

O N WEDNESDAY MORNING, JANUARY 8, 1902—
111 years ago—Train 118, the local from White Plains, was
late. It was due at Grand Central Station at 8:15 a.m., but,
already behind schedule, it was delayed at 110th Street for nearly five
minutes to let another southbound local, this one from Croton, pass
ahead of it. Incoming delays to Grand Central were nothing new.
After all, since the Park Avenue Tunnel was built in 1875, three railroad companies had shared the four-track main line down Manhattan's spine. By 1902, the three railroads carried 44,000 passengers
every weekday, or 16 million a year, on a total of 177,450 trains—one
every 45 seconds during rush hours.

SINCE 1991, THE TERMINAL'S SOUTH AND WEST
FAÇADES HAVE BEEN BATHED IN 136,000 WATTS
OF FLOODLIGHT AT NIGHT.

At the throttle of Train 118 was 36-year-old John M. Wisker. Even on the best of days, Wisker, the mustachioed son of German immigrants, was not a patient man. Although he had worked for the railroad for seven years, he'd spent most of that time as a locomotive fireman and had been promoted only the previous August to engineer, and even then he mostly filled in for full-timers. As an engineer, he usually piloted milk trains, early in the morning before the road became more congested. That week, he had no intention of piling up a record for tardiness, especially on what amounted to a tryout on a prestigious commuter route. Leaving the apartment he shared with his wife in the Bronx, he would ordinarily get to work while it was still dark, though this week, because he was on call, he slept on a bare wooden bench in the roundhouse in White Plains. That, he explained later, made him even more nervous than usual, coupled with the fact that the locomotive he was driving had a record of faulty air brakes.

On Sunday night, January 5, the regular engineer of Train 118 had called in sick. Wisker was recruited to replace him. On Monday, Wisker piloted a passenger train through the Park Avenue Tunnel for the first time. On Tuesday, Train 118 arrived at Grand Central promptly at 8:15. But on Wednesday, the train was already a minute and a half late when it left White Plains. Wisker was worried about making up lost time in between the seven stations on the 19-minute run. The unlit tunnel reeked of coal gas. It was not only smoky but also foggy that morning. "Unusually murky," was how one flagman described it. Outside, it was snowing. "It was just the kind of weather that would make smoke or vapor hang in the air a long time without being shattered," Thomas F. Freel, an acting battalion chief of the city's fire department, later recalled.

A crew member would testify that No. 118 was proceeding at a robust 20 mph, but a railroad official who was on the train later estimated that it was speeding through the tunnel at up to 35 mph. By this point, the train was five minutes late. Whether Wisker saw the green cautionary light (this was before green meant go), a flare, red lanterns, and other warning signals and simply ignored them was never definitively determined by railroad officials or by a grand jury. He insisted that he did not, nor did he hear the fireman's cry of "Green," although according to one version Wisker applied a brake at the last moment. When he saw the red light at 58th Street, where the mouth of the tunnel yawned into a vast open-air train yard two cross-town blocks wide and below street level, it was too late. One news reporter interviewed Wisker before his arrest and wrote, "The only explanation he can give is that he was trying to make up lost time." Wisker, a news report concluded, "was sober, but he was both ambitious and impatient of delay."

What is known for sure is that at exactly 8:20, without warning and despite the heroic efforts of a brakeman, Train 118 slammed into the rear car of a Danbury commuter train parked on the same track. The Danbury express was awaiting a signal that yard work had been completed so it could proceed to Grand Central, where it had been due at 8:17. Fifteen passengers, among the 60 who boarded in the last car at the New Rochelle station, were killed instantly. Most were crushed to death by the telescoping engine or scalded in a horrific mass of twisted wreckage, mangled limbs, and sputtering steam that remains Manhattan's worst railroad accident.

The last bodies were not removed for more than 10 hours. "The hissing steam and smoke made it seem that I was going to be cooked alive," said Richard H. Mollineux, 23, who fractured his right thigh and was among the 36 passengers injured. Two of these died within a week. Among the dead were Amanda F. Howard, who had been married only six months and worked at Standard Oil; Theodore Fajardo, a Spanish-born buyer for a Cuban importing firm, who left a widow and four young children; and Oscar Meyrowitz, general manager of E.B. Meyrowitz Opticians, established by his brother, Emil. "As slowly the harvest of death reaped in the hole under the New York streets is being garnered in the homes of New Rochelle," the *New York Times* reported, "the townsmen of the dead and the maimed are beginning to ask each other not how this thing occurred, but why."

J.H. Franklin, the manager of Grand Central, singled out John Wisker for blame. But the Reverend J.E. Lovejoy of the Mott Avenue

IMAGINE NAVIGATING THE PARK AVENUE TUNNEL WHEN IT WAS CHOKED WITH SMOKE AND SOOT FROM STEAM LOCOMOTIVES.

Methodist Episcopal Church, in his sermon the following Sunday, defended Wisker, his devout parishioner, and pointed fingers elsewhere. "It is easy to convict a poor man of almost any crime, but it is almost impossible to prosecute the rich man, who with haughty insolence jingles his dollars in his pockets and pulls powerful influences his way." A coroner's inquest lodged no formal charges, but a special state commission delivered a stinging rebuke to the railroad for gross negligence "in putting an engineer of such limited experience and unascertained capacity" at the controls of a passenger train at rush hour. No railroad officials were charged, however. Wisker was indicted for second-degree manslaughter because he "unmistakably violated the well-known rule which, under the conditions surrounding him, required him to stop his train."

THE CRASH OCCURRED AT 56TH STREET, not far from the Vanderbilt mansion on Fifth Avenue. Cornelius Vanderbilt III and Alfred Vanderbilt, great-grandsons of the Commodore, rushed to the scene in time to learn that Wisker had been arrested by the New York City police pending a coroner's inquest. Almost on the spot, they joined other railroad officials, including William J. Wilgus, the New York Central's chief engineer, in a decision that would change the face of New York. Given the state railway commission's subsequent findings, the grand jury's decision not to prosecute the railroad's chief executives this time was simply too close for comfort. "It was not enough that the New York Central Railroad had been maintaining for many years a defective signal system and that any day a serious accident might happen as a result of the maintenance of such a system," said William Travers Jerome, the district attorney (he was a nephew of Leonard

Jerome, who had been Cornelius Vanderbilt's stockbroker), "but it must have been found affirmatively, and beyond reasonable doubt, that this particular accident, with the ensuing deaths, occurred as the direct result of its defective system." The next time, a grand jury might do just that.

Even with the recent renovations, Grand Central Station, which was already outmoded the day it opened a generation earlier, would have to be razed. The rails would have to be electrified. The goat pastures and shanties that still dotted mid-Manhattan would be replaced by a colossal Grand Central Terminal. It would be a majestic gateway to the nation's greatest city, the catalyst for a new Midtown flanking a breathtakingly luxuriant boulevard, and a prototype for innovative transportation and urban planning imperatives across the country.

In short, the new Grand Central Terminal was built, in a way, by accident.

TERMINAL CONNOTES AN ENDING. For a century, Grand Central has been anything but. This book is Grand Central's biography. Nobody who has been there, no one who has witnessed the intricate choreography on the Main Concourse or eavesdropped on the crowd's collective voice, could doubt that a building, a supposedly quiescent pile of marble and stone, could embody a living organism. The terminal is the throbbing heart of a city. "As the earth cooled," Colson Whitehead wrote in *The Colossus of New York*, "Grand Central bubbled up through miles of magma, lodged in the crust of this island, settled here. The first immigrant. Still unassimilated. Ever indigestible. The river of skyscrapers flows around it. Travelers swim to it and cling, savoring solid handhold in roaring whitewater. Churches full up at regular intervals on a schedule laid out in the business plan. Like the best storms, rush hour starts out as a slight drizzle, then becomes unholy deluge."

The story of Grand Central mirrors the story of urban America.

It is a story that reveals the secrets of hidden staircases, mysterious underground vaults, a publicity-shy owner, and a secluded platform reserved for the president of the United States. It is a story about people, from Bryan Henry, a Metro-North cop who befriended the homeless, to Audrey Johnson, who fields customers' questions in the information booth, to Jacqueline Onassis, whose devotion to historic preservation saved the terminal from certain destruction.

Grand Central has been the wellspring of new beginnings for millions of people who arrived in New York to fulfill their dreams, heeded the siren call to go west, and returned lovesick to their hometowns. Unlike a station, a terminal conjures up a destination, not merely a place to pass through. Grand Central embodied that role, as the gateway to New York since 1913 and as the city's Gateway to a Continent. Between 1913 and the centennial of the New York Central in 1926, the number of passengers served annually by the terminal nearly doubled, to 43 million from 23 million. Today, the number is verging on a record, headed, for the first time, toward the 100 million passengers a year forecast when the terminal first opened a century ago.

ITS ROLE IN THE PEOPLING OF AMERICA would be reason enough to celebrate Grand Central's centennial and to mine its cavernous halls and subterranean lairs for historical lore. But there's more. The terminal has been the site of ransom demands and mail train robberies, of triumphal homecomings and hope-filled send-offs, the target of Nazi saboteurs and terrorist bombs. Its passengers have included presidents, living and dead, and foreign potentates. People have been born and have married and died there. Funeral corteges have carried statesmen and war heroes home from and to there. Kids left for summer camp and soldiers went to war. A steer once escaped from an East Side slaughterhouse and infiltrated the train yards. Four elephants, weighing 22 tons combined, wended their way through the waiting room in 1921 to board their sleeping car on Track 37 for the trip to Boston, where they were due for a matinee performance the next day.

The terminal houses six secret staircases. One goes to a top floor that officially doesn't exist but played a pivotal role on 9/11. Another leads to a secret subbasement, which was excised from the building's floor plans and would be constructed to convert AC to DC power and where one red button can shut down the railroad. A third accesses a secret train platform still protected by armed guards.

Time as we now know it originated in Grand Central. The 13-foot-diameter clock facing 42nd Street is described as the world's largest example of Tiffany glass, and the limestone sculptures of Minerva, Hercules, and Mercury were considered the largest sculptural grouping in the world. The Grand Central building would house CBS television studios where Edward R. Murrow would broadcast and *What's My Line* and *The Goldbergs* would originate. The Park Lane, an apartment hotel, would become home to Rudolph Valentino and Frederick T. Ley, who built the Chrysler Building. The 20th Century Limited and the Wolverine were among the storied trains that arrived and departed from the busiest train station in the coun-

THE PARK AVENUE VIADUCT, LOOKING NORTH TOWARD THE 60-FOOT-HIGH
ARCHED WINDOWS THAT FORMED WHITNEY WARREN'S TRIUMPHAL GATES.

try to and from points west. In 1947, 65 million passengers traveled
the rails from Grand Central. In 2011, Metro-North became the nation's busiest commuter railroad. Its annual ridership surpassed 82
million. And Grand Central is the world's largest rail terminal, with
43 platforms fed by 43 tracks, plus another 48 underground storage
tracks. It is about to grow even bigger with a Long Island Rail Road
connection and separate station.

    The terminal has threaded itself into popular culture. *Mad Men*'s
Roger Sterling gorged himself on oysters and martinis there. Cary
Grant called his mother from a phone booth before fleeing town on

the 20th Century Limited in *North by Northwest*. An art student finds a cache of diamonds there in James Patterson and Marshall Karp's *Kill Me If You Can*. Philippe Petit performed his tightrope walk under the terminal's celestial ceiling. *Holiday* magazine recalled the exploits of a newly married couple whose train to Niagara Falls was canceled; they honeymooned at Grand Central instead: "They got a room at the Biltmore Hotel, linked to the terminal by an underground corridor, dined, danced, took advantage of the terminal's shops and exhibition halls—and did all this without ever once seeing a train. Later, terminal officials heard the couple were planning to repeat the idea as an anniversary celebration."

"JUST WALKING THROUGH the vast main concourse of Grand Central Terminal—something that over half a million people do every working day—almost always triggers in me a spontaneous and quiet change in perception," Tony Hiss wrote in *The Experience of Place*. "I feel relaxed and alert at the same time." Some are mesmerized by the sound of hundreds of people simultaneously walking and talking in 11 million cubic feet of air. "This sound, pleasant in all its parts, regular in all its rhythms and humorous and good-natured, seemed also to have buttoned me into some small, silent bubble of space," Hiss wrote. "I felt that I wasn't quite walking but was paddling—or somehow propelling—this bubble across the floor."

Other people dream about Grand Central. Ami Ronnberg of the C.G. Jung Center in Manhattan was quoted as saying she had done so herself, and called the terminal a powerful symbol. "Just think of the name," she said. "It's the central place, where all things connect. It's underground, it's below what we know about and it's what we know about." Grand Central itself became the nexus of *Mad Men*'s second season promotional campaign because, Linda Schupack, the marketing chief at AMC, explained: "It works on multiple levels. It is, of course, so iconic to New York, but it's also a place of transition." Constantin Brancusi, the modernist sculptor, pronounced the terminal "one of the most beautiful specimens of modern architecture"—specimens so beautiful, he said, that they "give me as much pleasure as if I had done them myself." Henry-Russell Hitchcock, the architectural historian, dubbed it "one of the grandest spaces the early 20th century ever enclosed." Grand Central's survival spawned a preservation movement that spared other historic places all over America. The architecture critic Paul Goldberger proclaimed it "the poster building for every landmark in the United States."

EVERY INDIVIDUAL EXPERIENCES GRAND CENTRAL in a different way. Ben Cheever's Proustian memory is of his chaffed thighs, but he also marveled how even a small boy was not overwhelmed by the vast Main Concourse. "The counters are at the exact right height to lean or write on, the balustrades are for sitting, the dimensions of the marble slabs match those of the human body," Cheever wrote. "The building, like the body, is wonderful in its symmetry." Cheever, whose father was exalted as the "Chekhov of the Suburbs," called the terminal as inviting as "a rich person's house with the doors thrown wide. The concourse is larger than the nave of Notre Dame Cathedral and yet is strangely inviting; awesome, but in no way awful," he wrote. "Even as a child, on my dismal way to Brooks Brothers to be fitted for a flannel suit that would chafe the skin off my thighs, I did not feel diminished."

THE GLORIOUSLY REFURBISHED MAIN CONCOURSE STRIPPED BY THE MTA
OF CRASS COMMERCIALISM AND GAUDY SIGNAGE.

"The concourse is not just any room; it's my room," he wrote. "This half-acre of Tennessee marble is the stage on which I have many times appeared. 'Stand up straight. Take that paw out of your mouth' my father used to say, dragging my tiny, be-suited person across the echoing expanse. 'Admire the stars in the ceiling.' So I craned my little neck."

My own best memory is also of a visit to Grand Central with my father in the 1950s. I was standing with him on a platform, staring wide-eyed at a giant locomotive, when the engineer invited me into the cab. I even remember the locomotive's number: New York Central 371. As I remember it, he placed my hand on the throttle and the engine chugged forward a few feet. To me, it seemed like a mile.

• • •

OKAY, BE A STICKLER: Grand Central is not a station; it's a terminal. Trains *terminate* there. Railroad people like to recall the apocryphal rube who asked a conductor whether his New York Central train stopped at New York City. To which the conductor replied, "There'd be an awful crash if it didn't." The point is, David Marshall wrote in *Grand Central* in 1946, you couldn't tell that story about Pennsylvania Station, which, for all its splendor, one wag lamented, reduced New York "to a two-minute stop on the line from Long Island City to Rahway, New Jersey."

Two Grand Central *Stations* do exist in New York City—the post office on Lexington Avenue and the Interborough Rapid Transit subway stop that serves the Nos. 4, 5, 6, and 7 and the Times Square shuttle. There once was a railroad depot called Grand Central Station on 42nd Street in Manhattan, but it was razed a century ago to make room for this one. The dictionary says a terminal can be a station, but not every station is a terminal. "To 80 or 90 percent of the people of New York it's Grand Central Station," David Marshall wrote. "And so I have called it in this book—on the principle of Securus Judicat orbis terrarum" (or, as Augustine of Hippo would have said had he spoken English, "the verdict of the world is conclusive").

NEARLY 3 MILLION CUBIC YARDS of earth and rock would be excavated for the tracks, and construction would take 10 years and cost more than $2 billion in today's dollars. Atop the terminal's 48 acres sits some of the richest real estate and the most prestigious addresses in the world. Its construction established the legal principle of air rights, which created an ephemeral commodity worth billions of dollars. The threat of its demolition affirmed another legal principle: government precedence over private property to preserve a historic landmark. "Viewed urbanistically," architectural historians wrote in 1990, "Grand Central Terminal is without parallel." Their report continued:

> The urban design of the vast building vitalized and embraced its broader surroundings. Accommodating the city, the Terminal provided a circumferential roadway which circled it, underground passages which linked to buildings beyond it, corridors and ramps which led one through it, and tunnels for trains and subways to stop beneath it.
>
> The interior comfort and dignity of the traveler and commuter was of paramount consideration in the design of Grand Central Terminal. The elegant finishes and spatial quality throughout created a unified setting with a restful palette of neutral colors. The stark elegance of the uncluttered marble and stone walls and simple black-letter signs, the clarity of the programming and spaces, and the efficiency of the many services and amenities all serve the architect's original intent that the building "is not to be an art museum, or a hall of fame, but a place of dignified simplicity, easy of access and comfortable."
>
> Grand Central Terminal was the consummate civic monument—and yet it was even more. Commercially it stood as one of America's first multi-use buildings, incorporating shops, restaurants, stores and offices—in short, all the diversity of a city within the confines of one building.

In 1967, Grand Central was designated as a New York City landmark. A decade later, modernization of the old Commodore

Hotel, the first project in Midtown by Donald Trump, ignited a revival of 42nd Street. And 30 years later, a major renovation restored the station as an architectural gem and a destination not merely for train travelers, but also for shoppers, restaurant-goers, and other visitors. Grand Central anchored the revival of Midtown Manhattan, a revival that would spread west to Bryant Park, behind the New York Public Library, and Times Square and become emblematic of urban renewal at its best. Just recently, the Lincoln Building, originally named for the former president, was rechristened One Grand Central Place, in affirmation of the terminal's cachet and the city's resurgence.

THIS BOOK IS MORE THAN A STORY ABOUT TRANSPORTATION. It's about the expansion of the city of New York into a metropolis and the aggregation of metropolitan government, which mirrored the ruthless consolidation of corporate America and of the nation's railroads. The terminal was a product of local politics, bold architecture, brutal flexing of corporate muscle, and visionary engineering. No other building embodies New York's ascent as vividly as Grand Central. And no other epitomizes the partnership that melded the best instincts of government with public-spirited private investment, a model that is being mirrored all over America.

"It is a magical place with a history that captures the city's early growth, post-1970 crisis and subsequent rebirth," said Edward P. Glaeser, the Harvard economics professor and author of *Triumph of the City*. "I remember it as a place of danger and chaos in the 1970s, but thanks to its clever and effective public-private partnership it is a shining center once more. It is worth noting that the success of this partnership hinged in part on New York's abundance of generous, wildly successful people and that abundance is not available everywhere else in the country—think of the sorry state of Detroit's Michigan Central Station."

In listing the terminal on the National Register of Historic Places, the National Park Service suggested that even *gateway* was not magisterial enough for what Grand Central conjured up. *Gateway*, the architectural historians James M. Fitch and Diana Waite wrote, "is a totally inadequate term, suggesting a passive orifice under the open sky whereas the terminal must be seen as a mechanism, a great reciprocating engine for pumping a huge flow of pedestrian traffic through a whole series of valves and conduits into connecting systems—trains, subways, taxis, trolleys and elevated trains."

Despite the early segregation of immigrants and other undesirables underground and later efforts to discourage the homeless, Grand Central has been an egalitarian gateway. "When I first saw Grand Central Terminal close to 40 years ago—headed upstate with my mother and brother to visit Aunt Lillian—it was the quintessential public building, an astoundingly democratic place," Lee Stringer, the author of *Grand Central Winter: Stories from the Street*, wrote in 1998.

> The porters, Red Caps and conductors all treated us like first-class passengers, though we were traveling the equivalent of steerage. Twenty-odd years later, penniless, I ended up living in Grand Central, along with hundreds of homeless New Yorkers. It has since struck me how perfectly right it was that a great public building should serve, above everything else, as a refuge—in my case for 10 years. Grand Central was anything but beautiful or elegant the winter I first staked out a niche

on its lower levels—and certainly not grand. But in the thousand small acts of kindness tendered then by busy, bustling New Yorkers—acts as small as an encouraging word—I detected a whisper of the indomitable spirit that distinguishes this from any other mere compilation of brick and mortar that dares call itself a city. That New York, no matter what the human condition, shrugged and said: "It's cold. Come inside."

AN ENGINEER'S PERSPECTIVE ON THE LABYRINTHINE "LADDER" OF RAILS, WHICH MERGES INTO FOUR MAIN TRACKS.

No character like Brian Selznick's Hugo ever lived at the terminal, as far as we know (Selznick visited there, though, for inspiration). Still, Grand Central is a story about people, the people who built it, the people who are employed there and make the place work, and the people who arrive and depart there every day or come for an occasional visit. If the terminal reaches its target 100 million passengers in 2013, that number, combined with the estimated 21 million out-of-town tourists (*Travel + Leisure* magazine ranked it sixth not long ago in the list of world's most visited attractions, right after Niagara Falls, and ahead of the Statue of Liberty and the Metropolitan Museum of Art) and the more than 40 million who traverse the Grand Central subway station, would mean that in any given year, the equivalent of half the entire population of the United States passes through.

FOR ALL ITS GLORY, Paul Goldberger wrote in the *New Yorker* when the terminal was rededicated,

> The real brilliance of the place—for all its architectural glory—is the way in which it confirms the virtues of the urban ensemble. Grand Central was conceived as the monumental center of a single composition, with hotels and streets and towers and subways arrayed around it. When it opened, in 1913, it was New York's clearest embodiment of the essential urban idea—that different kinds of buildings work together to make a whole that is far greater than any of its parts. If Penn Station was built mainly to send a message about the splendor of arrival, then Grand Central was conceived to make clear the choreography of connection.

Every day, that choreography is performed on a gargantuan dance floor called the Main Concourse. "Are the people at Grand Central different?" Alastair Macaulay, the *Times*' dance critic, asked.

I cannot prove that the elegance of the place rubs off on people's behavior, but I sense that these same visitors would not carry themselves in quite the same way at Penn Station or the Port Authority. The immensity of the hall's space makes an impact at all times, surrounding people with drama. It keeps reminding me of a story my mother used to tell about the days when she worked as an au pair in France. Her employer had a maid from Milan to whom the employer once said politely, "I understand the cathedral in Milan is very beautiful." The maid replied: "Oh, but Madame! You should see the railway station!"

TO ALL THOSE WHO WITH HEAD HEART AND HAND TOILED IN THE CONSTRUCTION OF THIS MONUMENT TO THE PUBLIC SERVICE. THIS IS INSCRIBED

RAILS VS. RIVERS

THAT THE FIRST STEAM-POWERED LOCOMOTIVE operating in New York State was named the DeWitt Clinton must have been someone's idea of a bad joke. Governor Clinton, after all, had been the brains and the political maestro behind the Erie Canal, which, when it was finally completed with great fanfare in 1825, would link Manhattan's Hudson River waterfront with the Great Lakes and confirm New York as America's predominant port for years to come. Why would anyone in his right mind threaten the supremacy of the packet boats to Albany and the freight-laden canal barges by building a railroad just a few years later?

Maybe the early railroad pioneers weren't entirely in their right minds. After all, when the 9,000-pound, 13-foot-long DeWitt Clinton was cast at the West Point Foundry in Cold Spring, New York, and fitted at the foot of Beach Street in lower Manhattan, it was only the third or fourth steam locomotive built in the United States. But

CONSTRUCTION BEGAN ON THE NEW TERMINAL
IN 1903 IN LONGITUDINAL "BITES." THE OLD
STATION IS AT RIGHT.

the railroad men weren't completely crazy. They were shrewd enough to engage in a subterfuge sufficient to forestall a veto of railroad franchises by the state legislature, which the boatmen, including Cornelius Vanderbilt, all but owned.

Following experiments by the inventor Peter Cooper of New York on the Baltimore & Ohio and service on the Charleston & Hamburg line in South Carolina, John B. Jervis commissioned the DeWitt Clinton for the newly chartered Mohawk & Hudson Railroad, the first leg of what two decades later would become the New York Central. (Jervis, who had worked as an axman and later an engineer on the Erie Canal, would become instrumental in another aquatic project—providing freshwater from Westchester for New York City through the Croton Aqueduct.) Inauspiciously, the locomotive was delivered to Albany from the foundry by boat. On August 9, 1831—six years after George William Featherstonhaugh, a Schenectady cattle breeder, formed the railroad—the three-and-a-half-ton iron engine hauled several yellow stagecoaches crammed with passengers for a trial run over 16 miles of track between upstate Albany and Schenectady. It took 40 minutes. The Mohawk & Hudson tracks roughly paralleled the canal, but the trip by rail was much faster. One reason was the engine's speed, about 30 mph. Another reason was geographical: on that stretch of the water route, barges had to surmount more than a dozen locks on their circuitous 40-mile circumnavigation of the 90-foot-high Cohoes Falls on the Mohawk River.

Two years later, the Mohawk & Hudson set another promotional precedent that would quickly spiral out of control in the railroads' zeal to win converts to its cause: the first free railroad pass was issued to a public official, this one to Reuben H. Walworth, the chancellor of New York and the state's highest judicial officer. By the time his post was abolished nearly two decades later, the practice had proliferated. Free passes had been accepted by state legislators and even minor local functionaries as a political entitlement. By the end of the 19th century, good-government watchdogs would be hard-pressed to find a public official who, one way or another, did not own railroad stock.

THE FIRST RAIL LINE IN NEW YORK CITY also began operating in 1831, but with one big caveat. Its charter from the legislature specified that while it might parallel the Hudson, the tracks would have to be laid too far east of the river—between Third and Eighth Avenues—to threaten the steamboats' passenger and freight monopoly. Moreover, the charter wrung from lawmakers in the capitol left little room for future competition with maritime traffic to Albany and on to the Midwest. It allowed for a double-track railroad from 23rd Street, but only as far north as the Harlem River. Even at the groundbreaking, though, on February 23, 1832, the line's founders, including Thomas Emmet, whose younger brother, Robert, was the famous Irish revolutionary, barely concealed their ultimate goal. Before adjourning for toasts "drunk in sparkling Champagne with great hilarity and feeling," John Mason, the railroad's vice president (the president was dutifully attending to his day job as a congressman in Washington), acknowledged that "while the road's principal objectives were necessarily local, the higher importance was to encourage the building of another road to Albany, which is intended to commence where the present road (our New York & Harlem) terminates at the Harlem River."

The railroad industry in America was still so primitive that the first iron rails had to be ordered from England. After a visit, Charles

Dickens scorned some of the line's early carriages as "great wooden arks." And even before any track was laid, railroad officials realized that the terminus at 23rd Street was too remote from lower Manhattan. State legislators were importuned to grant an extension to the charter—but, pointedly, the extension was in the downtown direction, to Prince Street in what is now SoHo, and "through such streets as the mayor, aldermen and commonality might prescribe" (as a practical matter, that meant the railroad could be extorted by both state *and* city politicians). Another caveat was imposed after a locomotive boiler exploded, killing the engineer and injuring 20 passengers: no steam locomotives could be used to haul carriages south of 14th Street (by 1858, with the city bulging northward, steam power would be banned below 42nd Street). Only horsepower—literally—was allowed.

When the first stretch opened on November 22, 1832, between Prince Street and Union Square, the carriages, each pulled by two horses, more closely resembled streetcars than a railroad. The one-way fare was a penny. Horsecars would proliferate in the city and operate until 1917, but at least the Harlem's cars ran on rails—not on the deeply rutted unpaved avenues or jarring cobblestones, which prompted the *New York Herald* to describe a routine ride on a horse-drawn omnibus as "modern martyrdom." (Only about 25,000 of New York's 750,000 or so residents rode an omnibus daily by 1850, but the practice acclimated them to what the historian Glen Holt Jr. described, in transportation rather than sartorial terms, as the "riding habit.") Unfortunately, the inaugural ceremony did not go off without a hitch. A miscommunication between the drivers of the cars resulted in what the railroad historian Louis V. Grogan speculated was the first recorded instance of a rear-end collision in America.

This being New York, even the 12 mph horsecars provoked public controversy. (Below 14th Street the speed limit was a pokey 5 mph, about as fast as a hearty pedestrian could walk; the limit was rigidly enforced by an inspector, Henry Bergh, who would later found the American Society for the Prevention of Cruelty to Animals.)

Moreover, cabbies objected to the competition (and after one protest meeting at Tammany Hall vandalized some of the company's tracks). Storeowners feared the railroad would eventually usurp the entire width of Fourth Avenue (now Park Avenue and Park Avenue South), and landlords bordering the avenue, expecting an immediate bonanza in real estate values, worried instead that New York & Harlem would win further concessions from the city (which it did) and encroach upon their property. In 1833, the railroad purchased six parcels at East 26th Street and Fourth Avenue for a car barn and stables.

The reticence of the city fathers notwithstanding, the railroad was not about horses. It was about steam—even if steam, and the higher

WHAT BECAME PARK AVENUE WAS AN OPEN TRAIN YARD NORTH OF GRAND CENTRAL. THE YARD WAS SUNK BELOW STREET LEVEL AND FINALLY DECKED OVER.

speed it allowed, was still considered unsafe and even unnatural. While the horse-drawn streetcar business would enrich other entrepreneurs for decades, it was the potential of steam power that had inspired George William Featherstonhaugh to organize the Mohawk & Hudson. Steam power was what John Mason and other officials of the New York & Harlem fully believed would redeem their investment in an untested route between bustling lower Manhattan and the bucolic precincts north of 14th Street, much less the even more pastoral outpost of Harlem. By 1840, while the New York & Harlem still owned 140 horses to haul its 36 carriages on lower Fourth Avenue, the line had also placed six wood-burning steam locomotives in service.

Also by then, three developments foreshadowed the railroad's future success. In 1834, a rock cut was completed through Murray Hill and the line was extended north to East 85th Street in Yorkville. Three years later, railroad engineers completed a 596-foot-long brick and masonry tube between 94th and 96th Streets under Mount Prospect, or Observatory Place. (It is the city's oldest tunnel and still carries two tracks of the Metro-North Railroad.) The railroad was also extended farther south to Tryon Row, today the site of the Municipal Building in lower Manhattan.

By 1839, just seven years after service was inaugurated, the fledgling railroad could celebrate the completion of its original agenda: nearly seven miles of relatively rapid transit from the city to Harlem. Regular service to 125th Street and the opening of a hotel there inspired the *New York Herald* to predict that "this and other improvements will make Harlem a fashionable rival to Hoboken, New Brighton and other summer resorts."

Another feat took no less finesse. Dawdling by Gouverneur Morris's New York & Albany Railroad prevented it from laying tracks south from the Bronx into the New York & Harlem's Manhattan territory. The line had frittered away its franchise and, in 1840, the legislature granted the New York & Harlem the right to bridge the Harlem River and, in effect, lay track all the way to the state capital—actually, to Greenbush, across the river, until a Hudson River railroad bridge was built in 1866. (So much for progress: today, Amtrak's Albany stop is again on the wrong side of the river, in Rensselaer.) The Harlem line, originally confined by charter, but not by ambition, to the island of Manhattan, was poised to become the little railroad that could. By 1852, its tracks would stretch from New York's City Hall nearly 131 miles north to Chatham and connect to the last 22 miles toward Albany.

THE RAILROAD NOT ONLY FULFILLED A DEMAND. It created one. Brooklyn Heights is generally regarded as America's first suburb (for the record, historians say the city's very first commuter was Jacques Cortelyou, who surveyed New Amsterdam in 1660 for the Dutch West India Company and traveled to work from Long Island), but Brooklyn was reachable from Manhattan only by boat, which was undependable in bad weather. In winter, the East River might freeze for weeks at a time. Trains, in contrast, were considerably more versatile. They opened vast tracts of land to development, sending steel runners up the fertile plains of New York's Hudson Valley and southwestern Connecticut, where the railroad would advertise "villa plots for sale" conveniently near stations. From those nodes, new towns and even cities would take root. Suburbanization was not unique to New York City. Railroads also spread development beyond city lines in places like Boston and Philadelphia. Yet in New York, the tendrils of track seemed to proliferate farther from the city center and in virtually every direction.

In 1843, the New Haven Railroad had reached its namesake city from New York. A year later, the *New York Herald* prophesied that within two decades "the line of this road will be nearly one continuous village as far as White Plains." With Westchester's population ballooning by 75 percent in the 1850s alone, an English traveler marveled that suburban homes were "springing up like mushrooms on spots which five years ago were part of the dense and tangled forest; and the value of property everywhere, but especially along the various lines of railroad, has increased by a ratio almost incredible."

Reaction of rural residents who overnight evolved into suburbanites was profoundly mixed.

NOT LONG AFTER THE LINE linked the teeming city to country homes in Harlem, what would become the Bronx, and Westchester and to small Hudson Valley villages, a perceptive railroad superintendent remembered only as M. Sloat noticed a new class of customer: the repeat passenger, whose to-and-fro trips to work and home represented a potential marketing bonanza. Seizing the opportunity, the railroad originated an imaginative fare structure of tickets based not on a onetime passage or even a round trip, but on unlimited rides for six months or a full year at a steep discount from the single-fare rate. The full fare was *commuted*, and with one bold entrepreneurial stroke the railroad commuter—in name, at the very least—was officially

LOOKING SOUTH, A CHIMERICAL TELESCOPIC VIEW FROM THE 125TH STREET STATION IN HARLEM.

born. The first-class fare between downtown and Harlem was $35 for 12 months; a second-class ticket, for $25, was good only during prescribed hours and on local trains. Even with the discount, annual commutation rates from Westchester were too high for most wage earners, which forged the county's enduring identity as a verdant, affluent suburb. In a letter to the *Times* in 1873, a writer identified only as a blue-collar "brakeman" complained that given the high cost of commuting, "I confidently expect that, within the next 10 years, Westchester will be inhabited only by those who can afford to pay for the luxury, such as railroad directors, members of the Stock Exchange, and executors of large estates." But as Kenneth T. Jackson recalled in his book *Crabgrass Frontier*, even before the Civil War "the southernmost stations at Fordham, Morrisania, Tremont, and Mount Vernon were becoming centers of middle-class residence." Commuters' dependence on a reliable railroad would become manifest.

The advent of the commuter also produced an immediate and not entirely surprising corollary: the commuter complaint. Early on, a coalition of Scarsdale commuters threatened to sue the Central because "the poor train service has so discouraged people seeking real estate just south of White Plains that it has caused the market practically to collapse." The commuters complained that the haphazard service was especially hard on housewives. (Scarsdale riders griped: "It is almost impossible to keep servants, because they never know when they should have meals for their masters coming from New York, nor how long they will have to keep the meals warm.")

Similar complaints left commuters ripe for mockery. E.B. White perpetuated the stereotype in a 1929 poem:

> *Commuter—one who spends his life*
> *In riding to and from his wife;*
> *A man who shaves and takes a train*
> *And then rides back to shave again.*

But commuter revolts mattered only when riders had an alternative. And suddenly, another railroad offered one. In 1847, the Hudson

River Railroad Company had finally been organized, with John B. Jervis, who was instrumental in charting the original Mohawk & Hudson, as its chief engineer. Constructing a railroad adjoining the river—hemmed on the east by a steep embankment and punctuated by ponds that ebbed and flowed with the Hudson's tidal clock and had to be either bridged or filled in—presented a challenge. Jervis cast the project as an environmental bonanza for the shoreline: "rough points will be smoothed off, the irregular indentations of the bays be hidden and a regularity and symmetry imparted to the outline." (Some of the human impediments to construction were less obliging; the line paid $3,000 to settle property claims in upper Manhattan by John J. Audubon and $800 to Madame Eliza Jumel, a widow of Aaron Burr, "notwithstanding the defects" in her title.) But constructing a riprap river wall and leveling the flinty rock surface to lay gradeless track was an engineering challenge, not an operating one, and within two years the trains were running north past Peekskill from a terminal at West 32nd Street and Ninth Avenue (a route that would extend downtown to Chambers Street on Ninth Avenue, paralleling in some places the former elevated freight tracks that were transformed into what is now the High Line park).

By midcentury, the Harlem was facing fierce competition from what one of its advertisements warned were the "dangers and disasters incident to a road running on the margin of a deep river"— namely, the new Hudson River Railroad. The railroad's route proved to be a testament to the inevitable political ascendancy of rail over river. In a sense, though, it was less a matter of ascendancy than a case of meeting the enemy and discovering he is us.

THE COMMODORE

I N 1833, JUST AS THE NEW YORK & HARLEM RAILROAD was beginning service, a swashbuckling Hudson River boat mogul named Cornelius Vanderbilt boldly embarked on his first railroad trip. For a future railroad magnate, the trip could not have been more fraught with foreboding. The Camden & Amboy Railroad passenger car he was riding in rolled off an embankment in Hightstown, New Jersey. Vanderbilt was very nearly killed. He broke several ribs and punctured a lung. (If the accident alienated him from railroads in general, it also may have laid the groundwork for his later special antipathy toward the Pennsylvania, of which the Camden & Amboy was a component.) Needless to say, he was so unimpressed with the noisy, newfangled vehicle that even years later, when he was solicited to buy stock in the Harlem line, he would reply: "I would be a fool to sink my money in a business that sets out to compete with steamboats."

Vanderbilt was born in 1794 into a poor farming family on Staten Island, the great-great-grandson of a Dutchman who emigrated as an indentured servant from the village of Bilt in the Netherlands. He was 13 years old when Robert Fulton's *Clermont* first steamed up the Hudson. Three years later, Vanderbilt was captain of his very own flat-bottomed and oar-equipped piragua, on which he ferried passengers between Staten Island and lower Manhattan. Two decades later, as George Stephenson was engineering his first steam locomotive in England, Vanderbilt was building his first steamboat, after successfully challenging Fulton's monopoly on Hudson River shipping (first by landing at different piers to confuse the authorities).

Steamboats were still profitable, but something happened in 1847 that may have soured Vanderbilt on his identification with their fate. His coal-burning namesake steamboat, *Cornelius Van Derbilt*, was defeated in a round-trip boat race up the Hudson to Croton Point. Vanderbilt didn't abandon ships. But he also began investing in railroads. While he would forever be known universally as "the Commodore"—a self-styled sobriquet that celebrated his maritime coups—he was already gazing longingly on a new horizon and, by the late 1840s, was partnering with Daniel Drew, a devilishly clever sometime steamboat partner and Wall Street buccaneer. (Drew's reputation for bloating his cattle by quenching their thirst before delivering them to market and later for outwitting Vanderbilt by diluting Erie Railroad shares would give rise to the term *watered-down stock*.) Their first acquisition was the Boston & Stonington, which not only didn't compete with steamboats; it was practically in business with them. Its tracks provided the land link in the mostly maritime route between Boston and New York (in 1844, the Long Island Rail

Road had begun carrying passengers to Greenport, where they would board the steamboat to Stonington, avoiding the hilly Connecticut land route riven by the wide-open mouths of deep rivers). But while the Boston & Stonington didn't compete with Vanderbilt's steamboats, other railroads did. And while the railroads were initially less luxurious and offered few amenities, they could navigate the route to Albany during the four or so months a year that the Hudson would freeze north of where the Tappan Zee now spans the river.

Meanwhile, the New York & Harlem was falling on hard times. Its hilly inland route to the state capital—actually, only the 131 miles to Chatham, where it would connect with the future Boston & Albany—couldn't compete with the Hudson Railroads' water-level river route. Moreover, the line had been fleeced by one of its executives in 1854 and, in part, blamed Vanderbilt, whom the executive had inveigled into buying Harlem bonds. In the Panic of 1857, after Harlem stock plunged to $9 a share, Vanderbilt was invited in as a director (his stockbroker was Leonard Jerome, whose daughter would give birth to Winston Churchill).

By 1862, rumor had it that Vanderbilt again regarded the depressed price not only as an investment opportunity but also as a vehicle to outwit his on-again, off-again nemesis Daniel Drew. As Kurt C. Schlichting, a Fairfield University sociology professor, recalled it, Vanderbilt figured the Harlem's fortunes would improve with a franchise for a streetcar line up Broadway. But Drew thwarted Vanderbilt's strategy, probably by bribing the Common Council. Vanderbilt was undaunted. He continued to buy Harlem stock, which spurted to $150, and then he demanded $180—to the dismay of Drew and other short sellers, who were committed to deliver at $110 and therefore would lose $70 on every share they sold short.

Within a year, when Vanderbilt turned 70, he was president of the Harlem. Despite an occasional setback, such was Wall Street's faith in his acumen that the stock price promptly rebounded. As if to celebrate, three months after the South surrendered at Appomattox, Vanderbilt and his son William H., the vice president of the line, accompanied General Ulysses S. Grant on the Chatham leg of the general's well-deserved vacation to Saratoga on a train hauled, naturally, by a flag-festooned engine named W.H. Vanderbilt. At the end of the two-hour, 45-minute ride, a *Times* reporter pronounced the Harlem line "admirably adapted for rapid travel" and said it "afforded a rich treat to the tourist and lover of nature in the magnificent scenery to be found along the whole route."

The first-class Harlem railroad Vanderbilt envisioned would remain elusive, though. Initially, the most tangible increase was in the commuter fares, to $50 for an annual ticket to Harlem, $75 to Bronxville, and $150 to the end of the line in Chatham. Service gradually improved so that by 1867 regular commuters included Horace Greeley of Chappaqua, who commented in his *New York Tribune*:

> We lived on this road when it was poor and feebly managed—with rotten cars and wheezy old engines that could not make schedule time; and the improvement since realized is gratifying…With an underground track from the Battery to Harlem Flats, its passenger fares would be speedily doubled. Such a track 10 years ago would have kept thousands in our state who have been driven over to Jersey by the full hour now required

to traverse the space between City Hall and the Harlem River. With a good underground railroad, the census of 1880 will credit Westchester County with a population of at least half a million, whereof at least 50,000 will visit our city daily.

Greeley's demographic projection proved to be hyperbolic. Nonetheless, between 1860 and 1880, the population of Westchester and the southern portion of the county that would become the Bronx more than doubled. The railroad was mostly responsible.

HIMSELF: THE COMMODORE, CORNELIUS J. VANDERBILT, WHO SWITCHED FROM RIVER TO RAIL.

By 1851, the Hudson line reached all the way to Albany (actually, at first, to the ferry terminal in Greenbush). The New York train connected with the overnight express to Buffalo, a train that introduced the sleeping car—a vehicle so inferior that it inspired one rider from western New York, a carpenter named George Pullman, to devote the rest of his career to developing the perfect alternative. Whatever the defects of the sleeper from Albany, the daytime passenger business was booming. Within a year, the Hudson was claiming more than 1.1 million passengers annually.

On April 2, 1853, the state legislature authorized 10 New York railroads to consolidate into a single corporation. Ten days later, officers of the lines, including Erastus Corning and Russell Sage (a financier and often partner of Vanderbilt's nemesis Jay Gould), met to organize the New York Central, which covered the 300 miles of central New York from Albany to Buffalo and was already growing connecting tentacles to Boston, New York City, and the Midwest. Corning, though lame and quite ordinary in appearance, was the Central's preeminent personality (he accepted no salary, but his iron-works was awarded the exclusive contract to supply the line with track; in the 20th century, his great-grandson would serve as mayor of Albany for more than four decades). Once, a conductor failed to recognize him and barked, "Hurry up, old man; don't be all day about it. The train can't wait." Corning insisted he was not personally offended but fired the conductor anyway. "I'll keep no one in my employ," he said, "who is uncivil to travelers."

On February 27, 1860, Corning was at Cooper Union in Manhattan to hear Abraham Lincoln deliver the speech that catapulted him to the Republican nomination for president. The next morning, according to some accounts, Corning visited Lincoln at the Astor House and offered him $10,000 a year to be the New York Central's lawyer. "If Lincoln had accepted his offer," Edward Hungerford wrote in *Men and Iron*, "he unquestionably would have declined the presidency of the United States."

By midcentury, the Central owned 188 locomotives. *Harper's Weekly* proclaimed it a "great and perfect work" and Horace Greeley's *Tribune* anointed it "the Imperial New York Central Railway." In New England and the mid-Atlantic states, groups of as many as 200 migrants at a time would heed Greeley's advice to "Go West." With stagecoaches and Erie Canal packet boats all but defunct by then, they went west on the New York Central, either on cars with sofas of cut velvet or, in the case of poorer Irish and German newcomers, in "emigrant cars" that one observer belittled as "just slightly better than box cars with benches."

BY 1865, THE VANDERBILTS, father and son, owned both the Harlem and the Hudson. But not the Erie, which the elder Vanderbilt failed to acquire after being outmaneuvered by Jim Fisk and Jay Gould, who mysteriously produced $14 million worth of stock certificates and retained control. And not the Central, which chose to ship freight on the Hudson River Railroad in winter but defer to steamboats the rest of the year. During the winter of 1867, with the river solidly frozen, Vanderbilt pulled the plug: he severed the Central from all rail traffic between New York and Albany. Passengers and freight haulers who depended on the Hudson River Railroad were left to fend for themselves.

The steamboat lobby demanded a legislative investigation.

Wasn't it true, Vanderbilt was asked before an assembly committee, that he had some friends on the board of the fickle Central? To which Vanderbilt famously testified, "My personal friends, when they take such grounds as they did, I am afraid of; I am not afraid of my enemies, but, my God, you must look out when you get among friends." Vanderbilt's ploy worked. The Central begrudgingly capitulated. Vanderbilt became its president. And, by 1869 (the year he turned 76 years old and when the last spike was driven to complete the first transcontinental railroad), his Central absorbed his Hudson line.

"NOT ORNAMENTAL," was how Henry Adams described the Commodore, a man who "lacked social charm." A biography by a descendant, Arthur T. Vanderbilt II, recalled the Commodore's predilection to spit streams of tobacco juice and fondle the maids at social events. Mark Twain attacked him for "superhuman stinginess" and suggested he perform a single charitable act to place "one solitary grain of pure gold upon the heaped rubbish of your life." Gustavus Myers, a muckraker, wrote, "Each new million that he seized was an additional resource by which he could bribe and manipulate; progressively his power advanced; and it became ridiculously easier to get possession of more and more property...the mere threat of pitting his enormous wealth against competitors whom he sought to destroy was generally a sufficient warrant for their surrender."

Vanderbilt was cunning and brutal, a combination that served him well in vanquishing enemies, real and imagined. Confronted by two whom he believed had cheated him and had betrayed his trust, he was merciless. "I won't sue you, for the law is too slow," he supposedly said. "I'll ruin you." He was also quoted as acknowledging,

"I have been insane on the subject of money-making all my life." His son William Henry Vanderbilt became the richest man in the world. He also inherited the old man's charm. When a reporter asked about the possibility of lower fares for passengers, Vanderbilt barked that the railroad barely broke even on some routes, including the one between New York and Chicago, and maintained them only to keep up with the competition from the Pennsylvania.

"But don't you run it for the public benefit?" the reporter asked. To which Vanderbilt was quoted as delivering his immortal reply:

> The public be damned. What does the public care for the railroads except to get as much out of them for as small a consideration as possible? I don't take any stock in this silly nonsense about working for anybody's good, but our own because we are not. When we make a move we do it because it is our interest to do so, not because we expect to do somebody else some good. Of course, we like to do everything possible for the benefit of humanity in general, but when we do we first see that we are benefiting ourselves. Railroads are not run on sentiment, but on business principles and to pay.

William's father, the Commodore, once expressed a similar credo more succinctly: he neatly summarized Adam Smith's ideas in testimony before the New York State Legislature in 1867. "I have always served the public to the best of my ability," he said. "Why? Because, like every other man, it is to my interest to do so."

• • •

THE UNION PACIFIC AND THE SANTA FE would become romanticized cultural icons too. But the New York Central, which enjoyed the full energy and diligence of the Vanderbilts, would capture the imagination of the country like no other railroad. In one incarnation or another (by the 1920s, the New York Central Lines represented what were once 315 separate companies), the Central was responsible for innovations ranging from the lowly but beloved caboose (on the Auburn & Syracuse), from which crews oversaw mammoth freight trains snaking their way to market, to the J-Class 4-6-4 Hudson steam locomotives (immortalized by American Flyer and Lionel scale models), to the storied luxury of the 20th Century Limited, which whisked passengers between New York and Chicago. The water-level route from New York to upstate was the world's first four-track long-distance railroad. The Central's territory, beginning in the mid-19th century, the historian Alvin F. Harlow observed, "was producing men who did much to revolutionize the business of transportation."

Their names remain a litany of railroad and related business titans: Henry Wells, a Batavia leather worker, and William G. Fargo, a freight clerk from Auburn; John Webster Wagner and George M. Pullman, who would become competitors in the sleeping-car business; George Westinghouse, who as a boy was bewitched by the railroad cars that lumbered past his home in Schenectady. At its peak before the middle of the 20th century, the New York Central's tracks would stretch 11,000 miles across 12 states that were home to 50.3 percent of the nation's population.

IN 1869, VANDERBILT WAS OPERATING two lines in Manhattan with two separate terminals. For his Hudson line, he desperately needed a downtown freight complex (passengers were accommodated at Chambers Street and West 30th Street). With few other vacant tracts available, he seized upon the fashionable St. John's Park neighborhood in what is now Tribeca, a plot whose ownership would be contested for centuries. Trinity Church sold the four-acre parcel to the Hudson River Railroad (which held it until 1927, when it was razed for the Holland Tunnel exit). "Some New Yorkers who clung wistfully to the thought of open spaces with green lawns and stately trees here and there throughout their city protested, but they were laughed out of court," Edward Hungerford later wrote. "The trees were razed, the park leveled, and workmen were laying the foundations of the new freight house almost before New York knew just what was being done."

A heroic, 12-foot-tall bronze statue of the Commodore (twice life-size) was erected on an ornate 150-foot-long and 30-foot-high metal pediment that depicted his mastery of river and rail. The sculpture, by Ernst Plassmann, was commissioned by Albert De Groot, a Vanderbilt crony and one of the Commodore's

"THE PUBLIC BE DAMNED," WILLIAM H. VANDERBILT, THE COMMODORE'S SON, MEMORABLY DECLARED.

steamship captains. It was not universally acclaimed. *Scientific American* belittled the Commodore's sculpted overcoat as "ample to protect from frost a Siberian sledge driver." The diarist George Templeton Strong wrote, "Have inspected the grand $800,000 Vanderbilt bronze. It's a 'mixellaneous biling' of cog-wheels, steamships, primeval forests, anchors, locomotives, periaugas ('pettyaughers,' we called them when I was a boy), R.R. Trains, wild ducks (or possibly seagulls) & squatter shanties, with a colossal Cornelius Vanderbilt looming up in the midst of the chaos, & beaming benignantly down on Hudson Street, like a Pater Patriae—draped in a dressing gown or an overcoat, the folds whereof are most wooden. As a work of art, it is bestial."

On the East Side, meanwhile, the Harlem's main depot was becoming a dump. Built in 1857 and bounded by Fourth and Madison Avenues and East 26th and 27th Streets, it was the nation's first "union" depot, welcoming passengers from multiple lines, in this case the New Haven. But it was congested. Adjacent property owners who had been promised they would reap the rewards of adjacency to modern transportation were instead vexed by noise, sparks, and smoke. (Among the most vociferous opponents of steam was the Murray family, namesakes of Murray Hill, and whose Quaker ancestor, Mary Lindley Murray, legend has it, hospitably entertained William Howe, the British general, in 1776 long enough to let defeated American troops escape to fight again.)

Terrified pedestrians and drivers risked life, limb, and their vehicles by crossing the Fourth Avenue tracks. Complaints were met by this rejoinder from a railroad representative (which could just as easily have been issued by a tobacco company a century and a half later): "Railroads being the great means of commerce should be encouraged, not obstructed, and if the fuel of the pipe or the smoke of the locomotive was to be considered a cause of nuisance, that the steamboats should be banished from our seas and rivers, or silenced whenever they come so near a city to be heard."

Since 1830, though, New York City's population had soared from 200,000 to 1 million. Vanderbilt envisioned a single station for all three of his railroads, one whose grandeur epitomized the transportation empire he was aggressively assembling and one so accessible that, even as Manhattan's boundaries billowed, his primary passenger depot would always be central. He would build a station. The city would follow.

THE DEPOT

YOU DIDN'T NEED A CLAIRVOYANT to predict the burgeoning value of New York Central stock, but that didn't stop Victoria Woodhull and her sister Tennie C. Claflin. Both sisters claimed the ability to see visions of future events, a distinct advantage for a Wall Street broker (and one that gave a whole new dimension to Marshall McLuhan's maxim about the medium being the message). One investor later testified that when she asked his advice about stock purchases, Vanderbilt himself replied, "Why don't you do as I do, and consult the spirits?" Woodhull and Claflin (whom Vanderbilt proposed to marry) apparently found their inspiration, instead, from a less evanescent source, one with a proven track record. When they opened their brokerage business on January 22, 1870, on Broad Street, a portrait of Cornelius Vanderbilt prominently adorned one wall.

THE GRAND CENTRAL DEPOT, COMPLETED IN
1871. THE *TIMES* COMPLAINED THAT IT WAS
NEITHER GRAND NOR CENTRAL.

Five days later, on January 27, 1870, the spirits were willing. Vanderbilt presided over the first stockholders' meeting of the New York Central & Hudson River Railroad, capitalized at a dazzling $90 million. Three months later, the company paid a $3.6 million semiannual 4 percent dividend, which the *Times* breathlessly pronounced "the very largest single dividend ever paid in this country by any one great corporation or state." The New York Central was no ordinary corporation and its president was no ordinary man. "The creation of the New York Central & Hudson River stands as a historical landmark," T.J. Stiles wrote, "showing us where the era of big business—the Vanderbilt era—well and truly began."

VANDERBILT INAUGURATED HIS ERA by introducing two customs borrowed from British railroads: every employee wore a uniform, and tickets were punched before passengers boarded their trains. But a great railroad required a great station of its own, so he built Grand Central Depot. It stretched 249 feet wide on East 42nd Street and north to East 48th Street. Some of the land on which it stood was already owned by the railroad and was used for storing cars and as a "fuel factory," where a treadmill powered by horses teased with a wisp of hay operated the machinery that cut wood to power the steam locomotives that ran north of 42nd Street. Horses still pulled the streetcars south of 42nd Street through the tunnel under what is now Park Avenue from 33rd to 41st Streets, which is still used by automobiles. (As late as the mid-1870s, the line's stables on Fourth Avenue between 32nd and 33rd Streets could still accommodate 916 horses, and even that number was sometimes insufficient.)

The Commodore acquired the rest of the site, which was largely vacant or occupied by pastures and shanties, by negotiating with private landlords whom the 1850 General Railroad Law of New York State had placed under a crippling disadvantage: the railroads were empowered to appropriate property and let the courts appraise its value. When Peter Goelet, a member of the prominent real estate family, offered to lease Vanderbilt the block bounded by 46th and 47th Streets and Madison and Fourth Avenues, the self-confident Commodore replied, pointedly in the first person singular: "I never lease property—always buy." On November 1, 1871, less than two years after ground was broken, his $6.4 million depot and rail yard opened for business.

The land and construction cost well over $100 million in today's dollars, and Vanderbilt, who was 78 when it was completed, paid for the depot out of his own deep pockets. It was later revealed, however, that because he was well versed in the ways and means of Tammany Hall, the transaction inevitably involved politicians' pockets too.

A pair of court-appointed commissioners handed him Fourth Avenue between 42nd and 43rd Streets for a fire-sale price of $25,000 when the market price was closer to $350,000. Favoritism? Consider that just a year or two earlier, one of the Tweed ring's Supreme Court justices had gone so far as to issue an arrest warrant for Jay Gould when he sought to prevent Vanderbilt from seizing control of the Erie Railroad. But perhaps the commissioners were unaware that the ring was no longer beholden to Vanderbilt, having undoubtedly succumbed to a better offer. So when the commissioners delivered Vanderbilt a bargain for the Fourth Avenue parcel in 1869, even Justice Albert

Cardozo (the Tammany tool, whose son, the eminent jurist Benjamin Cardozo, proved how far an apple can fall from the tree) concluded that the deal was a sham that would "operate unjustly" to the city.

George Templeton Strong's unvarnished review of the Commodore's statue downtown might have been why Vanderbilt scrapped plans for a second such likeness. The *Times* said that another figure of the Commodore, this one also commissioned by his friend De Groot, weighing in at a half ton and flanked by a sailor and an Indian, was destined for the new passenger depot. Indeed, John B. Snook's new American Second Empire–style building, clad in red pressed brick and cast-iron trim, left a huge niche at the third floor. "But the niche remained empty," Christopher Gray later wrote in the *Times*— "perhaps the earlier japes had convinced Vanderbilt of the virtues of modesty." (Shortly after the opening of Grand Central, the *Times* took him to task over repeated accidents in the open railroad yards to the north, saying that any tribute in bronze should also include "the dismembered bodies of men, women and children.") The original massive statue of the Commodore finally came home to the viaduct around the south façade of Grand Central Terminal in 1929, where it still stands. "For now," Gray wrote, "he stands a hostage, in a haze of exhaust produced by the railroad's most potent enemy, the automobile."

John B. Snook's architectural imprint endures on the nation's first department store, A.T. Stewart's at 280 Broadway, and the cast-iron façades in what is now SoHo. Vanderbilt's depot was billed as the nation's biggest railroad station and, by one measure, was even larger than the world's biggest, London's Victorian St. Pancras, which had opened three years earlier. The imposing three-story building that fronted on 42nd Street was inspired by the palace of Versailles and the Tuileries. It rivaled the Eiffel Tower and Crystal Palace for its ingenious engineering, if not its grandeur. (It was largely overlooked on opening day, though; the New York newspapers were preoccupied by the Great Chicago Fire the night before.)

The depot was distinguished by five mansard roofs. But its most memorable architectural feature was a 652-foot-long arch-ribbed-vault train shed that was modeled on St. Pancras. Thirty-one iron trusses supported the depot's resplendent 60,000-square-foot semicircular glass roof. The half-cylindrical ceiling was 200 feet wide and soared 100 feet at its apex—the largest interior space on the North American continent and second as a tourist attraction only to the Capitol in Washington.

The effect was magical. It sparked the imagination of novelists. The depot was where Richard Harding Davis's Captain Royal Macklin, returning from his escapade in Honduras, reveled in buying a train ticket to his hometown in Dobbs Ferry. It was also there, in the afternoon rush one September in Edith Wharton's *The House of Mirth*, that Lawrence Selden began his stroll with Lily Bart—"a figure to arrest even the suburban traveler rushing to his last train. Against the dull tints of the crowd," Wharton wrote, her vivid head "made her more conspicuous than in a ballroom" as she threaded "through the throng of returning holiday-makers, past sallow-faced girls in preposterous hats, and flat-chested women struggling with paper bundles and palm-leaf fans."

The old station on 26th Street was sold to P.T. Barnum, who converted it into the Hippodrome, a showcase for circuses and other spectacles. In 1879, it was taken over by the Commodore's grandson, who renamed it Madison Square Garden. (The name endured four incarnations; the second one was where Harry K. Thaw, jealous over the alienation of his affection for Evelyn Nesbit, shot Stanford White in 1906 in a jealous rage; years later, after visiting the South Florida Mediterranean revival hotels, clubs, and mansions designed by Addison Mizner, Thaw lamented: "I shot the wrong architect." Well, everyone's a critic.) "Without much pretension to architectural elegance," a professional critic wrote of the new depot, "it is commodious and well adapted to the purposes for which it was designed, and perhaps we ought not to ask much more from a railroad depot."

The *Times* carped, though, that the depot "can only by a stretch of courtesy be called either central or grand"—particularly because 42nd Street was by no means the center of New York City yet. The remote depot was derided by another journal as "End of the World Station." The critic Lewis Mumford would later denigrate its "imperial façade." More than a century later, Christopher Gray would write in the *Times* that the station was "awkwardly up-to-the-minute, more cowtown than continental."

For reasons that were never made clear, Vanderbilt gave his tenant the New Haven the prime location, fronting East 42nd Street. The Harlem and the Central were relegated to Vanderbilt Avenue. Also lost to history was the reasoning behind the arrangement of the tracks. Because outbound trains left from the west side of the train shed and inbound arrived on the east side, trains had to cross each other's paths, which they did first at 53rd Street and later at Spuyten Duyvil along the Harlem River and Woodlawn in the north Bronx. Even with five platforms and 15 tracks, passengers complained that

FOR SOME REASON, THE NEW HAVEN, WHICH WAS MERELY A TENANT, ENJOYED THE MOST PROMINENT FAÇADE, ON EAST 42ND STREET.

they were jammed waiting at entrances for the 88 daily trains and resented the long hike to the platforms.

Each of the three railroads served by the depot had a separate waiting room, creating havoc for baggage-laden passengers transferring from one line to another and mingling long-distance travelers and commuters. Because the depot was in the middle of nowhere, passengers were "penned in like hogs" on the streetcars that ferried them from the depot to downtown. They were so crowded that the wait to board a commodious car could easily last an hour. The trip to City Hall, still the center of New York, could take another hour. "Without a single exception," the *Times* reported in 1871, New Yorkers "denounced the administration of affairs, not only in regard to the slow and wretched arrangement of time on the horse-cars, but also the inconveniences and outrages suffered by passengers at the Grand Central Depot." Dennis McMahon of Morrisania in the Bronx groused that he could get from the old station on 26th Street to Chambers Street in lower Manhattan in 25 minutes. The railroad promised that the new depot would save him seven minutes, but instead, "Now I never reckon on less than an hour." Complaining that "we lose one hour between the depot and City Hall," C.W. Poole of Mount Vernon invoked the ultimate threat, to "sell out and move to New Jersey."

The train shed itself was remarkably quiet and free of smoke, however. Ringing bells and blowing whistles were banned, and railroad cars minus locomotives coasted to the platforms by gravity. The *Herald* proclaimed it "the finest passenger railroad depot in the world," and it would play a vital role not only as a transportation hub, but also in the early development of Midtown. That development included the Vanderbilt mansions that the Commodore's children and grandchildren built for themselves on Fifth Avenue, prompting Edith Wharton to lament that their extravagances thoroughly retarded culture and confined them to a narrow corridor that conjured up the coastal passage in ancient Greece. "They are entrenched in a sort of

Thermopylae of bad taste, from which apparently no force on earth can dislodge them," she wrote.

When the Commodore died in 1877, he left nearly his entire fortune to William H., the son he trusted most. Within a few years, William's wealth more than doubled. William's sons, William K. and Cornelius II, would build Marble House and the Breakers, respectively, in Newport, Rhode Island. Their grandfather died on January 4, as were falling the first flakes of a blizzard that would shatter the glass roof of the Grand Central Depot. In total, the Commodore left $100 million—more money than was held by the U.S. Treasury. "Any fool can make a fortune," he once said. "It takes a man of brains to hold on to it after it is made." His last words were "keep the money together"—an admonition that went unheeded by his heirs.

"With the death of Cornelius II in 1899 at the age of only 56, the Vanderbilt dynasty at the New York Central really came to an end," Louis Auchincloss concluded, although Vanderbilt great-grandsons would remain involved with the railroad until the 1950s. "The 10 Vanderbilt mansions that once lined Fifth Avenue were never occupied by the next generation," Arthur T. Vanderbilt II wrote in *Fortune's Children*. "One by one, they fell to the wrecker's ball, their contest lost to the auctioneer's gavel." Only the grand depot and its glorious successor would endure as their legacy.

THE STATION

BY THE LATTER PART of the 19th century, commuting by train was no longer as unconventional as it had seemed just a few decades earlier. In 1873, New York City annexed the Westchester villages of Morrisania, West Farms, and Kingsbridge, nearly doubling its land mass and extending its north-south axis to 16 miles. Young couples weighed the trade-offs between a less frenetic and costly country life and the time and money spent commuting. An 1890 essay in the *Times* titled "Men Who Catch Trains" pointed out that commuting from the quaint and "ancient settlement of Yonkers," just 16 miles from Grand Central, could cost as little as 9 cents a day (compared to the regular one-way fare of 30 cents).

"'I must be able to reach my place of business inside of an hour's time,' declared the husband at the very beginning of the search for a suburban abode," the *Times* reported. "'Of course you must,' dutifully assented the wife, 'and we cannot afford to spend all of the difference

A QUICK FIX THAT TRANSFORMED THE DEPOT
INTO A NEO-RENAISSANCE CONCOCTION WAS
INSUFFICIENT TO MEET SOARING DEMAND.

in rent for railroad fares.'" For all the advantages of country living, commuting took its toll, as another *Times* writer estimated early in the 20th century. Figuring that it took him an hour to travel each way and that he had been commuting the 16 miles from Westchester for 14 years, he had averaged 9,600 miles and 600 hours annually for a grand total of 134,000 miles and 8,400 hours—or the equivalent of circumnavigating the globe five times over the course of nearly a full year. So much for George M. Cohan's proverbial *Forty-Five Minutes from Broadway.*

Thanks to the railroad, things weren't much better for Manhattan pedestrians. In 1839, a train from Grand Central had collided with a herd of cows at rural East 58th Street. By the time the Civil War ended, though, row houses had already reached the East 60s. With development came people and vehicles and an outcry against the New York Central. It was bad enough that the railroad had usurped public property, obstructing Fourth Avenue and the street grid with its depot, but the 600-foot-wide rail yard and the tracks beyond, from which locomotives spewed smoke, sparks, and cinders, irretrievably bisected a booming swath of Manhattan's East Side. Cross-town traffic was stymied altogether or shunted to a few bottlenecks.

In 1871, the *Times* all but shrieked that the city's "most fearful death-trap" was the nexus of tracks laid only a few feet apart in a no-man's-land two blocks wide and north of Grand Central in "this now populous quarter" of the city. "One has but to stand a few minutes in 45th Street, where the cars enter and pass out of the depot, to see the peril to which life is daily put," the paper continued, "and to wonder that more people are not wounded or killed for their temerity in attempting a crossing." The feverish news account presaged the dangerous congestion and constant tumult that not only vexed pedestrians, drivers, and neighbors, but would ultimately be the depot's undoing: "There is a continual ringing of bells and screaming of whistles that is confusing to the senses, awakened to the possibility of danger from an unknown or unseen quarter."

Mass meetings were called to protest the inconvenience and the threat to life and limb north and south of the new depot. "'Cross not Fourth Avenue at the peril of your lives,' is the dictum of the great Vanderbilt," one leaflet blazed in 1872. The perils posed by the railroad's "juggernaut" to pedestrians and horse-drawn conveyances even inspired a poem:

> *Sink your tracks, you railroad magnate!*
> *Arch it over well and strong,*
> *Do not wait the law's stern mandate*
> *And your nuisance thus prolong.*

One angry letter writer to the *Times* complained that "someone living on East 46th Street near Third Avenue, and wishing to go to 46th Street and Fifth Avenue, has to go to 42nd Street or 49th Street, making a detour of a half mile because this monopoly has made it unsafe to cross at any other point." Another resident, this one from East 50th Street, was apoplectic, writing, "There is no single thing on New York Island so dangerous to the community and prejudicial to its interests as this Valley of the Shadow of Death, which cuts the city in two its entire length, and stretches, unpaved, ungraded, and is given over to the hundreds of locomotives that continually dash up and down, through the richest district of New York."

With the community up in arms and the Commodore demanding that the right-of-way be widened to accommodate four tracks, compromise was inevitable. Beginning at 45th Street, the grade was lowered. A dozen bridges were commissioned to connect the two sides of Fourth Avenue between 45th and 56th Streets, where a Park Avenue Tunnel would begin (leading to a stone viaduct between 98th and 116th Streets where the land was swampy). Construction finally got under way in 1872. It dragged on for two disruptive years. Who would pay for the projected $6 million cost of a so-called Fourth Avenue Improvement? "All charitable persons pity Mr. Vanderbilt as a poor man who is compelled to spend his frugal income in lowering the railway tracks in Fourth Avenue, merely in order that people may not get themselves run over and killed by passing trains," the *Times* said sarcastically, adding: "The City of New York was rendered liable, with wonderful legislative promptitude, for the payment of several millions of dollars to assist Commodore Vanderbilt in paying the expenses of partially restoring Fourth Avenue to the public to whom it belongs." The collaboration was a marriage of necessity. Nonetheless, John Belle and Maxinne Leighton would later conclude, "In 1875, this was one of the earliest examples of collaboration between government and private industry."

Spurred by the growing public outcry and by the threat that newly emboldened legislators would impose a more onerous mandate, in 1873 the Central proposed to further mitigate the dangerous congestion by tunneling through solid rock all the way to 96th Street. The sunken tracks were flanked by iron fences and plots of grass—to justify the renaming of Fourth Avenue as Park Avenue north of Grand Central—and vents for the smoke and heat. (The name Park

IN THE 1870S, FORMING A PRECEDENT-SETTING PARTNERSHIP, THE CITY AND THE CENTRAL SPLIT THE COST OF SINKING THE PARK AVENUE TRACKS.

Avenue was first applied to the stretch in Murray Hill from 34th to 40th Streets in the early 1850s, then to 42nd Street in 1867 and in 1888, once the tracks were sunk, all the way to the Harlem River.)

The improvements did not totally ameliorate the nuisance but were palpable. When the depot first opened, the 100 trains that clattered over the Fourth Avenue tracks every day made such a racket that classes at Columbia College on 49th Street were disrupted. After the tracks were buried, though, Edith Wharton, who lived in a town house on Park at 78th Street, wrote to a friend in 1896 that in any given hour, "seven or eight trains passed without affecting our nervous system. What happens is a short roar & rumble, & a puff of white smoke. Some people might mind it very much—to me it would not be in the least disturbing, much less so than the jingle of a cable car, for instance."

THE TUNNEL PLEASED NEIGHBORS AND PEDESTRIANS, but not passengers of the three railroads served by the depot. By 1880, Manhattan's population would approach 1.2 million, and with Tammany politicians and their cronies profiting from paving contracts and real estate booms, the street grid that was first plotted on paper long before, in 1811, was finally wending its way north of what would become known as Midtown. By 1900, the population would top 1.8 million, and the grand depot, which had seemed so durable only three decades earlier and which the Commodore figured would suffice for a century, had devolved into a hopeless anachronism incapable of accommodating its 15 million passengers a year—much less future growth.

THE DEPOT'S HALF-CYLINDRICAL TRAIN SHED WAS MODELED ON LONDON'S ST. PANCRAS AND RIVALED NEW YORK'S CRYSTAL PALACE.

The stinging verdict on Grand Central Depot as the abject gateway to New York would be echoed nearly a century later by Vincent Scully, the Yale architecture professor, about the pathetic successor to New York's imposing Pennsylvania Station. "Nothing pertaining to New York City except its government has been so discreditable to it as its principal railroad station," the *Times* wrote. "The waiting rooms constituted an ordeal hardly second to that of the tunnel itself, a waiting in rooms crowded to the limit, heated to more than the temperature of the outer air and not ventilated at all...It was an ordeal so dreadful that the experienced shirked it at almost any risk." The depot was denounced as cramped, dark, repelling, ugly, and disgraceful, and, in the most unkind cut, as a station "which would be considered adequate in Sandusky, Ohio" (which was home to fewer than 20,000 people that year, compared to New York's population, which O. Henry would immortalize a few years later as "The Four Million").

IN 1898, the railroad settled on a quick fix. The three-story Second Empire structure was transformed into a six-story neo-Renaissance concoction covered in stucco and artificial stone. It was designed by Bradford Lee Gilbert, who became best known for designing the Tower Building, the first steel-framed curtain-wall structure, at 50 Broadway, which has also been called the city's first true skyscraper.

Gilbert installed a convocation of mammoth nine-foot-high cast-iron eagles (two of which, following a nine-decade absence, now adorn the terminal again). In 1900, the depot, by now commonly known as Grand Central Station, was enlarged again, this time by the architect Samuel Huckel Jr. The inconvenient separate waiting rooms for the three lines were merged into one that measured 100 by 200 feet. The

CHAUNCEY M. DEPEW (LEFT)
SURVIVES AS THE NAME OF A
PRIVATE STREET. THE FORMER
CENTRAL PRESIDENT CONFERS
WITH A SUCCESSOR, PATRICK
CROWLEY.

renovated head house on 42nd Street featured a 50-foot-wide concourse between Vanderbilt Avenue and Depew Place (named for the New York Central's president and simultaneously a U.S. senator) connecting the waiting rooms (fitted with rocking chairs and fireplaces) and the train platforms, and a rotunda flanked by more ticket windows and other marble-clad amenities, including a women's waiting room and a "retiring room." A separate "emigrants' waiting room" was installed in the basement, "thus relieving the main waiting room and rotunda of this class of passengers," the railroad's chief engineer boasted. The terminal passed its first test in the crush of summer vacationers in 1901.

"Anybody could before that have admired the spaciousness and the new architectural impressiveness of the new arrangement," the *Times* observed, "but nobody could have said with authority whether it was or was not adequate to its purpose." The new Grand Central Station was hailed again as "the largest, it is believed, in existence," with a waiting room 1,000 square feet bigger than Boston's South Union Station. Even so, by the turn of the century, Grand Central was handling 500 trains a day—three times the traffic of the 1870s. The station's shortcomings inconvenienced only passengers. The divide created by the tracks still vexed a broader constituency.

And as promising as the improvements seemed, the erstwhile *Times* editorialist, obviously writing from personal experience (someone once defined news as something that happens to an editor or, worse yet, to an editor's spouse), presciently cautioned that

> the work will not be complete until something is done to make traveling through the long Park Avenue tunnel less to be dreaded. In hot summer weather the thought of going through that hole in the ground hangs like a disheartening sword of Damocles over the mind of the poor commuter all day long and burdens his dreams at night. It is not pleasant in winter. But if the locomotive engines between 42nd Street and Mott Haven were driven by electric power and the interior of the tunnel were brightened by paint or kalsomine and illuminated by electricity, the traveler would have nothing more to complain of. The property owners along Park Avenue would be glad, too.

Sinking the tracks and covering them had mollified those property owners. The tunnel helped reduce traffic fatalities and congestion at street level. But it created havoc for riders trapped in the heat and fumes below. The *Times* railed against "the tortures daily inflicted upon large numbers of persons within the peace of the State of New York by taking them through four miles of the mephitic atmosphere of the tunnel from Grand Central Station to the Harlem River." While the tunnel improved the flow of traffic on the surface, it was compounded below, where steam, smoke, and cinders conspired to obscure the vision of locomotive engineers. Which is exactly what happened on Wednesday, January 8, 1902, to terrifying effect.

ENGINEER JOHN WISKER, "IMPATIENT OF DELAY,"
WAS BLAMED FOR THE 1902 FATAL COLLISION
THAT LED TO THE MODERN TERMINAL.

THE ENGINEER

HAD THERE BEEN ANY DOUBTS about the depot's adequacy even after the renovations, two events dispelled them as the new century began. The fatal crash in the Grand Central yards prompted demands that the engineer and even the New York Central's management be prosecuted for manslaughter and suggestions that the railroad be barred from Manhattan altogether and required to build a new terminus at its Mott Haven yards in the South Bronx instead. A month earlier, another event proved just as decisive: the Pennsylvania Railroad, the New York Central's chief competitor to points west, announced that it would challenge the Central's Manhattan monopoly by tunneling under the Hudson River from New Jersey and building a sumptuous station on the West Side.

As the New York Central & Hudson River Railroad's chief engineer since 1899, William J. Wilgus had supervised the recent costly renovation of Grand Central. Born in Buffalo in 1865, Wilgus

ROTARY CONVERTERS TRANSFORMED ALTERNATING INTO DIRECT CURRENT. JIM FRAWLEY, ENGINEER OF POWER, SUPERVISED IN NEW YORK'S DEEPEST BASEMENT.

studied for two years under a local civil engineer and later took a Cornell correspondence course in drafting. His creativity and expertise propelled him through the ranks of various railroads and finally to the New York Central. The fatal 1902 crash persuaded him that

ENGINEER WISKER, BROKEN, DAZED, BEARS BRUNT OF TUNNEL DISASTER.

Investigation Develops Important Facts Bearing on Question of Responsibility—Engineer Was Making His Third Trip on This Run—Clearly Violated Speed Rules and Failed to Heed Signals.

FIRST TRIP WITH FIREMAN FYLER.

District-Attorney Now Sure Accident Could Have Been Avoided—Secret Examination of Witnesses, Preparing for Inquest—Trial List Now 19—New Rochelle's Sorrow—Mass Meetings Called—Great Crop of Damage Suits Likely—Tunnel Test To-Day—Railroad Officials Silent.

JOHN M. WISKER, ACCUSED OF CAUSING THE 1902 CRASH.

the renovations, as impressive as they were, were insufficient to stem the rising tide of public outrage over the preposterous notion of running a chaotic railroad yard in what a few decades earlier had been a practically bucolic landscape but by now was becoming the very heart of the nation's largest city.

Already, prompted by the 1902 crash, the state legislature had extended the ban on steam-powered locomotives from 42nd Street all the way to the Harlem River, effective 1908 (imposing a $500-a-day fine unless the mayor "shall certify to the necessity for the use of steam locomotives arising from the temporary failure of other motive power"). Railroad officials briefly considered diverting commuter traffic to a "Grand Union Station" on the Harlem River in the Bronx, which would be accessible by subways and elevated trains. But Wilgus conceived another alternative.

"Suddenly, there came a flash of light," he recalled decades later. "It was the most daring idea that ever occurred to me." In a succinct three-page letter to W.H. Newman, the railroad's president, dated December 22, 1902, less than a year after the crash, the 37-year-old self-taught chief engineer recommended an audacious and extravagant remedy: raze the new Grand Central Station that had just been renovated and replace the egregious steam locomotives with electric trains, which had advanced technologically since they were first introduced on a main line by the Baltimore & Ohio in 1895 (four years later Wilgus himself had proposed an experimental trial on the Central; his plan was adopted but not implemented).

The technological advantages were clear-cut. Electricity required less maintenance. Unlike steam or, later, diesel locomotives, electric trains did not need the fuel or machinery to generate power on board. Electricity empowered trains to accelerate more quickly, a decided amenity for short-haul commuter service. Another advantage, an obvious one, in retrospect, provided the rationale that made Wilgus's suggestion so revolutionary and, in the end, so inevitable. Electric motors produced fewer noxious fumes and no obfuscating smoke or steam. That would help quell the public outcry and quiet the increasing vocal critics who re-

WILLIAM J. WILGUS, THE CENTRAL'S CHIEF ENGINEER.

garded the trains as a necessary evil, one that was needlessly dangerous and inconvenient, though. Moreover, as Wilgus explained, electricity "dispenses with the need of old-style train sheds," because it made subterranean tracks feasible.

Absent the smothering smoke, soot, and cinders, the depot could be expanded on the same footprint by delivering trains to platforms on *two* levels, the lower for suburban commuters and the upper for long-distance trains. For the first time, the entire rail yard all the way to 56th Street, to where the maze of rails that delivered passengers to the platforms coalesced into four main-line tracks, could be decked over. The "veritable 'Chinese Wall'" that bisected the city for 14 blocks could be eliminated. The air above the yards could be magically transformed into valuable real estate in the heart of Manhattan.

For starters, Wilgus envisioned a 12-story, 2.3-million-square-foot building above the terminal that could generate rents totaling $2.3 million annually. Those advantages not only benefited "humanity in general," as the Commodore would have put it, an ingratiating by-product, but also fulfilled the railroad's primary mission that "we first see that we are benefiting ourselves." Wilgus's overarching remedy to the "Park Avenue problem," he unabashedly proclaimed, "marked the opening of a remarkable opportunity for the accomplishment of a public good with considerations of private gain in behalf of the corporation involved."

"History," James Marston Fitch and Diana S. Waite wrote, "was to prove this an epochal scheme."

IF WILGUS DID NOT INVENT the notion of air rights and rivet the principle into real estate law, he surely applied it on a larger scale than anyone had ever imagined. "Thus from the air would be taken wealth with which to finance obligatory vast changes otherwise nonproductive," he said. And by capitalizing on those rights, rights to build towering hotels and office buildings and private clubs that just happened to have trains coursing through their subbasements, the railroad would reap enough revenue to recoup the costs of electrification. The terminal, he explained later, "could be transformed from a nonproductive agency of transportation to a self-contained producer of revenue—a gold mine so to speak."

In 1902, with the sprawling yards still flanked by pastures for an occasional cow or goat and by cheap tenements proliferating farther east, it would take a stubborn visionary to recognize that this blighted swath of Midtown could be converted into an iconic 140-foot-wide canyon bordered by brick, steel, and glass skyscrapers (and, in name, at least, join the stretches in Murray Hill, below 42nd Street, which had earlier been christened Park Avenue).

Wilgus envisioned other innovations: constructing an elevated roadway that would gird the terminal and no longer render it a roadblock in the middle of Park Avenue; reserving the upper level of the terminal for long-distance trains and the lower for the growing number of commuters; building loops on both levels, which would allow trains to turn around instead of wasting time backing out; and installing ramps that would obviate the struggle up and down stairs for passengers with baggage.

Years later, Wilgus would recall that his letter to President Newman got mixed reviews. "At first, he properly questioned the practicability of the scheme," the engineer recalled.

He felt that the office space would be a place only "for birds to roost"; that the proposed hotel on the vacant square bounded by Madison Avenue, 43rd and 44th Streets and Vanderbilt Avenue, would be as unpopular as railroad hotels in Europe; that hansom cab-men could not be driven to use Madison Avenue because of their addiction to the sights of Fifth Avenue;

and that underground horse cab-stands would be repulsive because of odors. My counter-arguments were that the rapidly increasing demand for office space in the vicinity would surely bring us tenants; that the use of electricity would obviate the features that made the European railroad hotels unpopular; that growing congestion would cause the cab-man to gladly avail himself of the new thoroughfares; and that the coming of the motor-car, then in its infancy, instead of the horse-drawn vehicle would obviate objectionable odors. It was also necessary to urge counter-arguments against the allegations of those who were not friendly to ramps in place of stairways and who opposed what they termed the "grocery store" idea of lending the station to revenue producing purposes.

Wilgus was asking the railroad's directors to accept a great deal on faith. His projected $35 million price tag for all the improvements, including a conservative estimate for electrification, nearly equaled half the railroad's revenue for a full year. Moreover, the railroad made most of its money hauling freight, not people. Why invest so much in a project that benefited only passengers? But the chief engineer was persuasive. He delivered his proposal on December 22, 1902. By January 10, the Central's board of directors had embraced the project and promoted him. Six months later, on June 30, 1903, the board—whose directors included the Commodore's grandsons, Cornelius II and William K. Vanderbilt, William Rockefeller, and J.P. Morgan—in a daring validation of the chief engineer's vision, formally empowered Wilgus to proceed with his bold agenda for a regal terminal that would be a gateway to the continent.

Once he was given the go-ahead, Wilgus still faced two daunting challenges: how to electrify the railroad (and how much of it to electrify); and how to build a new terminal and raze the old one without disrupting passenger traffic. He approached both quandaries with characteristic bravado. Rather than adhere narrowly to the mandate imposed by the state—to ban steam locomotives in Manhattan—Wilgus proposed to electrify the railroad the full 23 miles to White Plains on the Harlem line and all 33 miles to Croton on the Hudson line.

He gave two compelling reasons. One was that commuters accounted for a growing proportion of the railroad's passenger traffic and they would be reluctant to waste time transferring in the Bronx to steam locomotives. Moreover, as noted, electric motors allowed trains to accelerate more quickly than steam locomotives, a big advantage for commuter railroads that hopscotched between suburban stations. Theoretically, what Wilgus was proposing seemed sensible, and the decision, as he later described it, was "inescapable." But translating his hypotheses about the technological and commercial advantages of electricity into dependable motive power was something else altogether.

"No existing railroad electrification anywhere in the world," Kurt C. Schlichting wrote in his biography of Wilgus, "approached the scale of the Central's project or provided a model to duplicate."

AN ELECTRIC TRACTION ENGINE had made its experimental debut on the Ninth Avenue El in New York as early as 1885, but the sparks it generated and its slow speed doomed it for the time being. Using electricity to power trains over long distances was relatively untested.

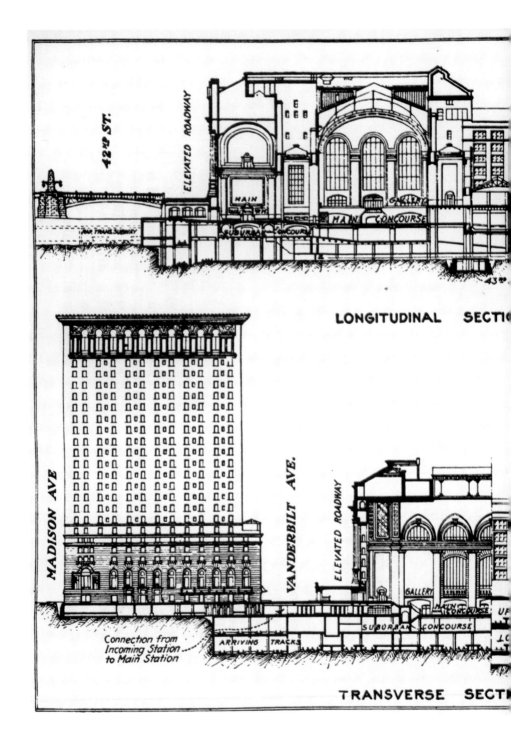

LONGITUDINAL SECTI

TRANSVERSE SECTI

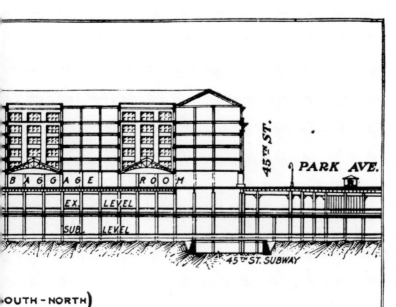

BAGGAGE ROOM

EX. LEVEL

SUB. LEVEL

45 TH ST.

PARK AVE.

45 TH ST. SUBWAY

OUTH - NORTH)

THE SHOTGUN MARRIAGE OF ARCHITECTURAL FIRMS YIELDED A GRAND DESIGN GREATER THAN THE SUM OF THEIR SEPARATE BLUEPRINTS.

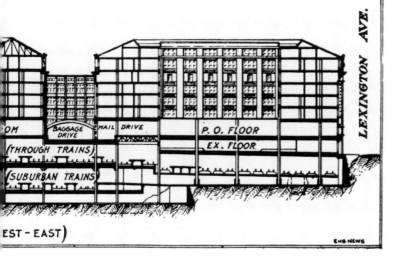

OM

(THROUGH TRAINS)

(SUBURBAN TRAINS)

BAGGAGE DRIVE

MAIL DRIVE

P. O. FLOOR

EX. FLOOR

LEXINGTON AVE.

EST - EAST)

ENG. NEWS

In 1897, Frank J. Sprague, an acolyte of Thomas Edison's, adapted an innovative device he had invented for elevators to railroad cars, allowing them to operate in tandem, each with its own electric motor.

Sprague approached the Central's directors with his vision, but the imperatives of electrification were not yet apparent. Still unresolved, too, was how best to generate electricity—through direct current, which was produced at a particular voltage and delivered to the user at the same energy but loses power over long distances; or alternating current, in which the charge periodically shifts direction and the high voltage is reduced before delivery. Given the commercial stakes, as more and more big-city and commuter railroads bowed to government pressure and began to electrify, Wilgus's dilemma sparked a reprise of the scientific debate a decade earlier over which version of current was most serviceable to execute felons condemned to death.

In 1890, Edison, an advocate of direct current, surreptitiously powered New York's first electric chair with George Westinghouse's alternating current, hoping to demonstrate that alternating current was generally so lethal that it should be reserved only for inflicting capital punishment. Edison proved his point: William Kemmler, a convicted killer, was executed (more or less successfully). The debate didn't end there, though. Westinghouse and Sprague angrily waged a war of words in the pages of the *Railroad Gazette.*

Eventually, Edison and Sprague carried the day. The New York Central, following the lead of the Baltimore & Ohio, opted for direct current traveling through a third rail that delivered power to each railroad car through a spring-loaded "shoe" extending from the motor. (Unlike the New York City subway system and the Long Island Rail Road, Metro-North trains now draw power from the *underside* of the third rail, which allows for insulation above to prevent electrocution and icing.)

In 1906, well in advance of the state-imposed deadline for electrification, the Central began operating electric cars from Grand Central. (The New Haven followed suit a year later, using direct current from the Central's third rail but switching to alternating current delivered from overhead lines on its own tracks in Connecticut, as it does today.)

• • •

A HUNDRED SWITCHMEN, INCLUDING TIM COUGHLIN, MANAGED THE METRO-NORTH LINE. NOW A DOZEN RAIL TRAFFIC CONTROLLERS DO THE JOB.

ON JUNE 19, 1903, the city granted subsurface rights to the New York Central between Lexington and Madison Avenues and East 42nd and 47th Streets for $25,000 annually in perpetuity. Work in earnest began on August 17, 1903. Unlike the depot built three decades earlier, the new Grand Central would actually define "Midtown." The center of the city had been inexorably advancing from downtown, mirroring the railroad's own brand of manifest destiny. That advance had been nominally cemented on the West Side with the advent of the 25-story Times Tower at 42nd Street and Broadway, then the second-tallest building in the city, which was still under construction. On December 31, 1903, 200,000 spectators would accept the *Times'* invitation to celebrate the new building and the New Year with a fireworks display from the roof at midnight (the ball drop down a flagpole on the roof would begin five years later).

The new Grand Central Terminal—and it would be a terminal, because New York Central horsecars would no longer ferry commuters from its train platforms to destinations downtown—would draw nearly as many people in a single day as Times Square did on New Year's Eve. Grand Central was designed to accommodate even more, maybe even as many as 100 million a year by the beginning of the 21st century, when the terminal would celebrate its centennial.

Even before the first spadeful of earth was turned, before the first boulder of Manhattan schist was blasted, a veritable forest of exclamation points began sprouting with what was dubbed the city's largest individual demolition contract ever. On 17 acres purchased by the railroad, 120 houses, three churches, two hospitals, and an orphan asylum would have to be obliterated, as would stables, warehouses, and other ancillary structures.

The *Times* admitted that "in describing it, the superlative degree must be kept in constant use." It would be the biggest, it would contain the most trackage, and, on top of that, it would be self-supporting.

Once the method of motive power was agreed upon, Wilgus's second challenge was how to build a terminal without inconveniencing the passengers on the railroad's hundreds of daily long-haul and commuter trains. To meet the challenge, the railroad temporarily relocated some of the station's functions to the nearby Grand Central Palace Hotel. Again Wilgus devised an ingenious construction strategy. The arduous process of demolishing existing structures, excavating rock and dirt 90 feet deep for the bilevel platforms and utilities, razing the mammoth train shed, and building the new terminal would proceed in longitudinal "bites," as he called them—troughs bored through the middle of Manhattan, one section at a time and proceeding from east to west. Construction would take fully 10 years, and by the time it was barely halfway finished, Wilgus would be gone and his guesstimate of the cost of the project would have doubled to about $2 billion in today's dollars.

JOHN WISKER, the man whose train accident in the Park Avenue Tunnel triggered the construction of Grand Central Terminal, did not live to see it completed. While no railroad officials were prosecuted, the accident sparked 30 lawsuits against the Central. One resulted in a record $60,000 jury verdict for the victim's widow (about $1.5 million in current dollars). Another verdict won by a Bronx stenographer, $1,250 for personal injuries, was tossed out by a judge who concluded that the "victim" quite possibly had not been a passenger on either train.

At Wisker's manslaughter trial, he was represented by Frank Moss (a dogged investigator who once provoked Richard Croker, the Tammany boss, to admit, "I am working for my pocket all the time, just like you, Mr. Moss"). On April 24, 1903, less than three months before ground was broken for the new Grand Central, the Manhattan jury delivered its verdict after only two hours of deliberations.

Wisker stood pale and trembling, according to contemporary accounts, "a shadow of the sturdy fellow who was arrested the day of the fatal collision." He collapsed into his seat and cried when the foreman pronounced him not guilty. Wisker was, apparently, accident-prone, though. Seven years later, operating a hoist for a coal company on the West Side, he fell into the Hudson River and drowned.

AS CONSTRUCTION ON THE TERMINAL progressed, the New York Central was keeping one very wary eye on what was happening just across town. Its archrival, the Pennsylvania Railroad, was challenging the Central's monopoly by finally providing direct service to Manhattan. The Central and the Pennsy were like Coke and Pepsi, perennial rivals for routes, passengers, and market share. The Pennsylvania was older (by name, at least) and bigger (by cargo tons carried), but the Central more than matched it in ego and glitz, as befitted their two home states. The Pennsylvania's keystone logo evoked the keystone state. The Central's was a distinctive, but not evocative oval. New York was in the name. Anything else was superfluous,

In the 19th century, the Pennsylvania was an also-ran in New York City. Without a Midtown station, passengers had to be ferried between Exchange Place in Jersey City and Manhattan by boat. Building a bridge across the river would have required a joint project with other Jersey railroads, but none was game. Electrification, though, would make a Hudson River tunnel feasible. On December 12, 1901, a little less than a month before the Park Avenue Tunnel crash, Alexander Cassatt, the Pennsylvania's president, announced that the railroad would bore under the river and run trains to a grand

PENN STATION CHALLENGED THE NEW YORK CENTRAL'S MANHATTAN MONOPOLY.

station of its own to be built on two square blocks bounded by 31st and 33rd Streets and Seventh and Eighth Avenues.

Ground was broken on May 1, 1904, for McKim, Mead & White's colossal gateway. The breathtaking pink-granite-colonnaded station—a "great Doric temple to transportation," the historian Jill Jonnes called it—was modeled on the public baths built in Rome 1,700 years earlier by Emperor Caracalla. It spanned seven acres and sat astride the tracks that continued under the East River to connect with the Long Island Rail Road and the Pennsylvania's Sunnyside Yards in Queens. The station would open in 1910 and, with the expense of the two sets of tunnels, cost $114 million, or about $2.7 billion in today's dollars. And if, by some measures, it was a bigger station than the proposed Grand Central, the New York Central's publicity department wasted no time in pronouncing its new depot the biggest *terminal* in the world. Despite its stark grandeur of girders and glass, Penn Station would never become the catalyst for planned development that Grand Central did.

• • •

WILLIAM WILGUS WAS AN ENGINEER, not an architect, but he hoped to impose his own aesthetic on the new terminal. He knew what he didn't like about the old depot: its "unattractive architectural design" and its "unfortunate exterior color treatment," as well as the "great blunder" of dividing the city for 14 blocks and by obstructing Fourth Avenue. Once he persuaded the Vanderbilts and the Central's other directors to accept his bold vision, they were intent on not repeating earlier mistakes, which had cost not only money, but goodwill as well.

In 1903, the Central invited the nation's leading architects to submit designs for the new terminal. Samuel Huckel Jr. went for

CONSTRUCTION OF THE TERMINAL TOOK 10 YEARS. MORE THAN 150,000 PEOPLE SHOWED UP FOR THE OFFICIAL OPENING ON FEBRUARY 2, 1913.

baroque, a turreted confection with Park Avenue slicing through it. McKim, Mead & White proposed a 60-story skyscraper—the world's tallest—atop the terminal (a modified version was later incorporated into the firm's design for the 26-story Municipal Building, completed in 1916), itself topped by a dramatic 300-foot jet of steam illuminated in red as a beacon for ships and an advertisement (if, even then, an anachronistic one) for the railroad.

Reed & Stem, a St. Paul firm (the name evoked landscape architects), won the competition. (Its successor, WASA/Studio A, still operates in New York City.) The firm began with two big advantages. It had designed other stations for the New York Central. Moreover, like the Central itself, Reed & Stem could count on connections: Allen H. Stem was Wilgus's brother-in-law. Yet in the highly charged world of real estate development in New York, another firm's connections trumped Reed & Stem's. After the selection was announced, Warren & Wetmore, who were architects of the New York Yacht Club and who boasted society connections, submitted an alternative design. It didn't hurt that Whitney Warren was William Vanderbilt's cousin.

The Central's chairman officiated at a shotgun marriage of the two firms, pronouncing them the Associated Architects of Grand Central Terminal. The partnership would be fraught with dissension, design changes, and acrimony and would climax two decades later in a spectacular lawsuit and an appropriately monumental settlement. In 1921, a referee found that Warren's accounting was "improper and erroneous" and awarded Stem, the surviving partner, the fantastic sum of $223,891.16—in effect validating Warren's maxim that "the standard of success in this country is the making of money, therefore, the architect should make money and be considered successful."

To Wilgus's dismay, the Warren & Wetmore version eliminated the revenue-generating office and hotel tower atop the terminal. It also scrapped the vehicular viaducts that would remedy the obstruction of Fourth Avenue created by the depot. (Some aspects of the original Reed & Stem design would later be restored.) But by any measure, the new terminal would justify its name. It would be grand.

Once the design was agreed upon, building Grand Central was a gargantuan undertaking. Wheezing steam shovels excavated nearly 3.2 million cubic yards of earth and rock to an average depth of 45 feet to accommodate the subterranean train yards, bilevel platforms, and utilities—some as deep as 10 stories. The daily detritus, coupled with debris from the demolition of the old station, amounted to 1,000 cubic yards and filled nearly 300 railway dump cars. The lower tracks were 40 feet below street level and sprouted "a submerged forest" of steel girders. Construction required 118,597 tons of steel to create the superstructure and 33 miles of track. At peak construction periods, 10,000 workers were assigned to the site and work progressed around the clock. Beneath the 770-foot-wide valley he created in Midtown Manhattan, Wilgus dug a six-foot-diameter drainage sewer about 65 feet deep that ran a half mile to the East River.

THE CENTRAL NOT ONLY MET the state's deadline to electrify the line in Manhattan, but did so two years early. The route was electrified for 17 miles, north to Wakefield and Kingsbridge in the Bronx. The first electric locomotive barreled through the Park Avenue Tunnel from High Bridge on September 30, 1906. Thirty-five 2,200-horsepower electric locomotives could accelerate to 40 mph; multiple-unit suburban trains could hit 52 mph. The Vanderbilts and the New York

THE COMPLETED TERMINAL WAS ORIGINALLY A SOLITARY PRESENCE ON EAST 42ND STREET, BUT NOT FOR LONG. DEVELOPMENT SPREAD EAST.

Central were immensely proud of their all-electric terminal and their mostly electric railroad. The maze of tracks and trains was commanded from a four-story switch-and-signal tower below 50th Street. On one floor was a machine with 400 levers, the largest ever constructed, to sort out the suburban trains. On the floor above, another machine with 362 levers controlled the express tracks. A worker was assigned to each battery of 40 levers, and tiny bulbs on a facsimile of the train yard would automatically be extinguished as a train passed a switch and illuminated again when it reached the next switch.

On June 5, 1910, the Owl, as the midnight train was known, left Grand Central Station for Boston. It was the last to depart from the old depot, which handled an impressive 100 trains a day when it opened but was incapable of servicing the hundreds of trains that arrived and departed daily four decades later. Demolition began immediately. The old station and yards spanned a little more than 23 acres. The new one covered more than twice that area. The station had a capacity of 366 railway cars. The new terminal could accommodate 1,053. The old depot handled 9,000 suitcases and trunks a day. The new one could handle 16,000 pieces of luggage.

WHILE PENNSYLVANIA STATION opened earlier and to rave reviews, it could not compare to Grand Central in magnitude. Penn Station and its yards spanned 28 acres. Grand Central covered 70. Penn Station had 16 miles of rails that converged into 21 tracks serving 11 platforms. The comparable figures for Grand Central originally were 32 miles, 46 tracks, and 30 platforms. Grand Central required twice as much masonry and nearly twice the steel that Penn Station did. Fifteen hundred columns were installed to support the street-level deck and the buildings that would rise on it. Another $800,000 was spent on steel reinforcement, not needed for the terminal itself, but to support a skyscraper that eventually might rise above it. The terminal alone cost $43 million to build, the equivalent of about $1 billion today, and the entire project set the Central back about $80 million.

Passengers' comfort was of paramount concern. When it was finally completed, Grand Central could boast a separate women's waiting room with oak floors and wainscoting and maids at the ready; a ladies' shoe-polishing room "out of sight of the rubbernecks" and staffed by "colored girls in neat blue liveries"; a telephone room for making calls; a salon gussied up with walls and ceilings of Carrara glass, "where none but her own sex will see while she has her hair dressed"; a dressing room attended by a maid (at 25 cents); and a private barber shop for men, which could be rented for $1 an hour, and a public version where "the customer may elect to be shaved in anyone of 30 languages."

No amenity was spared. "Timid travelers may ask questions with no fear of being rebuffed by hurrying trainmen, or imposed upon by hotel runners, chauffeurs, or others in blue uniforms," a promotional brochure boasted. Instead, "walking encyclopedias" in gray frock coats and white caps were available. Passengers would be protected from unwanted contact as well as glances. "Special accommodations are to be provided for immigrants and gangs of laborers," the *Times* reported. "They can be brought into the station and enter a separate room without meeting other travelers." Grand Central, the brochure proclaimed, is "a place where one delights to loiter, admiring its beauty and symmetrical lines—a poem in stone."

JUST HOW MUCH LOITERING could have been done on opening day is arguable. Railroad officials estimated that by 4 p.m. on Sunday, February 2, 1913, more than 150,000 people had visited the terminal since the doors were thrown open at midnight. The first train to leave was the Boston Express No. 2, at 12:01 a.m. The first to arrive was a local on the Harlem line. F.M. Lahm of Yonkers bought the first ticket.

Grand Central was billed as the first great "stairless" station, one in which the flow of passengers was sped by gently sloping ramps that were tested out at various grades and ultimately designed to accommodate everyone from "the old, infirm traveler, to the little tot toddling along at his mother's side, to the man laden down with baggage which he declines to relinquish to any one of the most cordial atten-

THE OYSTER BAR, HERE AROUND 1913, IS THE TERMINAL'S OLDEST TENANT.
IT SELLS SOME 5 MILLION BIVALVES ANNUALLY AND RETAINS ITS ELEGANCE.

dants, to the women trailing a long and preposterous train." (*Ramp*—
the very word was obscure, prompting *Munsey's* magazine to explain
to readers that Julius Caesar had built a long sloping earthworks to the
ramparts when he laid siege to a city.) The flow would now empty from
32 Upper Level and 17 Lower Level platforms (fed from as many as
66 and 57 tracks, respectively) into a Main Concourse that was 275 feet
long, 120 feet wide, and 125 feet high (spreading nearly 38,000 square
feet) and flanked by 90-foot-high transparent walls that were punctuated by glass walkways connecting the terminal's corner offices.

Its concave ceiling created a view of the heavens from Aquarius to Cancer in an October sky, 2,500 stars—59 of them illuminated and intersected by two broad golden bands representing the ecliptic and the equator. For several months, painters debated how to squeeze the heavens onto a cylindrical ceiling because the artist Paul Helleu's version seemed more fitting for a dome and experimented to find just the proper shade of blue. (Helleu was no stranger to the Vanderbilts. Proceeds from his wildly popular 1901 sketch of Consuelo Vanderbilt, the American-born duchess of Marlborough and William K.'s daughter, had helped support his extravagant Belle Epoque lifestyle.)

The ceiling designs were developed by J. Monroe Hewlett and executed largely by Charles Basing and his associates. As many as 50 painters under Basing's direction worked simultaneously to ensure that there was no differentiation in color tone. Lunette windows were ornamented with plaster reliefs of winged locomotive wheels, branches of foliage symbolizing transportation, and clouds and a caduceus (the short staff usually entwined with serpents and surrounded by wings and typically carried by heralds).

The finishing touches would not be complete for another year (the viaduct would not be opened until 1919 and the innovative Lower Level loop, which allowed arriving trains to depart more quickly, would not become operational until 1927). Among the last was the gigantic sculpture designed by a Frenchman, Jules Félix Coutan, above the central portal on 42nd Street. Coutan, who also designed the *France of the Renaissance* sculpture for the extravagant Alexander III bridge in Paris, created a one-fourth-size plaster model in his studio from which John Donnelly, a native of Ireland, carved the final 1,500-ton version from Indiana limestone at the William Bradley & Son yards in Long Island City, Queens. (Donnelly also worked on River-side Church and the U.S. Courthouse in Manhattan and the Supreme Court Building in Washington.)

The railroad described *Transportation*, the 60-foot-wide, 50-foot-tall sculpture, considered at the time the world's largest sculptured group, as representing "Progress, Mental and Physical Force," with Hercules embodying physical strength, the reclining Minerva wisdom and the arts, and Mercury, wearing a winged helmet and protected by a vigilant American eagle, science and commerce as the messenger of the gods. (Some second-guessers say Hercules is really Vulcan, the blacksmith, holding a hammer and emblematic of the iron horse. Also, while Whitney Warren interpreted the trio as mental and *moral* energy supporting the glory of commerce, a Metro-North guidebook demythologized the impact and attributed it to mental and *mortal* energy.)

"The three were meant to symbolize the grandeur of the Vanderbilts' New York Central Railroad, but surely these are the tutelary deities of all Manhattan, the city of the unquenchable entrepreneurial flame," the architectural historian Francis Morrone wrote. "As the historian Paul Johnson reminds us…so-called robber barons such as the Vanderbilts, ruthless though they undoubtedly were, not only left magnificent monuments in their wake but also created the vast national enterprises into which the teeming multitudes of immigrants were absorbed and uplifted by the engine of prosperity. To deny that this is what New York, in its essence, is about is to posit a fantasy city."

Contemplating a plaster model of the sculpture in his office, Warren later wrote that while the ancients entered cities through triumphal gates that punctuated mighty fortifications, in New York and other

THE FAÇADE WAS HAILED FOR THE LARGEST SCULPTURAL GROUPING IN THE WORLD AND THE BIGGEST DISPLAY OF TIFFANY GLASS.

cities the gateway is more likely to be "a tunnel which discharges the human flow in the very center of the town. Such is the Grand Central Terminal and the motive of its façade is an attempt to offer a tribute to the glory of commerce as exemplified by that institution."

Mike Wallace, the coauthor of *Gotham: A History of New York City to 1898*, described the terminal's construction as emblematic of the city's "intense quest for connectivity in the two decades between the consolidation of Greater New York and the First World War. The new Grand Central was imbued with the culture of connectivity. Not only did its expansion and electrification aim to boost the volume and velocity of passenger traffic, but it was a circulatory marvel."

When Grand Central was finally finished, the only thing lacking was adjectives. The *Times* produced a special section of the newspaper and hailed the terminal as "a monument, a civic center, or, if one will, a city. Without exception, it is not only the greatest station in the United States, but the greatest station, of any type, in the world."

A full century later, the journalist and novelist Tom Wolfe would write: "Every big city had a railroad station with grand—to the point of glorious—classical architecture—dazzled and intimidated, the great architects of Greece and Rome would have averted their eyes—featuring every sort of dome, soaring ceiling, king-sized column, royal cornice, lordly echo—thanks to the immense volume of the spaces—and the miles of marble, marble, marble—but the grandest, most glorious of all, by far, was Grand Central Station."

THE PARK AVENUE VIADUCT,
WHICH GIRDLED THE TERMINAL,
WAS COMPLETED TWO DECADES AFTER
IT WAS ORIGINALLY PROPOSED.

TERMINAL CITY

L OOKING NORTH OVER THE OLD SMOKY YARDS," William
Wilgus recalled years later, "I idly sketched one day in 1902
an annex of office buildings." What he envisioned would become Terminal City, or the Grand Central Zone. Whatever the name,
it was destined to be transformed within a decade into some of the
most valuable real estate in the world and an unlikely showcase for
the flourishing City Beautiful Movement that had captured the public's imagination through the model "White City" a decade earlier at
the World's Columbian Exposition in Chicago.

Among the movement's protagonists was the architect Daniel
Burnham, who had designed the beloved Flatiron Building off Madison Square in Manhattan and was invited to submit plans in the
competition to design Grand Central Terminal. Burnham's encom-
passing credo was "make no little plans. They have no magic to stir
men's blood and probably will not themselves be realized." (Whatever

their size in this case, no record of Burnham's plan survives.) Wilgus got the message. His captivating vision was consistent with the goals of a New York City Improvement Commission, which sought in 1904 and again in 1907 to devise a coherent and homogenous urban master plan, just as the city commissioners had sought to do a century before when they imposed the street grid.

But, as Robert A.M. Stern, Gregory Gilmartin, and John Massengale observed in *New York 1900*, the effort to establish a New York civic identity akin to that of Paris or Vienna failed because it materialized both too early and too late: "Too late, because by 1907 the great urban set pieces were in place or well under way: the public library, Grand Central and Pennsylvania stations, and the development of an 'acropolis of learning' on Morningside Heights. Too early, because the grand scale of the parks, parkways and boulevards would not seem urgently needed until the automobile became an everyday thing 30 years later."

Wilgus envisioned a civic center, opera house, hotels, office buildings lining a grand boulevard—a planned, harmonious city to replace the obstructive terminal and the chasm occupied by tracks and trains that were the logical extensions of an architecturally illogical city. "The changes which are to come about within a comparatively short time will entirely alter the complexion of the city," Mayor Seth Low said in 1903. His forecast barely scratched the surface. The *Times* proclaimed the new depot "more than a gateway, more than a terminal. The terminal proper, the great head house, and its accompanying buildings, are simply the heart and the cause of a group of buildings that has best been described as 'terminal city.'"

• • •

WHEN NEW YORK CITY released its real estate valuations in October 1913, Grand Central was already the highest-valued property, at $17.7 million (Pennsylvania Station was second, at $16.4 million, but the disparity would widen as the real estate around the terminal became even more desirable). By 1914, the assessed valuation of properties bounded by 41st and 57th Streets and Lexington and Madison Avenues had more than doubled, from $55 million, when construction on Grand Central began, to $117 million. A decade later, it would more than double again. By 1946, a peak year for long-haul passenger train traffic, the New York Central had a stake in 21 buildings, whose assessed value was more than $121 million.

What's so striking about Grand Central's impact on real estate development is that Penn Station had so much less. "While Grand Central was intricately interwoven into the city around it, Penn Station stood apart," the urban historian James Sanders has written. Penn Station spawned a hotel or two—the Pennsylvania, then the world's largest, across Seventh Avenue, and the New Yorker on Eighth Avenue and West 34th Street. But it never generated the critical mass and concomitant magnetism that would lure corporate headquarters from downtown to Park Avenue and beyond. Grand Central made Midtown.

"A combination of factors pushed the Grand Central area ahead: for one thing, it had a head start, since there had been a train station on the site since 1871, and both the first two Grand Centrals attracted high-end hotels, etc.," said Tony Hiss, the author of *In Motion: The Experience of Travel.*

For another, Wilgus's sinking and covering of the rail yard around Grand Central and his invention of air rights for this property led to a building boom in the Roaring '20s that far outstripped any development around Penn Station. So it was already a desirable neighborhood when it came to post-WWII office building redevelopment.

Another contributing factor may have been that, although it was home to the Long Island Rail Road, until the post–World War II consolidation and bankruptcies of New Jersey railroads, Penn Station didn't have a monopoly on commuters coming in from the west, many of whom went to Hoboken or Jersey City and got to the city on ferries or took the Tube, while, of course, Grand Central Terminal had all the traffic coming from the north right from the start. Also Grand Central to Wall Street is a straight shot on the subway for commuters.

Fully a century later, the West Side of Manhattan is developing largely in spite of Penn Station, not because of it.

EVEN BEFORE IT WAS FINISHED, Grand Central became the impetus for an extraordinary urban renewal and repurposing of nearby property. American Express's stables, the Steinway piano factory, and the F & M Schaeffer Brewery would give way to fashionable apartments, hotels (the Ambassador, Biltmore, Commodore, Ritz-Carlton, and Waldorf-Astoria, the new Grand Central Palace, the Roosevelt, the Barclay and Park Lane), a post office, and the Central's own offices—all lures for the multicolored cabs that, Thomas Wolfe wrote, now descended on Grand Central "like beetles in flight."

With Grand Central acting as an anchor, Park Avenue was elevated into New York's most prestigious address. "The story of Park

Avenue is the old story of Cinderella," Arthur Bartlet Maurice, an author and editor wrote, "yesterday a kitchen drudge of a street, today a resplendent Princess; and the Fairy Godmother who waved the wand and wrought the change was electrification."

By 1917, the Biltmore Hotel and the Yale Club graced Vanderbilt Avenue. Sloan & Robertson's Eastern Offices Building, better known as the Graybar Building (for Elisha Gray and Enos Barton, Western Electric's founders), opened on Lexington Avenue (the Graybar may be the only building decorated with rats; they're climbing up the cables that secure the canopy and resemble the ropes used to moor ships).

Within another decade, the Commodore Hotel, the 54-story Lincoln Building, the 56-story Chanin Building, and the 77-story Chrysler Building, which reigned for less than a year as the world's tallest, until it was eclipsed by the Empire State Building (it is still the world's tallest steel-supported brick building), rose on East 42nd Street. *Buildings and Building Management* magazine reported in 1920 that 100 millionaires lived at 270 Park Avenue. And just as Park Avenue would be glamorized within two decades all the way to 96th Street, East 42nd Street would be revitalized block by block by a progression of the Bowery Savings Bank, the Daily News Building, Tudor City, and eventually the United Nations headquarters, which, appropriately enough, replaced a row of slaughterhouses. Each building was home to more stories than merely the number of floors suggested.

THE BILTMORE, designed by Warren & Wetmore, opened on New Year's Day 1913 and was operated by Gustav Bauman of the fashionable Holland House on Fifth Avenue until he fell from a hotel window the following year. Its two towers flanked an Italian garden in the summer and an ice-skating rink in the winter. Graced by a grand ballroom that doubled as a roof garden, the Biltmore was where Henry Ford attempted to broker peace before World War I and where Scott and Zelda Fitzgerald honeymooned (and were evicted for disturbing the peace). The hotel later housed the Grand Central Art Galleries, originally located in the terminal. The Biltmore was, perhaps, most famous for its lobby meeting place "under the clock," where, among countless others, the reclusive J.D. Salinger would meet William Shawn, editor of the *New Yorker*.

The 34-story New York Central Building (later the Helmsley Building), also designed by Warren & Wetmore, straddled Park Avenue just across 45th Street from the terminal. "The design and ornamentation celebrate the prowess of the New York Central Railroad, which had its headquarters on the premises," Andrew Dolkart

THE FAÇADE: *CENTRAL* WAS DEFTLY EDITED TO *GENERAL* ON 230 PARK AVENUE, THEN OBLITERATED ALTOGETHER. HELMSLEY-SPEAR SOLD IT IN 1988 BUT INSISTED ITS NAME REMAIN.

and Matthew A. Postal wrote in their *Guide to New York City Landmarks*. "A sense of imperial grandeur is created by marble walls and bronze detail, which includes extensive use of the railroad's initials. The Chinese red elevator doors open into cabs with red walls, wood moldings, gilt domes, and painted cloudscapes." But even before the headquarters was finished in 1929, the *New Yorker* complained that "sunset comes to Park Avenue about two o'clock these days."

Still, the building and its ornate cupola became beloved. They endure as the sole remnant of the Court of Honor proposed by Charles Reed in 1903. (The steel frame was completed in 1928, just hours after Chauncey Depew, the legendary chairman of the New York Central, died. Depew is remembered most as the name of what is now a private street on the terminal's eastern flank and as an engaging after-dinner speaker. "I get my exercise acting as a pallbearer to my friends who exercise," he often said. Depew defined a pessimist as a man who thinks all women are bad. An optimist, he said, "is one who hopes they are.")

While Reed's concept for a vast civic plaza was never realized (he died in 1911) and no single architect would integrate all the buildings that flanked Park Avenue, "they nonetheless created a precinct of high-rise buildings in the city where a common aesthetic prevailed," the architect Deborah Nevins has written. The New York Central Building "and its broad arms and tower closed the vista from upper Park Avenue and created a monumental boundary to this unique architectural environment," she wrote. "The life of this enclave was brief, for it was soon to be replaced by the glass skyscrapers of the 1950s."

By 1926, 15,000 residents and 25,000 workers could reach their homes or offices through Grand Central without ever going outside. The zone was likened to "a gigantic rabbit warren," which not only connected them to the terminal, but accessed the Interborough Rapid Transit Lexington Avenue line and, after 1918, a shuttle to Times Square (along the subway's original route uptown).

GRAND CENTRAL TERMINAL was always about more than transportation. It was, as Whitney Warren imagined it would be, an exotic bazaar. Even during the Depression, *Fortune* magazine enthused, "More badly busy, more madly various than Coney Island are the

AN ELEVATOR INDICATOR IN THE ORNATE LOBBY OF 230 PARK. THE BUILDING PLAYED A ROLE IN *ATLAS SHRUGGED* AND *THE GODFATHER*.

station's 61 concessions. Kiddy Cars are sold at August Stumpf's, diamond rings at Samuel Kamerow's, shoe shines in the Union News Co. stands, orchids at J.S. Nicholas's, oysters at Mendel's Bar, shaves at J.P. Carey's, theater tickets, groceries, dress suits, sodas, electric light bulbs, books, lunches, radiograms, cigars, stamps. And from it all rolls into Central's pockets about $2 million-a-year."

As early as 1937, the Columbia Broadcasting System announced that the terminal would become home to experimental television studios directly above the main waiting room. CBS installed broadcasting equipment there two years later and the Chrysler Building across the street was fitted for a transmitter. Broadcasting was curtailed during World War II, but right after the war the technology and the talent coalesced. The network would broadcast from there until 1964 (despite the fuzzy images sometimes produced on television sets at home because of vibrations from the trains below). Among the programs that originated from one of four studios were *The CBS Evening News* with Douglas Edwards, Edward R. Murrow's *See It Now*, *The Goldbergs*, and *What's My Line?* In 1958, what was described as the first major videotape facility in the world opened there.

The *60 Minutes* creator Don Hewitt remembered his first visit to the CBS studio: "They had cameras and lights and makeup artists and stage managers and microphones just like in the movies, and I was hooked. I had been passing through Grand Central every day on my way to work and never knew that upstairs, over the trains and the waiting room and the information booth, was an attic stuffed with the most fabulous toys anyone ever had to play with." Hewitt continued, "I was mesmerized. As a child of the movies, I was torn between wanting to be Julian Marsh, the Broadway producer in '42nd Street,' who was up to his ass in showgirls, and Hildy Johnson, the hell-bent-for-leather reporter in 'The Front Page,' who was up to his ass in news stories. Oh my God, I thought, in television I could be both of them." The former studio is now a tennis court.

• • •

FROM 1922 TO 1958, the sixth floor of the terminal was home to Grand Central Art Galleries, which was founded by John Singer Sargent, Walter Leighton Clark, Edmund Greacen, and other artists, originally as a nonprofit cooperative. An estimated 5,000 people attended the opening in 1923, which featured paintings by Sargent, Wayman Adams, and Cecilia Beaux and sculpture by Robert Aitken and Daniel Chester French. The 15,000-square-foot gallery billed itself as "the largest sales gallery of art in the world."

The following year, the galleries opened an art school on the seventh floor. The galleries remained at Grand Central until 1958; their former display space is now the railroads' operations center. The terminal would also become home to a newsreel theater and restaurants. Its allure would spill onto 42nd Street, where two dozen skyscrapers connected to the terminal through underground passageways would sprout, and to Park Avenue, which would become synonymous with opulent living. It drew people like iron filings to a magnet, by 1947 handling more than 65 million passengers, or the equivalent of 40 percent of the nation's total population. And, after it experienced ups and downs like the railroads had themselves, the terminal's influence would reverberate into the next century too.

THE HOTEL, APARTMENT AND OFFICE TOWERS of Terminal City themselves typically would not reverberate, however, thanks to innovative insulation. H.G. Balcom, a structural engineer, was credited with conceptualizing supporting columns disconnected from the vibrating track floor and the viaduct for the 20-story Park-Lexington Building

THE CENTRAL'S STYLIZED LOGO WAS SUCCEEDED BY AN UPSIDE-DOWN ANCHOR AND, FOR THE CENTENNIAL, THE FAMOUS CLOCK.

(his portfolio would later include the Empire State Building, Rock-efeller Center, and the Waldorf-Astoria).

Many of the buildings on Park and Vanderbilt are separated from the sidewalk by a visible two-inch slot containing a vibration barrier. Moreover, the steel girders that support the tracks and the roof of Park Avenue are separated from the structural stilts, which support the buildings and were packed in layers of lead, asbestos, sheet iron, and other baffling at their base, deeper in bedrock. (When one apartment building on Park Avenue rattled nonetheless, the vibration was blamed on two protruding bolts that had lodged against a girder that supported the tracks and the street above.)

The seam between the sidewalk and the buildings mitigated the rumbling of trains in the bowels of Manhattan but didn't stop it entirely. Frederick Jack noticed the vibration in Thomas Wolfe's *You Can't Go Home Again*, and the assurances of the doorman of his building on Park Avenue were not entirely satisfactory. You might say Jack was rattled. "He would have liked it better if the building had been anchored upon solid rock," Wolfe wrote. "So now, as he felt the slight tremor in the walls once more, he paused, frowned and waited till it stopped. Then he smiled. 'Great trains pass under me,' he thought. 'Morning, bright morning, and still they come—all the boys who have dreamed dreams in the little towns. They come forever to the city. Yes, even now they pass below me, wild with joy, mad with hope, drunk with their thoughts of victory. For what? For what? Glory, huge profits, and a girl! All of them come looking for the same magic wand. Power. Power. Power.'"

IF ANY ONE MAN DESERVED THE CREDIT for Grand Central's success as a transportation hub and as the catalyst for creating Midtown, it was William Wilgus. He would never get it, though. In 1907, the 6:15 p.m. express from Grand Central to White Plains flew off the tracks as it rounded a curve at 205th Street in the Woodlawn section of the Bronx. Twenty commuters were killed instantly and another 150 were injured. Scapegoats were demanded. Wilgus was an obvious target. Officially, the railroad blamed a faulty rail, but Central officials—and

Wilgus—became convinced that the real flaw was "nosing," a tendency toward horizontal alignment of the locomotives, which the railroad and General Electric had been aware of and were trying to correct. Wilgus's meticulously documented conclusion about the cause would be devastating to the Central if it became public. He was advised by the railroad's chief counsel to destroy his evidence, which he did. But he later re-created his conclusions and included them in papers he would donate to the New York Public Library. His report would remain undisturbed there until after his death.

On July 11, 1907, after learning that the railroad was redesigning the locomotives without consulting him, Wilgus resigned. Replying to the departing chief engineer, who by then was making a very respectable $40,000 a year, W.C. Brown, the railroad's senior vice president, wrote, "The great work undertaken and practically completed by you, of changing the power within the so-called electric zone and the reconstruction of the Grand Central Station, was the most stupendous work of engineering I have ever known; and it has gone forward practically without a halt, certainly without a failure in any essential feature."

Wilgus, who was succeeded by George Kittredge, Edwin B. Katte, and George A. Harwood, would spend the rest of his life seeking the credit he deserved. In 1909, he received a measure of vindication when the Central's directors, while embracing Whitney Warren's resplendent concourse, restored two features that Wilgus and Reed & Stem had originally proposed: the elevated roadway that routed Park Avenue around the terminal, and the structural foundation for a revenue-producing tower that might someday be built over the building.

Four years later, though, as best as can be determined, Wilgus was never mentioned publicly when Grand Central was formally dedicated. Nor would his bold plan to bore 60 miles of rail freight tunnels to link Manhattan with Staten Island and New Jersey ever be realized. He would become deputy director general of transportation for the American Expeditionary Forces under General Pershing and was credited with the strategy that won the Battle of Saint-Mihiel in September 1918, which broke the German defensive line and facilitated the Americans' Meuse-Argonne Offensive.

Whitney Warren, too, merits a World War I footnote. Warren was chosen to rebuild the Louvain Library in Belgium, insisting that it bear the inscription "Furore Teutonico Diruta: Dono Americano Restituto" (destroyed by German fury; restored by American generosity). Warren, who became an admirer of Mussolini, lived long enough to see the library destroyed again, by the Nazis.

"GRAND CENTRAL ACHIEVED A GREATER IMPACT on the urban fabric of New York than any other building project in the first half of the 19th century, until construction began on Rockefeller Center," Kurt Schlichting wrote. Less than a decade after the terminal opened, *Railway Age* concluded, "It is doubtful if even the most optimistic participants in the work in question ever looked forward to seeing just how great an effect the electrification and terminal improvement were going to have on the development of New York City." William Wilgus had, and he was right.

ALL ABOARD

F ULLY TWO DECADES have elapsed since the last regularly scheduled long-haul run transported passengers more than 90 miles from 42nd Street in any direction. But for all the magic of the terminal building itself, it was the glamour of train travel during the first half of the 20th century that transformed Grand Central into a metaphor for cosmopolitan sophistication. The exoticness of the Orient Express, the magnitude of the Trans-Siberian, the exclusivity of Le Train Bleu, would spark imaginations for generations. In America, which offered the California Zephyr and the City of New Orleans, no train carried as much cachet as the New York Central's flagship No. 26—the westbound 20th Century Limited. In *The Art of the Streamliner,* Bob Johnston and Joe Welsh wrote that transportation historians consistently pronounced the 1938 version of the Century as "the world's ultimate passenger conveyance—at least on the ground."

WAITING FOR THE CENTURY IN THE ROARING
TWENTIES. THE CELEBRITY-STUDDED TRAIN WOVE
ITS WAY INTO POPULAR CULTURE.

• • •

RED CARPETS HAVE BEEN SYNONYMOUS WITH PRESTIGE since at least 458 BCE, when, according to Aeschylus, Agamemnon was welcomed home from Troy by Clytemnestra, who persuaded him to enter his palace on a "crimson path." In modern times, the "red carpet treatment" was popularized by the 20th Century Limited, which the New York Central inaugurated just before construction began on its new terminal. Like many of the named trains, this one was the brainchild of George Henry Daniels, a former Mississippi steamboat crewman and patent medicine salesman who turned his promotional skills to railroading as the New York Central's general passenger agent. It was Daniels who, in 1893, engineered a new world speed record on the crack Empire State Express between Buffalo and New York City. Hauled by Engine 999, built in West Albany, the express hit 112.5 mph east of Rochester.

The Empire was billed as the world's first high-speed passenger train, taking just seven hours and six minutes on September 14, 1891, to cover the 436 miles between New York City and Buffalo, as the first scheduled passenger train to travel regularly at more than 52 mph. The Empire also broke the record for going the longest distance between stops, the nearly 143 miles from New York to Albany. No. 999 was celebrated as a centerpiece of the World's Columbian Exposition in Chicago in 1893, was honored by a two-cent stamp issued by the post office, and inspired several songs. A streamlined version crafted in fluted stainless steel was christened in 1941. The timing could not have been worse: the service was inaugurated on December 7, which meant it was overshadowed by events that day in Hawaii; the locomotive is on display at the Chicago Museum of Science and Industry.

Daniels was credited with (or took credit for) naming the famed redcaps and originating other train names, including the Wolverine, the Commodore Vanderbilt, the Pacemaker, and the three dozen that constituted the Central's Great Steel Fleet, which hugged the Hudson and Lake Erie. (Daniels was not omniscient, though; in 1900, he famously declared that it was "safe to assume that it will hardly be possible to apply electricity to haul great passenger trains.")

IN 1920, WILLIAM K. VANDERBILT (LEFT) AND CENTRAL PRESIDENT CROWLEY JOINED ALBERT STONE, WHOM THE RAILROAD HIRED IN 1850, ON A CHICAGO EXPRESS.

Daniels's advertising and promotional genius extended well beyond railroading. He popularized the Thousand Islands in the St. Lawrence River as a tourist destination. He even helped create a literary hit, which evolved into a common catchphrase. In 1899 Elbert Hubbard published his "Message to Garcia" in the March issue of *Philistine* magazine. The story was about Andrew Summers Rowan, an army lieutenant who unhesitatingly braves the Cuban jungle to deliver a missive from the president of the United States to an insurgent general. Daniels promptly called the author and got permission to reprint more than a million copies of his short story with a bold advertisement for the Empire State Express on the back— presumably another example of pertinacity in transportation: Rowan delivered. So does the Central.

ON THE 20TH CENTURY LIMITED, guests, both famous and long since forgotten, received the special amenities they expected. Traveling on the Century halfway across the continent was comparable to crossing the Atlantic on the *Queen Mary*. The train ultimately had its own barbershop, secretarial services, concierge, manicurist, valet, a telephone connection (dial Murray Hill 9-8000 when the Century was in Grand Central, Wabash 2-4200 in Chicago), air-conditioning (which was not available on any of the Central's commuter trains until 1950), circulating ice water, two dining cars, its own post office (mail would be postmarked "N.Y. & CHI. R.P.O. E.D. 20TH CEN. LTD." and the train's number), radios that as early as 1924 reported presidential election results, and a luxury suite—shower included.

By the early 1900s, Pullman cars painted an emblematic forest green had replaced the wooden Wagner Palace sleeping cars that the

Central had originally used on longer runs. "The Water Level Route—You Can Sleep," advertisements for the Century crowed. Each train was equipped with eight Pullman cars containing roomettes, bedrooms, or suites; two dining cars; and a club car (railroaders call this the train's *consist*—the number and types of cars it consists of). The observation car included a room with two berths, club chairs, a shower, and an adjacent double bedroom. The Century offered carnations for men, perfume for women, and free morning newspapers (the *Chicago Tribune* or the *New York Herald-Tribune*) delivered to passengers' compartments. During Prohibition, booze was available, and even before the era of quiet cars, signs cautioned passengers, "Quiet is requested for the benefit of those who have retired."

ON JUNE 17, 1902, the inaugural run got to Chicago three minutes earlier than the 20 hours scheduled. That was an astounding four hours shorter than regular trains. No biggie, said the engineer, William Gates. "This schedule can be made without any difficulty," he boasted. The Central's insistence that no special effort was expended to maintain record-breaking on-time performance, that the Century was "a perfectly practical run," was a little disingenuous. That the nearly 1,000-mile run between Grand Central and Chicago's LaSalle Street Station eventually could be made in as little as 15 hours, 30 minutes, was no accident. The railroad even guaranteed passengers a partial rebate if the Century was late.

The train switched from an electric locomotive to steam at Croton-Harmon and ultimately could reach Chicago without refueling. Water to replenish the thirsty steam locomotives was scooped up at 80 mph by pans from troughs between the rails (giving rise to the stigma "jerkwater towns," where trains didn't stop). The Century "had the road," which meant all other trains had to yield to it, and it was exempted from the rule that trains could not pass a waypoint earlier than scheduled. As its chronicler, Lucius Beebe wrote, "the entire collective will power of the New York Central System seemed to focus on getting The Century through with the least possible delay. High priority freight might freeze to the tracks at Buffalo and other ranking trains go into the hole all the way from Cleveland to Elkhart, but extra gangs and flaggers, wedge plows and helper engines, diverted from other runs combined to get the line's crack varnish over the road with the least possible damage to its schedule." That schedule was so precise that the Century's progress could be timed to 30 seconds. No wonder it was originally promoted as a "train a century ahead of its time."

Advertisements in agate on the front page of the *Times* boasted that the train made the trip in 20 hours and, therefore, "is appropriately named" the 20th Century Limited. Other ads proclaimed it "The Busy Man's Train" and the "Fastest Long Distance Train in the World" and crowed, "It Saves a Day." In 1928, the Century grossed more than $11 million, setting a record for one train that was said to be unequaled. Ominously, though, that same year the Century was beaten to Chicago by a car driven by Erwin "Cannon Ball" Baker, who would become the first NASCAR commissioner.

THE CENTURY customarily left from Grand Central's Track 34, where the football field–length crimson carpet was ceremoniously rolled out on the 1,525-foot-long platform, the terminal's longest, each evening for departing passengers. Over six decades, they included tycoons and

RED CARPET TREATMENT AS A SYNONYM FOR LUXURY WAS POPULARIZED BY THE
20TH CENTURY LIMITED.

celebrities—among them, Enrico Caruso, J.P. Morgan, Theodore Roosevelt, Kate Smith, James Cagney, Rosalind Russell, and Walter Chrysler Sr. Tickets could be purchased at a special window (the fare in the 1920s was $32.70, plus $9.60 extra for the Century, and Pullman charges [$9 for a lower berth]; the total was $51.30, or about $700 in today's dollars). Because all of the cars were Pullman sleepers, the Century carried relatively few passengers.

MAYOR JAMES J. WALKER AND WILLIAM K. VANDERBILT JR. INAUGURATED
18-HOUR SERVICE TO CHICAGO IN 1932.

In 1938, the Central introduced its streamlined blue-and-gray-striped stainless-steel train, including a glass-enclosed observation car equipped with radio and speedometers for obsessive passengers and engineered by industrial designer Henry Dreyfuss, the Brooklyn-born genius who created a vast range of everyday appurtenances from the Princess telephone to the Big Ben alarm clock. His sleek, bullet-nosed, gun-metal-gray Art Deco locomotive with its distinguishing fin and the accompanying Pullman, dining, and observation cars have been described as the most famous American passenger train ever built. (Raymond Loewy was attempting the same for the Pennsy's Broadway

Limited, which began regular competition with the Century in 1912.) The engine's wheels were lighted at night for maximum effect, and Al Gengler, a train buff, wrote, "It had the self-assurance of a Wall Street banker's business suit, with blue chalk stripes and an Art Moderne drumhead glowing red and blue as it raced along the right-of-way." The distinctive and elegant logo that Dreyfuss designed, sleek horizontal bars underscoring the name of the train, adorned everything from the red carpet to the crockery.

The Century could reach speeds of 123 mph and make the 961-mile trip between Grand Central and Chicago in 960 minutes. The route of the Broadway Limited was 52 miles shorter, but more mountainous, crossing the Alleghenies (its Tuscan red trains are still evoked by the decorative mosaic tile in Manhattan's Pennsylvania Station subway stop). Comparing the two trains, *Time* magazine pronounced them "alike in contour as a brace of eels" but went on to contrast their dining cars—the Century's "informal but sober" (where a full dinner cost $1.75 in 1939 and $6.95 by 1967) and the Broadway Limited's "more splendiferous."

After World War II, when the Central focused more heavily on ferrying troops from the Midwest and Eastern Seaboard to embarkation points, Henry Dreyfuss introduced an even more modern diesel version. In 1948 General Dwight D. Eisenhower inaugurated the new train, and the actress Beatrice Lillie, echoing the ceremonial opening of the Erie Canal, christened the locomotives with water from the Hudson, Lake Erie, and Lake Michigan. But within a decade, the glamour of train travel was giving way to much greater speed, convenience, and independence—well before the era of long airport lines and security checkpoints.

The allure of the luxury trains would be eroded by both the airplane, which could travel from airport to airport (though not from downtown to downtown) in a fraction of the time that the speediest train could muster, and the automobile, which could stop anywhere at a passenger's whim. Train traffic peaked right after World War II, just before commercial air travel became more available and affordable. In 1947, 65 million passengers arrived at or departed from Grand Central on nearly 600 trains daily. (As the historian Francis Morrone astutely noted a decade ago, "at the height of its activity, in the years just after the Second World War, Grand Central served about the same number of passengers as the world's busiest airport does today, even though Grand Central uses only 1 percent as much land as the airport does.")

Less than two decades later, with the merged Central verging on bankruptcy and airlines providing what amounted to shuttle service to and from Chicago, the 20th Century Limited made its final run. It had descended more or less gracefully into threadbare elegance. It was slower and even more expensive than an airplane (one way by coach, the cheapest ticket, cost $43.26, compared to $43.70 by jetliner, and sleeping accommodations were costlier).

On some nights, the 80-man train crew outnumbered the passengers. On December 2, 1967, just a month after the *Queen Mary*'s final voyage, the Century left Grand Central for the last time. It departed precisely on time, at 6 p.m., from Track 34. A brakeman, Herbert P. Stevens, gave the highball signal that the track ahead was clear, but the train was only half-full, carrying 104 passengers. By the time it reached the environs of Ashtabula the following morning, it was no longer Train No. 25, because at 4 a.m. the railroad's new timetable took effect. As a conductor told a *New Yorker* correspondent who was researching the last run for Ernest M. Frimbo, the magazine's legendary railroad buff, "We're '25' until 4. Then we become '27,' and that's the end of the Century." (As it happened, the train was delayed by a derailment, and when 4 a.m. struck, the Century was still in Harbor Creek, Pennsylvania.) The Century was due in Chicago at 9:40 a.m., but by lunchtime it was only in Cleveland; Sunday blue laws in Ohio and Indiana barred the serving of liquor in the dining cars.

The train finally straggled into Chicago at 6:45 p.m., which meant the last run of the Century arrived nine hours late and took nearly five hours longer than the inaugural trip 65 years earlier. "I'm sorry that it couldn't have been on time," the engineer, J.A. McLain

NEW YORK CENTRAL "STREAMLINERS" EPITOMIZED MODERNITY AND LUXURY.

IN 1929, ONLY THE CENTRAL'S HEADQUARTERS TOWERED OVER THE TERMINAL.
THE COMMODORE HOTEL (NOW THE GRAND HYATT) IS AT RIGHT.

of Elkhart, Indiana, said. The timing provided a fitting validation of the prefix *late* before the 20th Century Limited. Ten days later, the Broadway Limited left from Penn Station for the last time.

IN 1989, AMTRAK, the federally financed passenger rail system, announced that it would abandon Grand Central altogether and consolidate its operations at the grungy hole in the ground on the West Side that had replaced the original Penn Station, which Amtrak by then more or less owned. Bypassing Grand Central would spare through passengers from Albany to Florida having to scurry across

Midtown Manhattan by foot or on public transportation. The shift would save Amtrak $600,000 in fees for electricity and other services paid to the Metropolitan Transportation Authority. But it would cost $100 million to lay 10 miles of new rails over a forsaken freight-track bed and past a colony of squatters and to renovate the Spuyten Duyvil Bridge, which spans the Harlem River and links Manhattan and the Bronx. The shift affected 20 trains a day serving upstate New York and Canada and as many as a million passengers a year.

"The world won't end," said Kent Barwick, the president of the Municipal Art Society, which had fought to save the terminal from demolition, "but who would have thought that in one fell swoop they could saw off Grand Central Terminal from the rest of America?"

On Saturday night, April 6, 1991, Amtrak did just that (unless you count Westchester and Connecticut as the rest of America). The stainless-steel Maple Leaf left for Toronto, hauling an antique private car, the Black Diamond, which 16 railroad buffs had rented to mark the occasion and to lament the loss, as one put it, of "the charm, the mystery and the mystique" of Grand Central. The head steward aboard was Jesse Mitchell, 73, who had been a porter on the 20th Century Limited and had whistle-stopped with three presidents: Franklin D. Roosevelt, Dwight D. Eisenhower, and Jimmy Carter. Grand Central's last long-distance train left at 8:35 p.m., the Rip Van Winkle, bound for Albany. The engineer, Jim Sweeney, waved a hand-lettered sign that read, "Last Amtrak Train Out of Grand Central Station." Overnight, the Gateway to a Continent devolved into a gateway to six counties in two states.

Still, even in its heyday, Grand Central sent not only trains across the country, but trends, too.

GATEWAY TO A CONTINENT

ODERN TIME BEGAN AT GRAND CENTRAL. Unlike any
other depot in the world—even busier ones—the terminal
became synonymous with a bustling urban ballet. The proverbial wisecrack "What is this, Grand Central Station?" in confront-
ing any jam-packed place became a universal metaphor for frenzy.
The metaphor was even invoked in the Warren Commission report
on President John F. Kennedy's assassination. An FBI agent, describing the chaotic crush of newsmen at police headquarters in Dallas,
observed that conditions were "not too much unlike Grand Central
Station at rush hour."

While popularizing the red carpet treatment on the Century,
the terminal's very name conjured up an egalitarian elegance, this
magnificent hub where subway riders, suburban commuters, the fa-

A STYLIZED VERSION OF THE FAMOUS OPALESCENT GLASS
CLOCK IS THE LOGO FOR THE TERMINAL'S CENTENNIAL
CELEBRATION. THE CLOCK WAS REPAIRED IN 1954.

mous and the infamous, first-class travelers and itinerant gawkers, might mingle. Perhaps more than any other public space, the terminal not only evolved into a household name, but also exercised a profound influence on American culture. Grand Central inspired song lyrics, a popular radio program, memorable movie scenes, literary works, television and theatrical performances, the civil rights movement, new visions of architecture for transportation, including airline terminals, the City Beautiful school of urban planning, the enormously profitable monetization of the empty space above private property, and the sometimes conflicting principle of historic preservation. All while whisking hundreds of thousands of people daily to and from their destinations.

GRAND CENTRAL, its predecessors on 42nd Street and its famous trains, emerged early on as a cultural touchstone emblematic of New York's magnetic glamour. One way a generation of Americans heard about it was through the popular radio soap opera on NBC *Grand Central Station*, which was broadcast nationally from 1937 to 1953. "To those of us who came from places where no one had heard of Lester Lanin and Grand Central Station was a Saturday radio program," Joan Didion wrote, "where Wall Street and Fifth Avenue and Madison Avenue were not places at all but abstractions ('Money,' and 'High Fashion.' And 'The Hucksters'). New York was no mere city. It was instead an infinitely romantic notion, the mysterious nexus of all love and money and power, the shining and perishable dream itself." Episodes in the dramatic radio anthology shared an exhilarating prologue: each began in Grand Central, with the announcer (George Baxter, Ken Roberts, or Tom Shirley) intoning,

As a bullet seeks its target, shining rails in every part of our great country are aimed at Grand Central Station, heart of the nation's greatest city. Drawn by the magnetic force of the fantastic metropolis, day and night great trains rush toward the Hudson River, sweep down its eastern bank for 140 miles, flash briefly by the long red row of tenement houses south of 125th Street, dive with a roar into the two-and-one-half-mile tunnel which burrows beneath the glitter and swank of Park Avenue, and then…Grand Central Station! Crossroads of a million private lives! Gigantic stage on which are played a thousand dramas daily!

The producers indulged in some poetic license. Sound effects for the show included the whoosh and chug of steam locomotives, which had been banned at Grand Central for more than three decades.

WHAT'S SO STRIKING is the range of movies in which Grand Central is cast as itself. The reason is that it is so recognizable, so suggestive of comings and goings simply by a familiar arch or signage. "In such details resides Grand Central's power as an almost universally recognizable 'place,' even as it offers a superb springboard for fantasy," James Sanders wrote in *Celluloid Skyline.* "How many other structures could be so universally identified by a few fragments of their graphics?"

"Nice city," says actor Percy Kilbride as he enters the Main Concourse in the 1950 film *Ma and Pa Kettle Go to Town.* To which daughter Kettle replies, "Pa, this is the station."

The movies captured the impressive grandeur of Grand Central. In Alfred Hitchcock's 1945 psychological thriller *Spellbound*, Ingrid

Bergman and Gregory Peck kiss and make their getaway from Grand
Central, where Bergman tells the amnesiac Peck to free-associate
when the clerk asks for their destination. He requests two tickets to
Rome. She explains that he means Rome, Georgia. Overheard, they
avoid police by taking a train to Rochester, New York, instead, where
her mentor (played by Michael Chekhov) opines, "Women make the
best psychoanalysts until they fall in love. After that they make the best
patients."

"In the montage that opens 'North by Northwest,'" James Sanders writes, "we see waves of New Yorkers rushing through the great
room—some on their way to trains and subways, others simply passing through, enjoying a covered shortcut from one part of Midtown
to another. No wonder that later in the film, Cary Grant—an in-
nocent man now become a fugitive—looks to the concourse and its
throngs to provide the anonymity he desperately needs." In the 1959
film, Grant and Eva Marie Saint banter on the 20th Century Limited:

> EVE KENDALL: I tipped the steward five dollars to seat you here
> if you should come in.
> ROGER THORNHILL: Is that a proposition?
> EVE: I never discuss love on an empty stomach.
> ROGER: You've already eaten!
> EVE: But you haven't.

(An original script by Ernest Lehman had Eve saying "I never
make love…," but it was dubbed to satisfy the censors.)

"Tell me," Roger asks his tablemate, "what do you do besides
lure men to their doom on the Twentieth Century Limited?" And

just before they escape their pursuers, Roger says, "If we ever get out of this alive, let's go back to New York on the train together, all right?"

EVE: Is that a proposition?
ROGER: It's a proposal, sweetie.

The Century figures in Bing Crosby's 1933 film *Going Hollywood*, in which, playing a Broadway star, Crosby gets a star-studded send-off complete with dancing porters, chorus girls, and a scrum of flashbulb-blinking photographers at Track 27. In what amounts to the round trip begun in *Going Hollywood*, two decades later Fred Astaire stars in *The Band Wagon* as a faded movie star who comes back to New York to lose himself "all alone in a crowd." By the time he dances up the Track 34 platform, though, he regains his confidence—reminding viewers that simply entering Grand Central is exhilarating and that the terminal is a place of new beginnings as much as endings.

Grand Central also is cast in cameos or starring roles in *Grand Central Murder*, *The Cotton Club*, *Men in Black II*, *The Prince of Tides*, *The Freshman*, *The House on Carroll Street*, *One Fine Day*, *The French Connection*, and Ang Lee's *The Ice Storm*. In *Carlito's Way*, a chase scene climaxes in a shootout during an interminable ride on the Grand Central escalators, which actually whisk pedestrians to and from the Met Life Building at 120 feet per second.

In *The Fisher King*, the chaotic tango of the crowd is transformed into a rhythmic gambol. "When Robin Williams, as a pure-hearted, emotionally unbalanced man, spots the quite plain woman of his dreams heading for her train," Caryn James wrote in the *Times*, "suddenly everyone in the room breaks into a waltz, as this grim, everyday place becomes a scene of glittering romance." In *Midnight Run*, the terminal is where bounty hunter Robert DeNiro departs with his quarry, Charles Grodin, because Grodin is afraid of flying. In *Superman*, Gene Hackman's Lex Luthor manages his evil empire from the bowels of Grand Central. Lex boasts of his Park Avenue address, to which his floozy secretary replies: "Park Avenue address? Two hundred feet below?" (In the new ABC series *666 Park*, the address is mythical, but apartment-dwellers may find the real estate machinations plausibly demonic.)

Even so, Grand Central projected the image of a more welcoming venue than the much-mourned Penn Station, which is why, Sanders wrote, the director Rouben Mamoulian chose Penn Station in his 1929 film *Applause* for an intimidating arrival of a vulnerable newcomer. "Compared to this place, Grand Central's concourse seems friendly, even relaxed," Sanders wrote. "This is simply overwhelming."

Brian Selznick photographed Grand Central and its secret compartments before he wrote *The Invention of Hugo Cabret*, which inspired the film *Hugo*. "Fantasy and reality mixed together to make the station in my book," Selznick said, "but it was dreaming of Grand Central that got much of it started."

A grand building also makes for a grand ruin. In *Beneath the Planet of the Apes*, the terminal plays itself as an ancient temple in post-apocalyptic New York. In *Armageddon*, dazzling special effects depict asteroids crashing into Grand Central. In *Revolutionary Road*, Leonardo DiCaprio commutes to Grand Central to work on his 30th birthday, his bobbing head indistinguishable from those of scores of other faceless men tethered to dispiriting work by their white collars. In *Madagascar,*

Melman, the neurotic giraffe, gets his head stuck in the information booth clock as animators created their own version of Grand Central from original blueprints and photographic essays. "It's such an icon," said Eric Darnell, one of the directors. "Even people who've never been to New York City know about Grand Central Station."

BEN HECHT AND CHARLES MACARTHUR'S 1932 farce *Twentieth Century* took place at Grand Central and on the famous train (it was adapted in 1978 as a musical, *On the Twentieth Century*). It was from Grand Central that Biff Loman embarked on his fateful visit to his father in Boston in *Death of a Salesman*, and where Holden Caulfield in *The Catcher in the Rye* stashed his belongings in a coin-operated locker, slept on an oak bench in the waiting room, and crossed the street to the Biltmore. While waiting to meet a date under the clock there, Caulfield engaged in some urban sightseeing ("Girls with their legs crossed, girls with their legs not crossed, girls with terrific legs, girls with lousy legs, girls that looked like swell girls," J.D. Salinger wrote).

Honking all the way through horrendous traffic, Grand Central is where Bill the driver delivers Tom and his mother in Lucy Sprague Mitchell's children's classic, *The Taxi That Hurried*. Grand Central is where Tom Rath, the hero of Sloan Wilson's 1955 novel *The Man in the Gray Flannel Suit*, stops to buy a clean white handkerchief and get his shoes shined, and where he sees "the dim figures of tired-appearing men in overalls occasionally illuminated by naked electric-light bulbs" as his train wends its way through the "dark caverns" under Park Avenue en route to Westport and his home on Greentree Avenue. As he walked through Grand Central one morning, "he looked up and for the first time in years noticed the stars painted on the blue ceiling there. They seemed to be shining brightly, and feeling slightly theatrical, he wondered if it were legitimate to wish on a painted star. He decided it would be all right to make a phony wish, so he wished he could make a million dollars and add a new wing to his grandmother's house, with a billiard room and a conservatory in which to grow orchids."

Grand Central was magical, its ramps calibrated to slope at precisely the most accessible angle, its platforms holding the promise of unfulfilled journeys and the proverbial light at the end of a tunnel. In 1950, Jack Finney, who later wrote the classic New York tale *Time and Again*, discovered a phantasmagorical third underground level of Grand Central in his short story of the same name that leads him back to 1894 and depot days.

> The presidents of the New York Central and the New York, New Haven and Hartford railroads will swear on a stack of timetables that there are only two. But I say there are three, because I've been on the third level at Grand Central Station. Yes, I've taken the obvious step: I talked to a psychiatrist friend of mine, among others. I told him about the third level at Grand Central Station, and he said it was a waking-dream wish fulfillment. He said I was unhappy. That made my wife kind of mad, but he explained that he meant the modern world is full of insecurity, fear, war, worry, and all the rest of it, and that I just want to escape. Well, hell, who doesn't? Everybody I know wants to escape, but they don't wander down into any third level at Grand Central Station.
>
> Sometimes I think Grand Central is growing like a tree, pushing out new corridors and staircases like roots. There's

probably a long tunnel that nobody knows about feeling its way under the city right now, on its way to Times Square, and maybe another to Central Park. And maybe—because for so many people through the years Grand Central has been an exit, a way of escape—maybe that's how the tunnel I got into... but I never told my psychiatrist friend about that idea.

Its sheer breadth makes Grand Central a universal metaphor. Sybille Bedford opens her *A Visit to Don Otavio* in New York where "the upper part of Grand Central Station is large and splendid like the Baths of Caracalla." The "mole people" who lived in a steamy "weedlot of steel" beneath the terminal figured in Colum McCann's *This Side of Brightness*. A Hungarian doctoral student who conducted research on the national symbols of suburban America concluded, "The Grand Central Terminal of New York is almost always the goal of traveling." And in novels, the movies, and even nonfiction, Grand Central has been a ubiquitous symbol for the commuter. In her book on shopping, the sociology professor Sharon Zukin draws on portrayals by journalist William H. Whyte, sociologist C. Wright Mills, and novelist John Cheever to invoke the corporate manager who "commuted home to the northern suburbs every evening on the 6:24 from Grand Central. The club car was filled with guys like these, loosening their ties and drinking gin and tonic, before they toddled home to their wives and children."

Cheever worked at home in Ossining and did not commute to Manhattan. But he knew Grand Central intimately because it was a real-life stage on which so many of his characters appeared and disappeared. He began his short story "Reunion" with this invitation to the reader: "The last time I saw my father was in Grand Central Station," and another story unfolded on the train in "The Five-Forty-Eight." In "O City of Broken Dreams," Cheever wrote of a family visiting Manhattan for the first time: "Alice noticed that the paving, deep in the station, had a frosty glitter, and she wondered if diamonds had been ground into the concrete."

Cheever's daughter, Susan, recalled that as her father grew older and became disoriented, the barely controlled chaos of the terminal terrified him, and even earlier, the terminal had morphed into a metaphor for beginnings and endings. She once wrote of her father that there "was something that would always lead him away and not only away but far away so that when he stepped from Grand Central into the traffic of 42nd Street and only then did he feel that he was free." "And at 3 a.m. I seemed to be walking through Grand Central Station," he wrote in 1956. "And the latch on my suitcase gives, spilling onto the floor the contents of my life."

The terminal figures in Mark Helprin's lush *Winter's Tale*, in which the protagonist, Peter Lake, secretes himself in a small compartment above the cerulean ceiling. ("What caused you to look up? No one else ever does," he demands of an intruder. "I don't know. When I saw the stars were on, I couldn't take my eyes from them.") A memoir by Elliot Vestner Jr., a retired lawyer, was titled *Meet Me Under the Clock at Grand Central* because in 1924 his parents, like so many other couples and potential partners, met on a date at that magical place (their second choice probably would have been across the street under the clock at the Biltmore Hotel).

"YOU SHOULD LIVE SO LONG," WAS ONE
ANSWER TO THE PROVERBIAL QUESTION,
"WHEN DOES THE LAST TRAIN LEAVE?"

In "Report on 'Grand Central Terminal,'" a short science fiction story by Leo Szilard, a Hungarian émigré physicist who helped develop the atomic bomb, researchers from another planet explore Manhattan after a neutron bomb destroyed all life. Their conflicting interpretations of what life was like climax as they investigate earthly artifacts in Grand Central. "What its name 'Grand Central Terminal' meant we do not know," the narrator acknowledges, "but there is little doubt as to the general purpose which this building served. It was part of a primitive transportation system based on clumsy engines which ran on rails and dragged cars mounted on wheels behind them."

Good guess, but the scientists are largely baffled trying to come to grips with the reasons behind pay toilets and the disks that must be deposited to enter them. One researcher concludes that "a system of production and distribution of goods based on a system of exchanging disks cannot be stable, but is necessarily subject to fluctuations vaguely reminiscent of the manic-depressive cycle in the insane." The narrator demurs, revealing that a spot check of lodging houses found no "depositories" equipped with "a gadget containing disks" and suggests that they are associated with a ceremonial act "connected with the act of deposition in public places, and in public places only." Never had so much profundity been expended on a restroom.

GRAND CENTRAL HAS BEEN A SHOWCASE for what the architects of its restoration pronounced "a fascinating fabric of cultural history." The North Balcony lured so many travelers seeking serenity and contemplation and "itinerant sophists" that it was dubbed the "Philosophers' Gallery." A prototype of the DeWitt Clinton locomotive was exhibited on the East Balcony, and in 1929 the Bremen, an all-metal monoplane with a 58-foot wingspan, the first to fly westward across the Atlantic, was suspended over it. Grand Central is the nation's living room and town square. The Main Concourse and Waiting Room could accommodate 30,000 people. A report completed in 1991 by Beyer Blinder Belle, architects of the restoration master plan, declared the concourse "the central hall, the lungs of the terminal, a place of public assembly without parallel in New York City." If the concourse evoked the broad aisle of a cathedral, it was fitting that in 1931 Episcopal Bishop William Manning launched a campaign from the North Balcony to raise $10 million to complete the Cathedral of St. John the Divine; a one-ton model was installed as a preview of the Gothic Revival structure rising uptown on Morningside Heights.

A year later, an estimated 5,000 well-wishers converged on the terminal to see off New York City Mayor James J. Walker on his way to Albany to face removal charges. (As he proceeded to the Ohio State Limited on Track 34, accompanied by his wife and her poodle, he encountered Joe Jacobs, the manager of Max Schmeling, who had lost his heavyweight title on a close decision to Jack Sharkey earlier that summer. "I hope they don't hand me the same kind of a decision you got," Walker quipped.) In 1934, 80,000 people turned out in a single day to inspect the Burlington Zephyr, a new speed king on the New York–to–Boston run. In 1912, 5,000 New Yorkers singing socialist anthems welcomed 100 children whose parents were striking the textile mills in Lawrence, Massachusetts, and in 1941, 10,000 cheering Brooklyn Dodger fans jammed the Main Concourse to welcome their heroes home from Boston with their first National League pennant in 21 years. And later that year, a week after Pearl Harbor, Treasury Secretary Henry Morgenthau Jr. inaugurated a drive to raise $10 billion in war bonds to prosecute the fight against Fascism. A 118-by-100-foot photomontage was installed depicting "What America Has to Defend and How It Will Defend It." More than 3,000 people attended the unveiling of the mural. The ceremony was also broadcast on radio nationwide—"again locating Grand Central as a center of American culture," as the restoration architects described it.

During the war, thousands of servicemen were deployed from the terminal, which was bedecked with patriotic posters. In 1945, 1,000 people an hour—nearly 15,000 in all—filed through a special seven-car train promoting Victory Loan war bonds to view the original German and Japanese surrender documents.

In 1952, an estimated 30,000 heard President Harry S. Truman speak from a Main Concourse balcony. (That same year, Walter Cronkite anchored the 1952 presidential election coverage from the fourth-floor studio.) In the early 1960s, thousands of spectators watched the CBS News screen above the New Haven's ticket window to follow the space flights of Project Mercury, whose namesake reigned from the terminal's façade. A spellbound crowd was glued to a video screen mapping Scott Carpenter's progress orbiting the earth in his *Aurora 7* capsule on May 24, 1962 (*As the World Turns*, the soap opera produced at the terminal's CBS studio, was preempted).

In 1971, hundreds of people queued up for two hours or more to place their wagers as the nation's first off-track betting parlor opened at Grand Central (commuters were already used to a long wait; appropriate to the place, one advertisement proclaimed: "Nothing Brightens the Rat Race Like a Horse Race"). In 1973, John Gallin & Son installed what was billed as the city's first automated teller machine at the Chase Manhattan branch beneath the 18-by-60-foot

Kodak Colorama. The Rolling Stones bestowed their imprimatur on the terminal for a new generation when they announced their Steel Wheels world tour there in 1989, the same year that Ringo Starr, who played the pint-sized Mr. Conductor, introduced Thomas the Tank Engine on public television's new *Shining Time Station* series there.

"IN THE EVENT OF A CRISIS," Ben Cheever wrote, "the big room behind and beneath the gods grows black with crowds." Three thousand "yippies" from the Youth International Party celebrated spring in 1968 by staging a chaotic "yip-in" on the Main Concourse. They were dispersed by nightstick-swinging police officers after they hurled firecrackers and spun the hands off the information booth's priceless, four-faced opalescent glass clock. (Another of its faces was later pierced by a bullet—apparently fired by a police officer in pursuit; that face is now at the Transit Museum.) More recently, Act Up and Occupy Wall Street have also staged demonstrations there.

Grand Central became the shelter of last resort—a terminal in every sense—for the homeless, whose encampments dotted the yards and tunnels beneath the streets and the terminal's public spaces. In *Subways Are for Sleeping*, Edmund G. Love wrote that Henry Shelby, a vagrant in 1953, would hunker down on the benches at Grand Central, where he could sleep prone and undisturbed for four hours between the regular police checks at 1:30 and 5:30 a.m. Shelby kept a ticket to Poughkeepsie in his pocket as insurance, so he could always claim he missed the last train. "On one occasion," Love wrote, "a station policeman escorted him to a 6:30 train and made certain he got on it. Shelby got off at 125th Street and walked back to Grand Central."

THE MAIN
CONCOURSE
IS AMERICA'S
LIVING ROOM.
THOUSANDS
GATHERED
THERE IN 1962
TO WATCH
JOHN GLENN'S
SPACE FLIGHT.

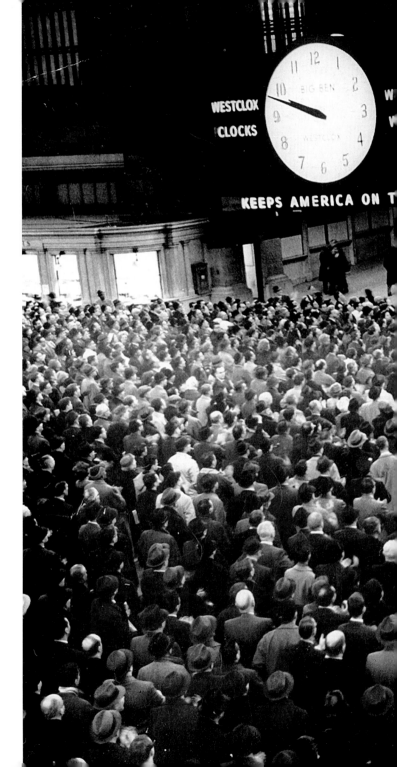

Some vagrants—when they were still quaintly called hoboes or tramps—had lived for years in subterranean dungeons beneath the Waldorf and other Park Avenue properties, in dank, rumbling, labyrinthine tunnels devoid of light except for the occasional naked incandescent bulb, but free from the interference, regulation, or danger associated with meddlesome public shelters.

They cooked their food on hissing steam pipes stripped of their asbestos covers and they emerged from sordid and sooty sanctuaries during the day only to panhandle for bare essentials. (A fire that began in the subterranean tunnels under Grand Central shut the terminal down in 1985, but police said squatters living in a boxcar were not to blame.) Jennifer Toth, who gave them faces in her book *The Mole People*, recalled a man named Seville who was panhandling in Grand Central when a commuter gave him a bag containing a loaf of bread and a pound of baloney. He thanked the man, then shouted: "Pardon me, sir, would you happen to have some Grey Poupon?"

By 1988, as Grand Central celebrated its 75th birthday, city officials estimated that as many as 500 homeless people were living in the terminal on any given night and that 50 or so had been encamped there for a year or more. "It's a metaphor for New York in 1988 in a shrine of such beauty to have such misery," said Robert M. Hayes, a lawyer who successfully sued the state in a right-to-shelter case and founded the Coalition for the Homeless.

HOW GRAND CENTRAL DEALT with the challenge also provided an object lesson for the rest of America. Drop-in shelters were created to steer homeless people to permanent homes. Sometimes, officers were forced to eject aggressive panhandlers, a solution that proved temporary and invited fire from advocates for the homeless (as did the removal of benches from the waiting room). The Metropolitan Transportation Authority hired the Bowery Residents Committee to provide outreach services, and transit officials also worked in concert with the Grand Central Partnership, an amalgam of property owners in a 50-square-block area around the terminal.

After Mobil Oil abandoned its East 42nd Street headquarters for suburban Virginia, those property owners convened an innovative self-taxing business improvement district in 1988 to spruce up the neighborhood and provide amenities that the city government could no longer afford. (Its 120 full-time employees, including 33 public-safety officers and 56 sanitation workers, and a nearly $13 million budget make it among the nation's largest such districts. The annual surcharge on 204 properties was initially 10 cents per square foot, or what amounted to an extra 1 to 2 percent in real estate taxes; it ranged from more than $250,000 for the Metropolitan Life Building to $154 for a nearby delicatessen.)

"The truth is," the architecture critic Paul Goldberger wrote then, "that the Grand Central neighborhood does not work as it is now—it is too dirty, too pressured, too troubled by a large homeless population and too lacking in amenity for everyone else." The partnership, he said approvingly, "is based on the idea that the terminal is not just a building, but the symbolic anchor of a neighborhood." Through Daniel A. Biederman, its president (whom the partnership borrowed from the wildly successful Bryant Park Restoration behind the New York Public Library on Fifth Avenue), and Peter L. Malkin, a lawyer and real estate investor whose office faced Grand Central (and whose father-in-law, Lawrence Wein, was once an owner of the

Empire State Building), the business improvement district spawned similar public-private partnerships across the country. A subsidiary of the partnership transformed a nearby former parochial school into a center where hundreds of homeless people who congregated around Grand Central could be fed and could shower, receive counseling, and even stay overnight. "Enlightened self-interest and then some," said Robert Hayes, the advocate for the homeless (although the partnership was later criticized when some outreach workers aggressively rousted vagrants in and near Grand Central).

In New York City alone, 67 such business improvement districts invest $100 million collectively in public amenities. In addition to installing uniform signage and removing litter, the Grand Central Partnership raised more than $1.5 million to floodlight the terminal's south and west façades. Since 1991, the terminal has been bathed in 136,000 watts of floodlight from buildings across the street. The blue and magenta tints were designed by Sylvan R. Shemitz, a lighting engineer whose goal, he said, was to make New York "a lively, friendly and joyful place."

IN ITS FIRST CENTURY, Grand Central has played a prodigious role in the annals of urban planning, beginning with William Wilgus's ingenious monetization of air rights (the ability to transfer those rights between adjacent properties was also introduced in New York in 1916 in the nation's first zoning ordinance). The skyrocketing value of those rights nearly doomed Grand Central until the U.S. Supreme Court delivered another victory to the terminal by upholding its landmark status and a municipality's right to confer it. But Grand Central's influence on planning, as profound as it was, went well beyond establishing air rights and historic preservation as fundamentals of real estate law and development.

Recounting the cycles of building, obsolescence, and denser rebuilding that characterized Manhattan's inexorable march uptown, James Marston Fitch, a Columbia architecture professor, and Diana S. Waite, a researcher for the state's parks department, concluded, "Only three projects in Manhattan's history have been able to slow down, much less to stop or reverse, this remorseless process of expansion and decay": Central Park, Rockefeller Center, and Grand Central Terminal. Pointedly, they did not include Pennsylvania Station, which, for all its glory, spawned a few nearby hotels but never became a catalyst for further development (only now are the Hudson Yards west of the station fulfilling their potential).

Those three megaprojects shared a number of epochal characteristics, not the least of which was they each defied the inviolable street grid that city commissioners had presciently mapped in 1811 from Houston Street all the way uptown to 155th Street. "They are significant," Fitch and Waite wrote, "for having served to polarize the forces of growth, thus acting to stabilize the whole center of the island rather like the electro-gyroscopes employed on large ocean liners. They have not been passive containers of urban activity; instead they have acted as generators of new urban energies, infusing the urban tissues around them with nourishment and strength. This capacity is a mysterious one in urban affairs, not much analyzed and never adequately explained."

Attempting to do just that, the authors concluded that Wilgus's perspicacity converted the terminal complex "from an inert obstacle to urban development into a dynamic reciprocating engine for urban activity." The railroad air rights that Wilgus pioneered have produced a private and public development bonanza. In Manhattan alone, profits were plucked from thin air by Riverside South, where 10,000 apartments were built over the old New York Central West Side yards; the Hudson Yards project over the tracks west of Penn Station; and the Atlantic Terminal development, including the Barclays Center arena.

GRAND CENTRAL FUNCTIONED as a metaphysical gateway in other respects. For decades, only two jobs held out much promise for black men. They could either apply for work with the post office or hope to be hired as Pullman porters. At one point, when its ranks swelled to 20,000, the Pullman Company was the largest single employer of black men in the United States. Their chief patron was A. Philip Randolph, who arrived in Harlem in 1911, would become the president of the Brotherhood of Sleeping Car Porters, would be denounced

as the most dangerous black man in America, and would lead the historic 1963 March on Washington for Jobs and Freedom. Because porters traveled routinely between the North and South, they were instrumental in awakening southern blacks to the Great Migration. And they were pioneers in the battles for equal rights.

"If Martin Luther King was the father of the civil rights movement," wrote Larry Tye, author of *Rising from the Rails*, "then A. Philip Randolph was the grandfather of the civil rights movement." The porters

A. PHILIP RANDOLPH, "THE MOST DANGEROUS BLACK MAN IN AMERICA."

were always civil but had few rights. Their pay was poor, and they depended heavily on tips. ("Tipping is objected to by austere and frugal American moralists upon the ground that it undermines the manhood and self-respect of the tippee," the *Times* opined. "But this proposition loses all its force when the tippee is of African descent.") Regardless of their given names, they were condescendingly referred to by most passengers as "George," the first name of the Pullman Company's founder and inventor. (Pullman's second president was Robert Todd Lincoln, Abe's son; the company would continue producing railroad cars and prototypes until 1987, when it was absorbed by Bombardier.) In 1914, presumably as a joke, a group of white men, many of them named George, formed a Society for the Prevention of Calling Sleeping Car Porters George. Whatever its motives, the Pullman Company responded by placing a sign in each car with the given name of the porter on duty. As it turned out, only 362 of 12,000 porters surveyed were named George.

The sleeping car porters union was organized in New York in large part by Ashley L. Totten, a Virgin Island–born porter for the New York Central, after periodic rebuffs by Pullman and its lopsided company union, the Pullman Plan of Employee Representation (which left porters with a basic work month of 400 hours or 11,000 miles and a $7.50 wage hike to $67.50 a month). In June 1925, Totten approached the 36-year-old Randolph, then editor of *The Messenger*, a black political and literary magazine, on 135th Street in Harlem and invited him to address the Pullman Porters Athletic Association.

Totten later recalled that he was looking for someone "who had the ability and the courage, the stamina and the guts, the manhood and determination of purpose to lead the porters on." Meeting secretly in Harlem on August 25, 1925, Totten and several hundred other porters from the New York Central and neighboring railroads voted to organize. They invited Randolph, an avowed Socialist and an outsider immune to company pressure, to be their president. Randolph, whose brother was a former porter, eventually agreed. "As history had shown, no Pullman porter could survive the attempt," Jervis Anderson wrote in his biography of Randolph. "Randolph's preeminent credential was that he could not be picked off by the Pullman Company." The porters were in a fighting mood by then, and their motto, "Fight or Be Slaves," bore no hint of Stepin Fetchit servility. Totten was fired by Pullman and became the brotherhood's secretary-treasurer. Benefiting from New Deal labor legislation, the porters finally signed their first collective bargaining agreement with the Pullman Company in 1935 and won a charter from the American Federation of Labor that same year—the first black union to do so.

The union's agenda wasn't limited to wages, though, or only to its members. In 1941, Randolph threatened a march of 100,000 blacks on Washington unless the government banned discrimination by defense contractors. On June 25, 1941, President Franklin D. Roosevelt did so and created the Fair Employment Practices Committee.

PERHAPS THE TERMINAL'S MOST ENDURING EXPORT is about time. Until 1883, virtually every town in the country set local time by the sun. Typically, noon would be regularly signaled so people could synchronize their clocks and watches. (A ball drop down a flagpole was considered most reliable, ringing a gong less so, given the slower speed of sound. In New York the daily ball drop downtown alerted mariners and delivered a telegraphic notification to the city's more than 2,000 jewelry stores so they could adjust their time pieces.) Whatever the method, the divergent definitions wreaked havoc on timetables as the railroads spread geographically and gained speed. Suddenly, every minute and second counted. But efforts to standardize time were uneven at best and disconnects were common. In *On Time*, Carlene E. Stephens recounted the epochal experience of Richard Cobden, the British calico baron, who was traveling by train from Boston to Providence in 1835:

> First, his train was delayed. Eventually it set off, but the passengers had to get out and walk at a stretch where the track was unfinished. Finally, the car caught fire—twice—and the travelers not only suffered more delay but received a dousing in the frenzy to put out the flames. By the time Cobden arrived at his destination, the hour was so late that all the inns in town were full. He bedded down on chairs in a public hall. Noting the elaborate instructions in the railroad regulations for what to do when delays occurred, we may conclude that such experiences were common.

Kind of puts your daily commute in perspective.

BY THE 1850S, Henry David Thoreau was proclaiming that trains on the Fitchburg Railroad in Massachusetts, which passed Walden Pond, were so precise "and their whistles can be heard so far, that farmers set their clocks by them." But each railroad imposed its own standard, usually depending on where it was headquartered. Professor J.K. Rees of Columbia estimated that by 1883, the number of local standards, once as many as 100, had been halved to a still considerable and confusing 53. Meanwhile, the trackage that crisscrossed the country had expanded exponentially, from a mere 73 miles in 1830 to 9,000 by midcentury and more than 30,000 just one decade later. Cities served by multiple lines were especially vulnerable to chronological chaos. Buffalo's station, for example, displayed three clocks: New York time for the New York Central, Columbus time for the Lake Shore & Michigan Southern, and Buffalo local time.

A passenger traveling from Portland, Maine, to Buffalo could arrive in Buffalo at 12:15 according to his own watch set by Portland time. He might be met by a friend at the station whose watch indicated 11:40 Buffalo time. The Central clock said noon. The Lake Shore clock said it was only 11:25. At Pennsylvania Station in Jersey City, New Jersey, one clock displayed Philadelphia time and another New York time. When it was 12:12 in New York, it was 12:24 in Boston, 12:07 in Philadelphia, and 11:17 in Chicago. "Had there been stretched across the Continent yesterday a line of clocks extending from the extreme eastern point of Maine to the extreme western point on the Pacific Coast," the *Times* mused, "and had each clock sounded an alarm at the hour of noon, local time, there would have been a continuous ringing from the east to the west lasting three-and-a-quarter hours."

An amateur astronomer, William Lambert, proposed to Congress as early as 1809 that with the nation growing westward, time be standardized. His proposal languished for half a century, even as England, Scotland, and Wales (which covered a much smaller band longitudinally than the United States) uniformly adopted Greenwich Mean Time in 1848. In 1853, an inaccurate watch led to a crash on the Camden & Amboy railroad in New Jersey. Three days later, a

Providence & Worcester train carrying spectators to a yacht race at Newport and speeding to make a steamboat connection collided on a blind curve of a single track, killing 14 passengers. A brakeman, acting as the conductor, calculated that he had enough time to switch to a siding but was relying on a watch borrowed from a milkman that was running slow. "Our columns groan again with reports of wholesale slaughter by Railroad trains," the *Times* fumed. As a result, railroads in New England adopted a single standard.

The need for a national standard was hastened by the commercial development of the telegraph and, in 1862, when Congress authorized the building of the first transcontinental railroad. A year later, a rash of collisions spurred the Reverend Charles F. Dowd, co-principal, with his wife, of Temple Grove Ladies' Seminary in Saratoga Springs, New York (a girls' boarding school, which later became Skidmore College), to suggest multiple regional time zones.

He sketched out his proposal in 1869 and the following year presented it to railway superintendents in New York. He elaborated in a pamphlet proposing four zones 15 degrees longitude wide (the sun moves across 15 degrees every hour). Railroad trains "are the great educators and monitors of the people in teaching and maintaining exact time," said William F. Allen, editor of the *Traveler's Official Railway Guide*. But "there is today scarcely a railroad center of any importance in the United States at which the standards used by the roads entering it do not number from two to five. The adoption of the system proposed will reduce the present uncertainty to comparative if not absolute certainty."

In 1882, Connecticut bowed to a Yale astronomer, Leonard Waldo, and enacted a standard time that replaced the separate times set by railroads to synchronize their schedules separately with the clocks in Boston, Hartford, New Haven, New London, and New York. A national standard was something else entirely. As Allen wrote, "How can this reform be accomplished? It is on record that a small religious body once adopted two resolutions as a declaration of its faith. The first was, Resolved, that the saints should govern the earth. Second, Resolved that we are the saints."

A version of Dowd's proposal was finally embraced by the General Railway Time Convention in 1883—representing most of the lines that controlled 93,000 miles of rail—to take effect nationwide a month later at noon, Sunday, November 18. For the first time, a traveler going cross-country could rely on the minute hand of his watch telling the correct time, with only the hour changing as he passed from one time zone into another. No longer would clocks be chiming continuously for three and a quarter hours. Instead, they would ring in each hour simultaneously, even if the hour would be different in each time zone.

In New York, they would strike noon approximately 3 minutes, 58 seconds, and 38 one-hundredths of a second earlier than they had the day before. All over the country, Americans greeted the change with Y2K trepidation and with not a little resentment that the railroads were once again impinging on their daily routines. A local prophet in Charleston, South Carolina, warned that toying with time would provoke divine displeasure (sure enough, a major earthquake struck there three years later). Pittsburgh, Cleveland, and Detroit refused to comply, and Cincinnati delayed adoption of standard time for seven years. The mayor of Bangor, Maine, rejected the new standard, declaring that "neither railroad laws nor municipal regulations have the power to change from the immutable laws of God."

CLOCK MASTER WILLIAM STEINHAUSER MAINTAINED THE 13-FOOT-DIAMETER
TIMEPIECE. THE VI PANE OPENS FOR A PARK AVENUE VIEW.

Boston's commissioner of insolvency, Edward Jenkins, refusing
to comply with the new standard, declared Horace Clapp in default
on November 19, 1883, because he got to court a minute late by local
time but 15 minutes early under standard time. Massachusetts Superior Court Justice Oliver Wendell Holmes ruled that while the standard had not been adopted by the state legislature, the popular
community consensus—standard time, as imposed the day before in
Boston by the city council—applied.

J.M. TOUCEY, general superintendent of the New York Central, announced that beginning November 18 all trains would run on "New
Standard, 75th median time, which is four minutes slower than the
present standard." The official timekeeper at the time was the Western Union Company at 195 Broadway. There, in Room No. 48, James
Hamblet, the superintendent of the Time Telegraph Company,
planned to stop his regulator clock at 11 a.m. New York time, pause
the requisite 3 minutes, 58 seconds, and start it again on standard
time on the 75th meridian as verified with observatories in Washington, D.C., Cambridge, Massachusetts, and Allegheny, Pennsylvania.

The first noon under standard time would be signaled by the regular dropping of the 42-inch-diameter, 125-pound copper time ball from a 22-foot-high staff atop the Western Union Building, triggered by a signal from the U.S. Naval Observatory in Washington that tripped a magnetic latch. Trains across the country would be stopped to adjust their timetables to standard time. A crowd gathered in front of the Western Union Building to celebrate the "Day of Two Noons" and to watch the time ball drop twice—first on local time and four minutes later on the new eastern standard time. Despite the public apprehension about changing times, the *New York Tribune* dryly concluded, "There was no convulsion of nature, and no signs have been discovered of political or social revolution."

Even earlier, at 10 that morning in New York, a horological revolution took place. Grand Central became the first railroad station in the nation to adopt standard time. Seeking to minimize the disruption, the New York Central figured earlier was better. To accommodate the Central, Hamblet stopped the pendulum of his regulator clock at 9 a.m. instead of 11.

Following the American example, countries around the globe adopted time zones too. "No crisis forced the railroads to alter the way they kept time, no federal legislation mandated the change, no public demand had precipitated it," the historian Carlene Stephens wrote. "The railroads voluntarily rearranged the entire country's public timekeeping, albeit under the threat of government interference if they did nothing. The country, for the most part, went along without too much reluctance."

Industrialization and urbanization were taking their toll on spontaneity, even as travel became speedier and leisure time increased.

Americans were becoming "increasingly attentive to and accountable for living and working in synchronized ways," Stephens wrote, although it would take until 1918 for Congress to formally establish standard time and daylight savings time.

Today, Grand Central's master clock is located on the Lower Level near Track 117. It looks like an oversize blue refrigerator and is synchronized every second by a signal from the atomic clock at the Naval Observatory in Bethesda, Maryland, where time is measured by the vibrations of a cesium atom. The master clock controls every official timepiece in the terminal, from the four-faced golden ball clock atop the information booth in the Main Concourse to the clock on the 42nd Street façade. Still, one clock in the terminal, in the Graybar Passage looking west toward the Main Concourse, sometimes sends mixed messages. The hands are always correct, but the sign beneath it is wrong for nearly half the year. The Central was so proud of its role in inaugurating time zones that the builders of Grand Central carved "Eastern Standard Time" into the marble under the clock in 1913, five years before Congress imposed daylight savings time.

Western Union's shift to standard time in New York was overseen by William Allen, the *Railway Guide* editor, whose name, the *Times* declared, "will be forever connected with the successful accomplishment of one of the most useful reforms possible to the heretofore often bewildered traveler." How long Allen was remembered is arguable. The Reverend Charles Dowd faded from public memory even faster, though. Dowd died underneath the wheels of a Delaware & Hudson locomotive at a grade crossing in Saratoga, New York, in 1904. History does not record whether the train was on time.

SAVING GRAND CENTRAL

THE TEMPLE OF DENDUR was built in Egypt 19 centuries before Grand Central Terminal. It celebrated a river, not a railroad. And it stood 6,000 miles from the middle of Manhattan. But the Temple and Grand Central had one very important person in common, a woman whose prestige led to their salvation. Momentum for what might very well have been the end of Grand Central came to a screeching halt with a surprise telephone call in 1975 to the Municipal Art Society. "There's a woman on the phone," Laurie Beckelman, a dubious 22-year-old assistant, told her boss, Kent Barwick, "who claims to be Jackie Onassis."

Onassis was no newcomer to historic preservation. Her love affair with the Temple of Dendur started while her first husband was president and she was restoring the White House. The Egyptian

PRESERVATIONISTS RALLIED ON THE
VIADUCT OVER PERSHING SQUARE UNDER
THE COMMODORE'S APPROVING GAZE.

✧   159   ✧

government offered up a smorgasbord of monuments to the United States in gratitude for gifts from the Kennedy administration to save the temple and other antiquities from flooding caused by construction of the Aswan Dam. Onassis immediately chose the temple. Years later, she moved into a Fifth Avenue apartment that provided a stunning vista of the salvaged temple, which was installed in a glass jewel box at the Metropolitan Museum of Art across the street. By special arrangement, the museum would illuminate the temple at night so she could show it off to guests.

Onassis's call to the Municipal Art Society was prompted by an article in the *Times*. A few days before, on January 21, 1975, State Supreme Court Justice Irving H. Saypol had voided the designation of Grand Central Terminal as a city landmark. The decision went well beyond the realm of aesthetic criticism, although Saypol gratuitously belittled the terminal as leaving "no reaction here other than of a long neglected faded beauty." Without ruling on the constitutionality of the decade-old landmarks law, he decided in favor of the Penn Central Railroad, owners of the terminal. By not allowing the railroad to place a revenue-producing 59-story skyscraper above the terminal, Saypol said that the city was causing "economic hardship" so severe that it amounts to "a taking of property"—the property, in this case, being the very air rights that William Wilgus had conceived of seven decades earlier. Deep inside the *Times* story on Saypol's decision was a paragraph that caught Onassis's eye: "It was learned last night that the Municipal Art Society would announce within the next week the formation of a citywide committee to work for the preservation of the terminal and to support the city in its expected appeal."

• • •

IN A WAY, you could blame the whole landmarking mess on William Wilgus. Arguably, his very conception of Grand Central Terminal provided the deep roots for its potential destruction. As the Central's chief engineer, in 1903 he, in effect, created the intangible legal principle of air rights, which the successor railroad—bankrupt and hemorrhaging—wanted to transform into an office building that would generate hefty rental revenue. Unwittingly, another Wilgus innovation also laid the groundwork for the terminal's threatened demolition. He originally envisioned a revenue-producing tower atop the depot. While it was never built, the structural support for a future skyscraper was installed as the six-story bases off the four corners of the main concourse. The tower proposal largely lay dormant for 50 years.

BY THE END OF THAT HALF-CENTURY, long-distance passenger traffic was plummeting while deficits from passenger service were ballooning. The Suburban Concourse, now known as the Lower Level, was closed altogether by midcentury. By 1954, the Central was sending only 18 long-distance trains weekdays from Grand Central to upstate and the West, compared with 32 in 1947. The Central's president, Alfred E. Perlman (he later joined Howard Newman at the Western Pacific Railroad, but there is no evidence that he inspired the *Mad* magazine character), threatened to shutter Grand Central altogether and leave passengers to fend for themselves on public transportation from the Bronx or Westchester. Even from as far north as Croton-Harmon, Perlman said, "they can get into New York the way they do when they fly into Idlewild Airport." (He also suggested integrating the city's subway system and the Central's Park Avenue tracks, which, he said, would be far less costly than building a proposed Second Avenue subway.)

In 1954, the Central announced that it was mulling construction of the world's tallest building on the site of its terminal, which railroad officials claimed was running a $24 million annual deficit. The Central's spectacular Hyberboloid, an ambitious 108-story, nearly 5-million-square-foot tower, designed for William Zeckendorf by I.M. Pei, would be topped by an observation tower that would boost its height to 1,600 feet, well beyond the 1,250-foot Empire State Building. The proposal, and a subsequent alternative (ironically by a successor firm to the terminal's original architects), generated an outcry. *Architectural Forum* published a letter signed by 220 architects pleading that the terminal's Main Concourse be spared. They called the concourse "probably the finest big room in New York" and continued their paean:

> It belongs in fact to the nation. People admire it as travel carries them through from all parts of the world. It is…one of those very few building achievements that…has come to stand for our country. This great room is noble in its proportions, alive in the way the various levels and passages work in and out of it, sturdy and reassuring in its construction, splendid in its materials—but that is just the beginning. Its appeal recognizes no top limit of sophistication, no bottom limit. The most exacting architectural critic agrees in essentials with the newsboy at the door.

The *Times* added tentatively that "before the plans reach rigid crystallization, there is a chance that public opinion can persuade the heads of these railroads to consider some scheme whereby, without arresting the desirable progress implicit in their project, this great

GRAND CENTRAL LOOKING NORTH, WHEN MOSTLY HOTELS AND POSH APARTMENT BUILDINGS STRADDLED PARK AVENUE.

piece of civic architecture could be spared." Four years later, Pei's proposal had morphed into Grand Central City, an octagonal skyscraper that would become known as the Pan Am and later as the Met Life Building, a massive 2.4-million-square-foot hulk—surpassed in bulk at the time only by the Pentagon and the Chicago Merchandise Mart. The tower was sandwiched between Grand Central and its corporate headquarters but spared the terminal itself. The humongous building's 45,000-ton steel frame was supported by 200 existing columns and another 95 sunk into bedrock, 55 feet below the surface. Some concessions to Grand Central were proffered. The bulk was cut from 3 million square feet. The axis was rotated to east-west, to give the New York Central Building a little more breathing room. Still, the *Times'* architecture critic, Ada Louise Huxtable, wrote:

> Many planners agree that this addition to an overbuilt New York is one more rapid step toward the certain strangulation of the city, and its eventual reduction to total paralysis. However, as long as private enterprise controls city land, use and economics and legislation offer no incentives to improved urban design, such buildings are inevitable, and neither developer nor designer is to blame. The blockbuster building is here to stay, a singular symptom of one of the most disturbing characteristics of our age: A loss of human scale that seems irrevocably tied to a loss of human values.

Developed by Erwin S. Wolfson and designed by Emory Roth & Sons with Walter Gropius and Pietro Belluschi, the tower replaced the six-story Grand Central Terminal Office Building just north of the terminal. Grand Central City was hailed by Governor Nelson A. Rockefeller as emblematic of the genius and creativity of the free enterprise system. *Harper's* magazine begged to differ. "When Commodore Vanderbilt, surely a champion of free enterprise, organized the Grand Central area, enterprise was free enough to create order in the grand manner of Versailles, on the grand scale of the railway age. What is happening now is hardly more than what happened in Rome in the Dark Ages—men tear down great works to put up the best they can."

The critic V.S. Pritchett was even less forgiving. Noting that the Pan Am Building was financed by his fellow Brits, he observed (in an uncredited bow to William Wilgus), "No other city I can think of has anything like the undulating miles that fly down Park Avenue from 96th Street to Grand Central blocked now though it is by the brutal mass of the Pan Am Building—a British affront to the city spoken of as a revenge for Suez."

The Central hoped that an anticipated $1 million in rentals would help stanch its bleeding. Instead, the new building touched off a simmering dispute with the New Haven Railroad over who owned the terminal and adjacent property. It also whetted the deficit-ridden Central's appetite to develop even more real estate. In 1961, the railroad's request to install a three-level bowling alley over the main waiting room, which would have lowered its ceiling from 60 feet to 15, was rejected by the city's Board of Standards and Appeals (because it was located in a restricted retail area, a bowling alley would violate zoning regulations). But prominent architects and civic groups warned that the victory was just a skirmish before an inevitable epic battle over the terminal's future.

THAT SAME YEAR, across town, the Pennsylvania Railroad had optioned the air rights over Penn Station, fulfilling a dream of Alexander Cassatt, the line's president when Penn Station was being built (he was dissuaded by his architect from placing a hotel atop the station because the railroad owed the city a "thoroughly and distinctly monumental gateway"). The Beaux Arts–style station, flanked by 84 Roman columns, had faded even less elegantly than Grand Central, its junior by three years, since demolition was announced in 1961. It was seedy. And grimy. The roof was leaking. Maintenance costs were draining its corporate parent.

Despite protests from preservationists, demolition began on October 28, 1963, with the staccato sound of jackhammers tearing into the station's granite skin and the lowering of a stone eagle. "Just another job," said John Rezin, foreman of the wrecking crew. His assessment was echoed by Morris Lipsett, president of the demolition company: "If anybody seriously considered it art, they would have put up some money to save it."

The detritus of a great station would be ignominiously dumped in the Secaucus Meadows as landfill for what would become the Meadowlands. "The message was terribly clear," the *Times*' Ada Louise Huxtable wrote. "Tossed into that Secaucus graveyard were about 25 centuries of classical culture and the standards of style, elegance and grandeur that it gave to the dreams and constructions of Western man." A banal office building and the fourth incarnation of Madison Square Garden rose in its place. Indeed, if Pennsy passengers and Long Island Rail Road commuters felt claustrophobic, they were justified. The ceiling of the old station's awesome main waiting room was 150 feet high. In the new one, it would barely reach 25 feet. Vincent Scully memorably summed up what had been lost. "One entered the city like a god," he wrote. "One scuttles in now like a rat."

• • •

VIEWED FROM THE WEST BALCONY, THE MAIN CONCOURSE WAS COMMERCIALIZED UNTIL THE METROPOLITAN TRANSPORTATION AUTHORITY INTERVENED.

BUT PENN STATION WOULD NOT DIE IN VAIN. In a city that never valued its history as much as Boston or Philadelphia did ("History is for losers," Ken Jackson, the Columbia history professor, japes), where relatively sparse prime space is periodically recycled to produce bulkier and taller buildings, razing Penn Station fueled an unexpected backlash. "I really believe Grand Central Terminal was saved because of what happened at Penn Station," said Peter Samton, an architect and civic leader who lobbied to save them both. Earlier in 1961, even before the wrecking crew went to work and with development threatening other historic landmarks, such as Carnegie Hall and the Alexander Hamilton Grange, Mayor Robert F. Wagner appointed a committee to research the applicability of the Bard Act, first suggested in 1913, the year Grand Central Terminal opened, and finally passed by the state legislature in 1956.

The act empowered localities to create special zoning or land-use protection for historically or aesthetically distinguished places. "As time marches on," wrote Francis Keally, past president of both the Municipal Art Society and the New York chapter of the American Institute of Architects, "it behooves all of us to keep a watchful eye on any changes that would affect the aesthetic possessions of New York, and, when necessary, our voices should be heard in combating any such attempts to destroy the cherished remembrance of the past."

In April 1963, before the demolition of Penn Station began, Wagner formally endorsed the recommendation of his committee and named a 12-member Landmarks Preservation Commission. The commission came too late for Penn Station, though, prompting the New York chapter of the architects institute to lament, "Like ancient Rome, New York seems bent on tearing down its finest buildings. In Rome, demolition was a piecemeal process which took over 1,000 years; in New York demolition is absolute and complete in a matter of months. The rise of modern archaeology put an end to this kind of vandalism in Rome, but in our city no such deterrent exists." Two years later, the city council overcame the objections of real estate developers and codified a permanent commission armed with police power and the right of eminent domain. The law also provided tax abatements to hard-pressed property owners.

THE MAYOR'S TEMPORARY COMMISSION had already identified 700 sites that were considered valuable enough historically or aesthetically to be preserved. Community Planning Board No. 5 in Midtown voted overwhelmingly against landmark status for Grand Central, but surprisingly little controversy was generated at a commission hearing on May 10, 1966. Three witnesses appeared in favor. Virtually the only opposition was mustered by lawyers for the railroad itself. Robert Tinsley, representing the Municipal Art Society, unabashedly proclaimed the terminal "the most magnificent railroad station in the world." He described it as "purely an American building bearing the full stamp of the American Renaissance" and said Jules Félix Coutan's sculpture on the 42nd Street façade "is the best of its kind of the 20th Century anywhere."

Another speaker, William Lynn McCracken Sr., of Staten Island, referred the commission to a 1959 essay by Henry Hope Reed. In his *The Golden City* (a book that Jacqueline Onassis described as "like finding a long-sought friend or mentor"), Reed waxed rhapsodic about the "colossal Mercury who motions to us to view the splendor that transportation has created" and unequivocally concluded, "No Picturesque Secessionist terminal can even attempt to rival the Grand Central or any other of our great classical terminals, because today's designer refuses to recognize the theatrical, nay, operatic, qualities of art."

Methodically working its way through hundreds of potential sites deemed worthy of preservation, on August 6, 1967, the permanent commission declared 11 structures—including Carnegie Hall, Hamilton Grange, the Metropolitan Museum of Art, the Highbridge Park water tower, and Grand Central Terminal—New York City landmarks, bringing to nearly 200 the structures it had designated during its first two years. Grand Central was described as "a magnificent example of French Beaux Arts architecture; that it is one of the great buildings of America, that it represents a creative engineering solution of a very difficult problem, combined with artistic splendor; that as an American Railroad Station it is unique in quality, distinction, character; and that this building plays a significant role in the life and development of New York City."

The terminal "evokes a spirit that is unique in this city," the designation added, and "combines distinguished architecture with a brilliant engineering solution, wedded to one of the most fabulous railroad terminals of our time. Monumental in scale, this great building functions as well today as it did when it was built." Grand Central, the commission concluded, "always has been a symbol of the city itself."

But the terminal's reprieve was only temporary. Within a few weeks, the beleaguered New York Central was inviting architects to submit plans for a 2-million-square-foot building as tall as 45 stories atop Grand Central's main waiting room.

BY THEN, the New York Central was virtually bankrupt and was running out of alternatives to generate revenue. The railroad had already wantonly commercialized the terminal by monetizing every square inch it could (including the Colorama, which was billed as the world's largest photograph transparency, and the 13.5-foot-diameter replica of the Westclox Big Ben clock over the south concourse). The clutter manifested itself in nonmaterial ways too. In 1949, the railroad experimented with daily canned Muzak broadcasts from more than 40 loudspeakers and accompanied by 240 commercials over 17 hours (which netted the railroad $1,800 a week, against what it said was then an $11 million annual deficit to operate the terminal).

Leading the charge against the audio intrusion was Harold Ross, the editor of the *New Yorker*, who figured that any interference with people's ability to concentrate on a book or magazine was bad for business—his. "If they get away with this, nobody will be able to read on any means of conveyance in the United States," he complained.

Appearing before a state Public Service Commission panel, the railroad's lawyer challenged Ross's assertion that the broadcasts made his ears ring. He was asked whether his own hearing was good. "It is perfect," Ross testified. "It is too good. Under the circumstances I am thinking of having an ear drum punctured." Ross denied that he had urged the magazine's readers to complain, but the railroad lawyer produced a "Talk of the Town" item that exhorted readers to do just that. To which Ross, unfazed, replied: "I beg your pardon, I guess I must have read that in Grand Central Terminal."

At the hearing, James F. Johnson, a former Secret Service agent, recalled how he had lost his ailing mother-in-law in the terminal because his wife became befuddled by the hubbub, which was compounded by the fact that the paging service had been discontinued in favor of lucrative commercials. James L. Fly, a former chairman of the Federal Communications Commission, declared that "the forced feeding of advertising" destroys a listener's right not to listen. Harold J. Harris, a psychiatrist, cautioned that the noise pollution could unleash behavior triggered by "suppressed rage." Another witness, Virginia L. Rowland, warned of even more dire consequences. "It is not too fantastic," she testified, "that one of those employed in the terminal might go berserk and start shooting up the customers." A month later, the Central capitulated, halting the broadcasts and acknowledging, without saying so in as many words, that its experiment was unsound.

• • •

BUT IF COMMERCIALS weren't enough to drive away passengers, long-distance rail travel was doomed by airplanes and the construction of a concrete web of interstate highways. Railroads were under assault, especially passenger service, which couldn't compete and which the lines subjugated to more profitable freight. (Robert R. Young, the Central's chairman, memorably observed that until 1946, pigs huddled into freight cars could cross the country without changing trains, but passengers could not.) The Central's passenger revenues plummeted from $135.5 million in 1948 to $106.5 million in 1954 and a mere $55 million a decade later.

"I live in the twilight of railroading, the going down of its sun," E.B. White wrote in 1960. "For the past few months I've been well aware that I am the Unwanted Passenger, one of the last survivors of

NINETY-FIVE COLUMNS WERE SUNK INTO BEDROCK 55 FEET BENEATH PARK AVENUE FOR WHAT BECAME THE PAN AM BUILDING.

a vanishing and ugly breed. Indeed, if I am to believe the statements I see in the papers, I am all that stands between the Maine railroads and a bright future of hauling fast freight for a profit."

Moreover, while automobiles and airplanes achieved dazzling speeds, the trains he rode to and from New York and his farm in Maine maintained their "accustomed gait" of just over 30 mph. "This is an impressive record," he concluded. "It's not every institution that can hold to an ideal through 55 years of our fastest-moving century." The Pennsylvania Railroad was in a similarly precarious position. Real estate ventures like Penn Plaza, which replaced Penn Station, and the Pan Am Building had bought time for the railroads but were insufficient to cover mounting costs and diminishing revenue. On February 1, 1968, the unthinkable happened. A worst-case scenario loomed as the only remaining option for survival. The New York Central and the Pennsylvania Railroad merged to form the Penn Central. The combine, which became the country's biggest real estate company and the owner, through Madison Square Garden, of the New York Knicks and the New York Rangers, would last two years before declaring bankruptcy itself—the nation's largest. (In 1976, the railroad was folded into Conrail, which was created by the federal government to run failing freight lines; the former Penn Central Corporation morphed into American Premier Underwriters, part of Carl Lindner's American Financial Group.)

By then, the Long Island Rail Road, which the Pennsylvania had controlled since 1900, would have been sold off to New York State for $65 million. New York and the Connecticut Transportation Authority would buy or lease the Central's tracks from Grand Central to Connecticut and pay Penn Central to operate the commuter service. A similar arrangement would produce Metro-North in 1983, leading

Joseph R. Daughen and Peter Binzen, who wrote *The Wreck of the Penn Central,* to conclude, "Thus, close to a quarter of a million commuters in the nation's largest city ride trains that are state owned or are heavily subsidized by public agencies. If this isn't 'nationalization' it is something quite close to it."

FIVE MONTHS AFTER THE MERGER, the new company proposed building a 55-story cast-stone and granite slab designed by Marcel Breuer and developed by Morris Saady, which, as the builders described it, would be "floated" above Grand Central and rise 150 feet higher than the Pan Am Building. One design called for the tower to be cantilevered above the terminal to preserve the façade. An alternative would raze one side of the terminal to create a uniform front but preserve the Main Concourse. The tower known as 175 Park Avenue would generate at least $3 million annually for the Penn Central from air rights alone. Neither version was embraced by city officials or by many prominent architects.

"Horrible—terrible," said Richard Roth, who was the principal architect of the Pan Am Building. "We put the Pan Am Building way back from the main part of the terminal, replacing an ugly structure over the train shed. It formed a gracious backdrop for the terminal itself." Architect Philip Johnson declared the proposal an "outrage," adding, "I was against the Pan Am Building, against the idiotic idea of putting bowling alleys in the waiting-room space when that was brought up a few years ago, and I'm against this new thing. It's wrong in every possible way."

The City Planning Commission had no jurisdiction because the proposed building did not require any zoning variances. That didn't stop Donald Elliott, the commission chairman, from pronouncing the proposal "the wrong building, in the wrong place, at the wrong time." Ada Louise Huxtable weighed in a few days later and was no less unequivocal. She called Breuer's blueprint "a bizarre scheme that could only be conceived in and for New York." Worse still, it created a heads-they-win, tails-you-lose dilemma. "Designation by the Landmarks Commission does not insure preservation," she acknowledged. "All the railroad has to do is show that the building is enough of a losing proposition to prove 'hardship' under the landmarks law and permission must be given to demolish after certain procedures have been satisfied. This is having your landmark, but taking a certain calculated risk of dooming it."

In one version or another, the historians James Marston Fitch and Diana S. Waite later wrote, "The Breuer scheme had several architectural merits and two insuperable drawbacks." The merits, such as they were, included the preservation of the concourse, the waiting room, and the façade. "But," they wrote, "the negative aspects of the proposed alteration are profound and are ambiental in nature"—that the tower would suck up all the air from the remaining sky space and place an impossible burden on already overloaded public transportation.

On September 20, 1968, under its chairman, Harmon H. Goldstone, the landmarks commission rejected the developer's claim that the project would have "no exterior effect." That touched off a full year of verbal jousting and counterproposals—including a promise by the developer to preserve the Main Concourse if the commission allowed him to construct the tower. (The commission's jurisdiction extended only to the exterior.)

On August 26, 1969, the commission voted 8 to 0 to deny the Penn Central permission to mongrelize the terminal. Its rejection of a certificate of appropriateness derided the two plans as so massive that they "would reduce the landmark itself to the status of a curiosity" and declared that "to balance a 55-story office tower above a flamboyant Beaux-Arts façade seems nothing more than an aesthetic joke." The second alternative was even worse, the commission concluded. "To protect a landmark, one does not tear it down. To perpetuate its architectural features, one does not strip them off."

Moreover, the commission said that the terminal's aesthetic value had to be considered in its physical context in a city that, unlike Paris, had few "dramatically terminated vistas." Echoing V.S. Pritchett, the commission wrote that New York had "Trinity Church at the end of Wall Street, Washington Arch at the foot of Fifth Avenue and the RCA Building at the end of the Rockefeller Center gardens. Yet none of these have the sweep that Park Avenue still provides for the Grand Central Terminal from the south." To mitigate any hardship claim by the railroad, the commission empowered the Penn Central to transfer the air rights to other developers at nearby sites.

Instead, less than two months later, the Penn Central sued.

THE RAILROAD ARGUED in the State Supreme Court in Manhattan that the commission's rejections were unconstitutional because they went "beyond the scope of any permissible regulation and constitute a taking of plaintiff's private property for public use without just compensation." The suit, seeking $8 million for each year development was delayed, even challenged the landmark character of Grand Central as "highly debatable and at best doubtful." "The aesthetic

A RARE VIEW OF THE REAR OF THE TERMINAL AS THE STEEL FRAMEWORK WAS BEING
INSTALLED FOR THE PAN AM BUILDING.

quality of the south façade is obscured by its engulfment among narrow streets and high-rise buildings," the Penn Central's lawyers from Dewey, Ballentine, Bushby, Palmer & Wood contended. "It is hardly seen at all except for a short distance to the south on Park Avenue, and even there the view of the façade is intersected by the encircling roadway and by the tall buildings that line Park Avenue. Furthermore," the railroad's lawyers argued, in what amounted to a stinging architectural indictment of the Penn Central's earlier air rights venture, "the terminal is set against the backdrop and contrasting lines of the Pan Am Building, which appears to hang over the terminal and to dwarf it." (This argument was a little like the defendant accused of parricide begging for mercy because he is an orphan.)

The Municipal Art Society intervened as a friend of the court and mustered a veritable who's who of legal talent on behalf of Grand Central. (Among those who contributed to the society's brief were former mayor Wagner, and other legal luminaries, including Bernard Botein, Whitney North Seymour Sr., Francis T.P. Plimpton, Samuel I. Rosenman, and Bethuel M. Webster.) A trial was conducted before Justice Irving Saypol, who would take more than two years to deliver his decision. (Saypol was perhaps best known for having prosecuted Julius and Ethel Rosenberg for espionage conspiracy in 1951, a case in which he had decided the defendants were guilty nearly a year before the jury rendered its verdict.)

Saypol invalidated the Grand Central designation, delivering a second blow to the landmarks law in less than a year (the designation of the J.P. Morgan mansion on Madison Avenue had been voided the previous July by the state's highest court, the Court of Appeals). He declined to address the constitutionality of the statute but ruled that by preventing the railroad from earning rent on the air rights for the proposed tower, the commission created "economic hardship" which "constitutes a taking of property."

He also concluded that a city compromise, which would have permitted the transfer of air rights from Grand Central to the adjacent Biltmore Hotel site, was uneconomical. Ada Louise Huxtable wondered whether the delay had been a blessing in disguise, given the downturn in the city's real estate market. "Did Penn Central and the developer really lose all that money they are claiming damages for (that will help sink the city), or did the city's delaying action perhaps save their shirts?" After two years of "municipal breath holding," those questions, she suggested, finally would be addressed in an appeal of a case so disturbing because of "the gravity of its effect on the city's heritage."

But while Deputy Mayor Stanley M. Friedman said the city was "99 percent sure" to appeal the decision, an appeal, it turned out, was by no means certain. In fact, the city's chief lawyer was arguing against it. Without ruling on the constitutionality of the law, Saypol had delivered a thinly veiled warning to city officials that designating a landmark did not come without cost. "The point of decision here," he wrote, "is that the authorities empowered to make the designation may do so but only at the expense of those who will ultimately have to bear the cost, the taxpayers."

That cautionary note was not lost on W. Bernard Richland, the city's corporation counsel. With the Penn Central claiming that landmarking the terminal had cost it $60 million so far, Richland was worried that the city, already verging on a fiscal crisis of catastrophic proportions, would be liable for damages. Richland recommended to Mayor Abraham D. Beame that the city not appeal Saypol's decision.

"Bernie wanted us not to appeal," John Zuccotti, the former chairman of the City Planning Commission, remembered. "He had some thought that we were exposed. He was very concerned. I remember the Penn Central people coming to see us and they urged us not to appeal, too. We debated the issue in front of Abe and he said appeal." Exactly what changed Beame's mind may never be known. But by the time he reviewed the subject with Zuccotti and Judah Gribetz, a deputy mayor, he had received a poignant appeal from Jacqueline Onassis.

. . .

THE LEGAL APPEAL—and the threat that the city would fold—galvanized a pantheon of prominent New Yorkers, spearheaded by the Municipal Art Society. Frederic Papert, Ashton Hawkins, and Brendan Gill, all ardent preservationists, figured prominently (Gill was succeeded as architecture critic at the *New Yorker* by Paul Goldberger, who later wrote that while Gill "alone did not save Grand Central Terminal, he did as much as anyone to establish the climate that made that possible, through his writing and his civic activism and his behind-the-scenes wheeling and dealing"). Gill had been Grand Central's guardian for decades. In 1958, he railed against a "living billboard"—a platform over the ticket windows on which fashion shows were staged—and warned that Madison Avenue's hidden persuaders "will eventually find a way to make those twinkling constellations spell out your favorite smoke, like a constellation should." At Gill's memorial service in 1998, George Plimpton said: "The only things Brendan hadn't been able to save in his lifetime were the Polo Grounds, Ebbets Field, the Maisonette, Alger Hiss, the Reichstag, the Edsel, and the passenger pigeon." The preservation movement had other heroes, too, including Dorothy Miner, who was the landmarks commission lawyer.

If Jacqueline Onassis needed any prodding, she got it from her good friend Karl Katz (a board member of the Municipal Art Society, he took her to an exhibit he designed at Grand Central to dramatize the potential demolition of the terminal), and possibly from Babe Paley, whose husband, Bill, had advised Beame's predecessor, John V. Lindsay, on urban design (Babe Paley's involvement would have been poetically just; she was a descendant of Commodore Vanderbilt). Laurie Beckelman, who answered the pivotal phone call

from Onassis (and would later go on to become chairwoman of the Landmarks Preservation Commission), passed the phone to Kent Barwick, the Municipal Art Society president, at its tiny offices on East 65th Street. "I took the call and it was unmistakably Jackie," Barwick recalled. Papert, a former Kennedy advance man, later recruited her to the Municipal Art Society board, where she would diligently advocate on behalf of Columbus Circle, St. Bartholomew's Church, and other preservation projects. (In 1982, she publicly planted a kiss on City Comptroller Harrison J. Goldin's cheek, which was said to have sealed his vote to save Lever House.) Her handwritten plea to Mayor Beame

FRED PAPERT OF THE MUNICIPAL ART SOCIETY, JACQUELINE ONASSIS, AND PHILIP JOHNSON JOINED TO SAVE GRAND CENTRAL.

dated February 24, 1975, probably carried the day for Grand Central. She appealed to his nobility, recalled how much President Kennedy had intervened to block a federal office building in Washington's Lafayette Square, how he loved Grand Central, and added plaintively:

> Is it not cruel to let our city die by degrees, stripped of all her proud monuments, until there will be nothing left of all her history and beauty to inspire our children? If they are not inspired by the past of our city, where will they find the

strength to fight for her future? Americans care about their past, but for short term gain they ignore it and tear down everything that matters. Maybe, with our Bicentennial approaching, this is the moment to take a stand, to reverse the tide, so that we won't all end up in a uniform world of steel and glass boxes.

"HAVE I GOT A CASE FOR YOU," Bernie Richland told Nina Gershon, a senior appeals lawyer in the corporation counsel's office, once he was persuaded to pursue the appeal. Gershon, who would later be appointed to the U.S. District Court in Brooklyn, said that once the decision to appeal was made, the city was gung-ho:

> There were some in the preservation community who questioned the city's resolve to pursue, through appeal, the fight to preserve Grand Central Terminal as a landmark, after a devastating loss in the trial court, which had not only rejected, with derision, the findings of the Landmarks Preservation Commission regarding the significance of the Terminal but found that the designation of the Terminal as a landmark was unconstitutional; ominously, the trial court had also severed and kept open the request for damages for a "temporary taking." But when Bernie became convinced of the merit of the city's position, he did not stint in his support of the appeal.

Preservationists made their case before the Appellate Division of the State Supreme Court and in the court of public opinion. Onassis joined with Philip Johnson, Mayor Wagner, Bess Myerson (the city's former consumer affairs commissioner), the author Louis

Auchincloss, Thomas P.F. Hoving (the Metropolitan Museum of Art director), Representative Edward I. Koch, and Manhattan Borough President Percy Sutton, among others, on a star-studded Committee to Save Grand Central Station. "Europe has its cathedrals and we have Grand Central Station," Johnson had declared, on January 31, 1975, at a press conference. Diane Henry wrote in the *Times*, "Although the audience cheered Mr. Johnson's eloquence, it was most fascinated by the presence of Mrs. Onassis, who rarely lends her presence and name to a public cause."

IN DECEMBER 1975, the Appellate Division reversed Saypol. In a 3 to 2 ruling signed by Presiding Justice Francis T. Murphy, the appeals panel wrote that the only question before it was whether the Penn Central had persuaded the court that the law "as applied to them in this case, imposes such a burden as to constitute a compensable taking. Put another way, while the exercise of the police power to regulate the private use of property is not unlimited, it is for the one attacking such regulation in any given case to establish that the line separating valid regulation from confiscation has been breached." Penn Central's burden, the court said, "is to establish that they are incapable of obtaining a reasonable return from Grand Central Terminal operations, not that they are not receiving it." The court concluded that the burden had not been met.

"Structures such as the Brooklyn Bridge, the Metropolitan Museum of Art, the New York Public Library and Grand Central Terminal are important and irreplaceable components of the special uniqueness of New York City," the judges wrote. "We have already witnessed the demise of the old Metropolitan Opera House and the

original Pennsylvania Station. Stripped of its remaining historically unique structures, New York City would be indistinguishable from any other large metropolis...The need to preserve structures worthy of landmark status is beyond dispute; and the propriety of the landmark designation accorded Grand Central Terminal is essentially unchallenged."

The judges were more than wary of Saypol's warning that landmark designations may be made only at taxpayers' expense: "Such language suggests that any regulation of private property to protect landmark values constitutes a compensable taking. Such holding would surely, as the amicus brief submitted hereon states, 'eviscerate New York's Landmarks Preservation Law.'"

Eighteen months later, in a case argued by Gershon's successor, Leonard Koerner, the Court of Appeals, the state's highest court, again affirmed Grand Central's status as a landmark. When times are flush, seizing landmark properties by eminent domain and compensating the owners might be desirable or even required. But, the judges concluded, especially when a city is in financial distress, "it should not be forced to choose between witnessing the demolition of its glorious past and mortgaging its hopes for the future."

The preservationists' victory parties were short-lived. Penn Central appealed to the U.S. Supreme Court. When the Court heard oral arguments on April 17, 1978, advocates chartered an eight-car Landmark Express (including Car 120, the vintage Pennsylvania, which played host to first-class passengers at the turn of the century) to make the round-trip from New York to Washington, where they were met by Senator Daniel Patrick Moynihan. "A big corporation shouldn't be able to destroy a building that has meant so much to so many for so many generations," Onassis said. "If Grand Central Station goes, all of the landmarks in the country will go as well." She added, "If we don't care about our past, we cannot hope for the future."

The stakes were enormous, for preservationists and for property owners. Ada Louise Huxtable was driven to hyperbole by this point, warning that everyone except "the Penn Central and some unreconstructed real-estate types" considered the proposed piggyback tower that would render Grand Central "the filling in a Pan Am–office tower sandwich" to be "architecturally and environmentally revolting."

• • •

PENN CENTRAL TRANSPORTATION CO. V. NEW YORK CITY was the first case in which the High Court considered historic preservation. The Court issued its decision on June 26, 1978. The 6 to 3 opinion by Justice William Brennan affirmed the New York Court of Appeals ruling that landmarking was constitutionally within a municipality's police powers and that this designation in particular did not constitute an indefensible "taking" of property by the government. "The designation as a landmark not only permits but contemplates that appellants may continue to use the property precisely as it has been used for the past 65 years: as a railroad terminal containing office space and concessions," the court concluded. Brennan wrote:

> The Landmarks Law no more effects an appropriation of the airspace above the Terminal for governmental uses than would a zoning law appropriate property; it simply prohibits appellants or others from occupying certain features of that space while allowing appellants gainfully to use the remainder of the parcel.
>
> The Landmarks Law, which does not interfere with the Terminal's present uses or prevent Penn Central from realizing a "reasonable return" on its investment, does not impose the drastic limitation on appellants' ability to use the air rights above the Terminal that appellants claim, for, on this record, there is no showing that a smaller, harmonizing structure would not be authorized. Moreover, the pre-existing air rights are made transferable to other parcels in the vicinity of the

Terminal, thus mitigating whatever financial burdens appellants have incurred.

Justice William Rehnquist wrote for the minority that the Landmarks Commission's refusal to sanction the tower above the terminal violated the Fifth Amendment's ban on taking private property for public use without just compensation. "The City of New York, because of its unadorned admiration for the design, has decided that the owners of the building must preserve it unchanged for the benefit of sightseeing New Yorkers and tourists," Rehnquist wrote.

"JACKIE ONASSIS WILL SAVE US," Philip Johnson had predicted, and no one involved in saving Grand Central doubted that her presence and eloquence contributed mightily to the public groundswell that undergirded the verdict and to subsequent victories by preservationists. "Jackie, the great arbiter of good taste in fashion, food and architecture, raised the consciousness of the nation to the importance of historic preservation," wrote Roberta Brandes Gratz, an architectural historian. "The implications of Penn Central for advocacy are so great," the architecture critic Paul Spencer Byard wrote, "that the public perception will shift from seeing preservation as a matter of pleasure to seeing it as a public necessity."

But the court victory was partly Pyrrhic. After all, as Rehnquist wrote, the city does not "merely prohibit Penn Central from using its property in a narrow set of noxious ways. Instead, appellees have placed an affirmative duty on Penn Central to maintain the Terminal in its present state and in 'good repair.'"

Problem was, the Penn Central was bankrupt.

THE
RESTORATION

J USTICE IRVING SAYPOL'S DECISION to void the landmarks designation of Grand Central Terminal could not have come at a better time. "The station is probably in no immediate danger," the *New Yorker* noted imperturbably. "Who's going to start putting up another office building this year?"

In 1975, when Saypol issued his decision, New York City was teetering on the brink of municipal bankruptcy. Public works projects were halted midway, leaving the steel skeletons of new schools to rust. Another landmark—the elegant but disintegrating Tweed Courthouse behind City Hall, which was to be razed and replaced with a parking lot—was spared only because the city could no longer afford to tear it down. Private developers also packed away blueprints and placed planned construction on hold. (William Wilgus's original plans

WORKERS TACKLED THE TERMINAL'S EXTERIOR
AFTER MOST INDOOR RESTORATION WAS DONE.
LUIS CABRERA FIXED JOINTS IN 2004.

KODAK'S MAMMOTH 18-BY-60-FOOT COLORAMA, A 15-FOOT MUTANT VERSION OF WESTCLOX'S BIG BEN ALARM CLOCK, AND A MERRILL LYNCH BOOTH DOMINATED THE CONCOURSE.

for a tower over the terminal might have been scrapped because of similar economic qualms on the eve of World War I; he wrote later only that they "fell by the wayside.")

Three years later, when the Supreme Court saved Grand Central, precisely what had been saved since the landmarking process began must have provided grist for some serious second thoughts. By then, the interior of the terminal had been festooned with advertising and even a Merrill Lynch, Pierce, Fenner & Smith investment booth in the Main Concourse; the giant baleful clock, which by now was advertising Manufacturers Hanover; and a Chemical Bank branch, perched obtrusively under the Kodak sign. "Right now, this space looks like—like St. Patrick's lit up for television," Philip Johnson fretted. "Grand Central has become honky-tonk, with its extra-dimensional advertising displays and its tendency to adopt the tactics of a travel broker," E.B. White groused, complaining that "the great hall seemed to me one of the more inspiring interiors in New York, until Lastex and Coca-Cola got into the temple." Paul Goldberger, then the *Times*' architecture critic, agreed, arguing that the concourse should serve as "a discreet background for human movement, not a room with movement of its own."

MEANWHILE, THE GRAND CENTRAL PALACE on Lexington Avenue between 46th and 47th Streets, the city's premier exhibition hall, was razed for a 47-story office building. The 1,900-room Commodore Hotel, which the Penn Central said was losing more than $1 million a year, abruptly closed in May 1976, throwing its 500 remaining employees out of work. The *C* and *T* in the name of the 34-story New York Central Building at 230 Park Avenue, the railroad's sublime and historic gem of a headquarters since 1929, were ignominiously chiseled into a *G* and an *E* when the building was sold to General Tire & Rubber (a ninth-floor office in 230 Park had been the scene of the mob execution of Mafia boss Salvatore Maranzano in 1931; appropriately enough, in *The Godfather* the meeting of the five Mafia families was filmed in the Central's 32nd-floor boardroom, with its mural of Engine 999; it was also described as Dagny Taggart's Transcontinental Railroad Building in Ayn Rand's *Atlas Shrugged* and later became the Helmsley Building).

Since the Penn Central had gone belly up in 1970, operation of the terminal was turned over to Conrail (and, in 1983, to the Metropolitan Transportation Authority's Metro-North). In still another retrenchment, the railroad recommended the cancellation of all nine predawn passenger trains (only a decade before, there were 30), sending musicians, bartenders, printers, and other graveyard-shift workers scurrying to find alternative routes home. In 1973, for the first time in its modern history, Grand Central was shuttered every night from 1:30 to 5:30 a.m., ostensibly to facilitate cleaning, but also to recapture the terminal from the growing proliferation of homeless people and other "undesirables" who congregated in its public spaces and encamped in the train yards beneath it.

Vanderbilt Avenue had become a haven for drug dealing, and surging crime seemed even more dangerous on dim and claustrophobic passageways and platforms. In 1977, the landing gear collapsed on a helicopter that had just alighted atop the Pan Am Building, killing six people, including a pedestrian below, who was struck by one of the copter's 20-foot blades. The accident doomed regular copter service from the roof.

STILL, A COCKEYED OPTIMIST could point to a few hopeful signs for the deteriorating terminal and its beleaguered neighborhood. By 1978, Philip Morris was eying the southwest corner of Park and 42nd Street for a sleek corporate headquarters. (Its building, three-and-a-half stories higher after the company acquired 75,000 square feet of air rights from Grand Central, would help doom the classic image of the Main Concourse bathed in shafts of sunlight streaming from most of its southern lunette windows.) The railroad had profitably sold off the Barclay, Biltmore, and Roosevelt hotels. Penn Central also dumped the adjacent Commodore Hotel in a complex deal involving tax breaks, leasebacks, and other investment arcana among the city, the state Urban Development Corporation, Donald Trump, and the Hyatt Hotel Corporation. In addition to restoring the hotel inside and out, the deal was intended to generate $2 million to clean Grand Central's exterior. "As an investment," Ada Louis Huxtable wrote presciently, "this could well be seed money for far greater returns in the start of a revitalized 42nd Street."

Something else had changed too. The city was slowly rebounding from the depths of a demoralizing fiscal crisis, and a new mayor, Edward I. Koch, was leading the charge as cheerleader in chief. (When asked in 1975 whether the demolition of Grand Central was inevitable if it could not support itself, Koch replied characteristically: "Central Park doesn't support itself. God forbid we should ever think of it in that way.") If New York still could not afford to build grand new projects, it could at least muster the will to salvage its Gilded Age gems. Year later in the *New Yorker*, Tony Hiss explained it another way:

> While many of the links that connect places and experiences and health have yet to be traced, some people have started treating their own experiences of places in a mid-19th century-clean-water fashion, by taking action to protect experiences that are important to them—for example, fighting the demolition of places like Grand Central Terminal...The people involved in this work speak, often, not just of architectural beauty but of the character of a place, or its essential spirit, or the quality of life there, or of its livability, genius, flavor, feeling, ambience, essence, resonance, presence, aura, harmony, grace, charm or seemliness. These are probably allusions to an actual direct experience of some place.

The architect Philip Johnson noticed the change that Jacqueline Onassis and other prominent champions of Grand Central had wrought. "When they tore down Pennsylvania Station, there were just six of us trying to save it," he recalled. "We stood outside the station as people went in and out, and they all wanted to know if we were kooks or what. We told them we were trying to save the station. 'What station?' they said. That won't happen this time."

BY THE TERMINAL'S 75TH BIRTHDAY, IN 1988, the Brobdingnagian advertising timepiece (billed as the world's largest indoor clock), second as a target for architectural purists only to the Kodak sign, had been removed. "In any other place the Kodak Colorama sign in Grand Central Terminal would be a preservation issue," Christopher Gray of the *Times* acknowledged. But, he concluded, the sign, which greeted millions of passengers with pastoral farm scenes and Alpine idylls, was, like the proposed skyscraper atop the terminal, simply in the wrong place at the wrong time. Kodak was paying a hefty $450,000 a year to promote itself, but Metro-North, signaling an enduring and—for a government agency—unusual commitment to enlightened self-interest, refused to grant a long-term lease. The sign was removed early in 1990.

Still, pessimists, too, had ample grounds to dismiss Grand Central's physical condition as, well, terminal—it was like that of an aging convict suffering from an incurable disease but given a reprieve from execution. The punch list for the building's neglected interior was miles long.

"Grand Central had been spared the wrecking ball, but was far from saved," according to the MTA's own official history of the ter-

SINCE 1983, THE MTA HAS INVESTED OR COMMITTED NEARLY $1 BILLION TO MAINTAIN AND IMPROVE THE TERMINAL.

minal. "After decades of deferred maintenance, the building was crumbling. The roof leaked; stonework was being chipped away; structural steel was rusting. Pollution and dirt had stained surfaces. Commercial intrusions blocked out natural light."

Early in 1982, offices and the stairway to the 43rd Street exit were closed because of leaks and cascading plaster, apparently caused by the gut renovation of the Biltmore Hotel across Vanderbilt Avenue. A month later, commuters dodged falling plaster and dripping water, which forced officials to close a waiting room and the terminal's sole locker room. When Metro-North was created in 1983, among its first priorities were the copper roof and the porous deck over Park Avenue. "By sealing the roof first and stopping the water from coming in,"

WHEN THE MTA TOOK OVER FROM CONRAIL, THE FIRST PRIORITY WAS THE ROOF, WHICH JIMMY CERMINARO AND HUGO NACCARATO REPAIRED IN 1987.

said Wayne Ehmann, the railroad's chief architect, "we can then start tackling interior problems."

Fixing the roof was not your average $4.5 million home repair job. The roof suffered not only from decades of neglect, but also from a basic misunderstanding about metal fatigue. Particularly at its fringes, the plates were frayed and fractured by repeated expansion and contraction caused by changing temperatures. The 55,000 square feet of copper had to be replaced by eight-foot-long panels nailed to

GLASS CATWALKS SANDWICHED BETWEEN THE DOUBLE-PANED WINDOWS OFTEN SILHOUETTE
OFFICE WORKERS. THE DESIGN PROVIDED LIGHT, VENTILATION, AND ACCESS TO OFFICES.

wooden strips 20 inches apart. The six-foot-high frieze needed repairs.
Eight 24-foot-square skylights blacked out during World War II had
to be scraped of peeled paint or have new panes installed. Only then
could preservationists, architects, and engineers tackle the interior.

IF JACQUELINE ONASSIS DESERVES CREDIT for saving Grand Central
from rapacious developers and shortsighted railroad managers, Peter
E. Stangl, the president of Metro-North in the 1980s, saved the

terminal from itself. Stangl, a former college economics teacher from Connecticut who once quit a high-level job to hustle pool for nearly a year, became the first president of the Metro-North Commuter Railroad in 1983 (under MTA Chairman Richard Ravitch) when it was created by New York and Connecticut from the cadaverous remains of Conrail's bankrupt metropolitan passenger service. Three years earlier, on September 23, 1980, the city landmarks commission extended its protection of Grand Central to the interior spaces after a pro forma hearing in which one witness spoke in favor and no speaker bothered to dissent (although a tenant, the Metropolitan Transportation Authority, reluctant to be constrained, expressed reservations in writing).

When the terminal turned 75 in 1988, Stangl outlined three goals: "First and foremost, we want Grand Central to be a terrific train station again. Secondly, it's important to restore the building's architectural integrity. And thirdly, we want to improve the way we use space for retail purposes." Eight years later, Stangl was named chairman of the Metropolitan Transportation Authority by Governor Mario M. Cuomo. It was Stangl—who commuted daily from a 1792 farmhouse in Chappaqua—who insisted that no legitimate expense be spared in salvaging the aging terminal and transforming it into a shrine to what government at its most enlightened can accomplish. His reverence for Grand Central bordered on the divine. "Some mornings you'll see light flooding into the terminal," he said. "It's almost religious."

And if there was one person on whom Stangl depended (beside Frederick Harris and Susan Fine, directors of the MTA's real estate department), whose counsel he sought and whose vision he embraced, it was John Belle, a Welsh immigrant, whose firm, Beyer Blinder

Belle, would be tapped to restore the Ellis Island Immigration Museum and was recruited in the late 1980s to supervise the restoration of Grand Central and develop a master plan.

"Grand Central is magnificent architecture, but it is brilliant urbanism, an object lesson in the integration of a monumental work of architecture into the larger urban fabric of buildings, streets, viaducts and ramps," the architecture critic Paul Goldberger wrote in the *Times* in 1990. "The genius of the original architects was to create a noble building that did not stand aloof, but was a superbly functioning part of everyday life in New York, and the master plan recognizes this and enhances it."

A generation later, Belle, still at it, credits Stangl as "the godfather of this project; he was the best thing that an architect needed—a patron." The joint partnership of public and private works produced a Grand Central—one that is serving a very different constituency in a very different city than when it opened a century ago—that is even grander than the original. The redevelopment generated millions of dollars in rentals to defray the costs of maintenance. Working from a cache of architectural renderings discovered by accident in the terminal's southeast tower, Belle and his colleagues, including Frank J. Prial Jr. and Maxinne Leighton, painstakingly chronicled the terminal's embryonic beginnings and adapted them to meet the metamorphosis from the nation's premier long-haul passenger depot to America's biggest and busiest commuter terminal. The architects meticulously catalogued the peeling and cracked plaster, the chipped and spalled marble, the stained

FOLLOWING SPREAD: REMOVING GRIME FROM THE CELESTIAL CEILING AND RESTORING IT REQUIRED LOTS OF CLEANING FLUID BUT ONLY FIVE GALLONS OF PAINT.

artificial Caen stone panels and "ad hoc commercial accretions—retail and advertising signs, for example—which are inconsistent with the terminal's original architectural dignity."

In April 1990, Metro-North announced a $425 million master revitalization plan conceived by Beyer Blinder Belle and intended to transform Grand Central into, as Stangl described it, "a destination in its own right." With the Metropolitan Transportation Authority perennially strapped for funds, the renovation budget was quickly pared, to about $240 million. But through creative accounting by visionary bureaucrats and a bond issue backed by retail revenue, the full $400 million and more (actually, closer to $800 million, including repairs, new passageways, and platforms, utilities, and other improvements) has been spent since 1983 on enhancing and ennobling Grand Central. "We figured out a scheme that allowed us to buy a building losing a fortune," Susan Fine remembered, and ultimately redeemed "the value of public entrepreneurship—taking risks beyond the MTA's core mission and trusting staff to get it done."

As they embarked on the renovation, the Beyer Blinder Belle architects and historians declared, "The many functions and services of Grand Central Terminal and its brilliant architectural and urbanistic design form a whole that is far greater than the sum of its parts. Good architecture, as defined by Vitruvius, integrates 'commodity, firmness, and delight.' In its extraordinary balance between usefulness, endurance and beauty, Grand Central emerges, on the brink of the 21st century, as a triumph of architecture."

The deal depended, though, on who controlled the terminal. "The key initial obstacle to the Grand Central master plan is getting clear title to the building," said Fred Harris, the MTA's director of

DETAIL OF THE ORNATELY CAPPED LUNETTE WINDOWS 125 FEET ABOVE THE FLOOR OF THE MAIN CONCOURSE.

real estate. That obstacle was overcome in 1993 when the Penn Central Corporation of Cincinnati extended from 60 to 110 years its lease with the Metropolitan Transportation Authority and its Metro-North division. The MTA agreed to pay Penn Central $2.4 million annually—up from $377,000—a relatively low sum, except that the state authority also assumed liability for known environmental hazards in the train yards and along the right-of-way.

The long-term lease meant that plans could proceed for a restoration of the transcendental ceiling, installation of an awe-inspiring staircase to the East Balcony matching the one on the west, increasing retail space to 155,000 square feet from 105,000 square feet, creating a 43rd Street Passage into the terminal from Lexington Avenue, between the Grand Hyatt Hotel and the Graybar Building, and removing office space that had been crammed in above the ramps to the Oyster Bar.

FIVE CHANDELIERS FESTOONED WITH BARE BULBS HANG FROM THE CEILING
OF THE OLD WAITING ROOM, NOW VANDERBILT HALL.

The lease included another vital proviso to a public investment
in the reconstruction project: Penn Central relinquished any right to
develop the air space over the landmark, to demolish the 42nd Street
façade, or to drive columns through the Vanderbilt Hall waiting room

on the terminal's south side. The MTA negotiated an agreement with LaSalle Partners Inc. and William Jackson Ewing to implement the revitalization, which Jennifer Raab, then the chairwoman of the Landmarks Preservation Commission, described as "not just a cosmetic plan, although it will have great cosmetic impact."

CONSTRUCTION BEGAN IN 1996 with the nearly $5 million restoration of the barrel-vaulted constellation-dappled ceiling over the Main Concourse. The original, with its 2,500 stars, 10 major constellations, and zodiacal signs, had been conceived by Whitney Warren and painted with tempera onto the plaster. Less than a decade later, it began to deteriorate. In 1944–45, it was scraped, four-by-eight-foot asbestos and cement Flexboards were attached to the steel-truss ceiling with 600 galvanized iron wires, and the mural was repainted by Charles Gulbrandsen. By the early 1990s, art historians concluded, the ceiling was "but a shadow of its past glory"—peeling, darkened by pollution, and punctuated by a five-inch-wide hole.

To clean and restore the ceiling without interrupting the flow of 500,000 people below required a 120-ton aluminum Erector set that could inch along tracks at the top of the scaffold and just below the terminal's attic. "It didn't take rocket science or Euclidean deduction," John Belle said, but it did take innovative engineering and perseverance and a mammoth polyester shroud. "We want to be as invisible as we can be, without our workers looking down or commuters looking up," said Steven H. Sommer, vice president of Lehrer McGovern Bovis, the primary contractor for the restoration. For nine months, restorers armed with cheesecloth and Simple Green dabbed decades of dirt away, revealing the universe. The grime was thought to be the eight decades' accumulation of soot and diesel fumes, but on closer examination it was determined to be tar that had wafted sky-high from the billions of cigarettes puffed by passengers passing through the terminal. Beneath the filth, the sky was in such good shape that only five gallons of paint were needed to restore it.

To clean decades of dirt off the walls, they were painted with plastic. When it was pulled off, the grime came with it. The floor was less problematic. In four or so predawn hours every day, the restoration architects wrote, "all temporal vestiges are swept away and the great floor becomes a lake of smooth stone under a sky of gilt stars. Perhaps this is why the Main Concourse endures so memorably—not in its architectural eccentricities or complexity—but in its tenacious capacity to bear the brunt of change through changing times." John Belle summed it up more succinctly: "It makes you feel like Fred Astaire. You just glide over it." The rest of the oak benches were removed from the Main Waiting Room, which was converted into Vanderbilt Hall, a public exhibition and special event space (you can still feel furrows in the floor where waiting passengers shuffled their feet).

The restoration was so widely applauded that architecture critics ran short of superlatives and metaphors. In 1996 in the *Times*, Herbert Muschamp described the looming transformation as a "sex change" for "New York's most cherished landmark"—one that embodied "architectural gender-bending": "Most people recognize that the workplace has been altered by the changing status of women. The city, in effect, is one big workplace. So it shouldn't be surprising to find similar alterations taking place on an urban scale. Grand Central was built 83 years ago as a temple to the manly cult of work: hustle, bustle, button-down collar, the high-powered rhythm of the 9 to 5. It will reemerge as a shrine to rituals traditionally associated with domesticity: dining, shopping and keeping up the house."

The restored terminal was rededicated on October 1, 1998, just in time for a gubernatorial election, but before the renovation was fully complete (work on the finishing touches extended well into the 21st century). While dismissing the "gargantuanism" of the Metropolitan Life Building and the "vulgarity" of the Grand Hyatt, the *New Yorker* gushed that John Belle and the MTA, by transforming the terminal from a "covered version of Times Square," had "managed the trick of making Grand Central look virginal while making it more commercial."

Improvements are still being made, including a centennial corridor to honor Jacqueline Onassis and other heroes of the preservation campaign. Metro-North is transforming Grand Central into a terminal that fulfills a 21st-century mission. Passengers typically don't wait for hours any more for trains to depart. They no longer arrive bedraggled from an overnight train ride in need of a shave or a steam bath. The new terminal would be brighter, freer, with less segregation between short- and long-haul passengers—in short, more egalitarian. "We democratized it," Belle said. "Your train to New Haven or to Poughkeepsie became just as important as the 20th Century Limited." Belle admitted, though, to one personal regret about a bygone era: "I would have loved to be in Grand Central when they rolled out the red carpet," he said.

THE CHARACTERS

N O. 93 IN POLICE INSPECTOR Thomas F. Byrnes's encyclopedic *Professional Criminals of America* was named Peter Lake. He was described as five feet seven, weighing a stout 165 pounds, with graying black hair and dark hazel eyes. He typically sported a bowler, rakishly cocked. His arrest record dated roughly to 1870, and while he was accused as many as 50 times after then, he was seldom convicted. In 1886, Byrnes described Lake, better known as "Grand Central Pete," as "one of the most celebrated and persistent bunco steerers there is in America, 'Hungry' Joe possibly excepted." ("Hungry Joe" Lewis famously swindled Oscar Wilde while he was on a lecture tour in New York in 1882, prompting Byrnes to remark unapologetically that Wilde, who "reaped a harvest of American dollars with his curls, sun flowers and knee-britches," was no less a swindler then Lewis, "only not quite so sharp.")

RAFAEL GUASTAVINO, A VALENCIAN ARCHITECT,
PATENTED THE DESIGN FOR THE SELF-SUPPORTING
TERRA-COTTA TILE CEILINGS.

Peter Lake (his name would be evoked in Mark Helprin's novel *Winter's Tale*) earned his moniker by loitering at the depot looking for arriving rubes. He found yet another one as late as 1907, prompting the *Times* to opine about Pete and his fellow bunco artists:

> Of late years confidence games of far larger size than these worthies ever attempted have monopolized public attention, but people with good memories can recall when New York could get quite excited over a little thing like the beguilement of a pocketbook containing $32.87 from a rustic visitor. But, though such exploits have lost their zest through cruel comparison with the achievements of high, or higher, finance, it seems that they are still the limit of "Grand Central Pete's" humble ambition. Not only is he still attempting them on his old hunting ground; he is succeeding with them quite in the old way. And this despite the fact that he is now 72 years old!

By the time Peter Lake died in 1913, the same year that the new Grand Central opened, some would see poetic justice in the fact that the House that Vanderbilt Built was immortalized in the nickname of the nation's number-two-ranked con man, who was considered "so tough that his spit bounced" and is credited by some with the maxim "There's a sucker born every minute."

DURING ITS FIRST CENTURY, Grand Central has witnessed the arrival and departure of celebrities, of draftees on their way to military training, and of kids going to summer camp. Walter Prendergast, a deputy city sheriff, estimated in 1940 that over the two decades that he had been escorting prisoners to Sing Sing on the Ossining train, at least

135 of them were executed. The terminal has often been defined, too, by its anonymous regulars, the stereotypical passengers whose billions of footfalls at rush hour have burnished the Main Concourse's Tennessee marble floor. For all the well-earned encomiums bestowed on the terminal's physical being, its character has always been shaped by the people associated with it: the commuters and the travelers who arrived or departed for the long haul; the avuncular conductor who's been greeting the same passengers for decades; the black-shirted Ecuadorean shoe shiners in the Graybar Passage who, like the redcaps before them, work at menial jobs to pave the way for the first generation in their families to attend college.

The muted whispers and full-throated roars of people speaking to themselves or greeting friends collectively form the cacophonous voice of the Main Concourse, and that voice, David Marshall wrote in the mid-1940s, "born of a thousand human lips and the shuffling of a thousand human feet upon marble, is never still. Never a buzzing sound, not even a roar, it's a wide-open, spacious sound like the autumn wind in a forest, or the sea breaking on the rocks; and through it runs—unnoticed by the tone-deaf and the unobservant—a rich variety of overtones, a kind of accidental music that forever achieves little patterns and loses them again; a wild, fugitive music, like the tune fragments that race through the ringing of the rails and the clicking of wheels over the joints."

RUSHING TO CATCH A TRAIN might strike some people as pedestrian. To others, it is a mesmerizing daily ballet that defies the linear foundation of train travel and the street grid outside. (Trains, Thane Rosenbaum, a Fordham law professor, once wrote, are perfect for type

A personalities. In contrast to buses, a train "runs on a track, rarely deviates from a straight line, operates entirely with tunnel vision and is primarily goal-directed as it races to get its passengers to their next appointments.") Alastair Macaulay, the *Times*' dance critic, analyzed the choreography:

> Before 8:15, almost everyone is in motion, part of one busy stream or another: it's populous but remarkably quiet. Between 8:30 and 10, movement and stillness are continually juxtaposed: a good many people are stationary—waiting, watching, handling luggage, standing in line for tickets or information, making calls on their cellphones—adding a strong element of visual contrast to the still flowing, though lessening, lines of human traffic. By 10, the hall has largely become a tourist site, with more than 10 people at any one moment taking photographs. Although passengers certainly still come and go, they no longer dominate…Between 8:30 and 10 a.m., enough people stand

BEFORE THE 1990S, COMMUTERS ALTERED THEIR CHOREOGRAPHY
ON THE CONCOURSE TO SIDESTEP THE HOMELESS.

still, some in groups, to make the floor look like an Italian piazza: those painted by Piero della Francesca come to mind. Earlier, a dancegoer could easily feel the resemblance between the incessant streams of people and the first movement of Jerome Robbins's ballet "Glass Pieces," but now the view recalls the scene in the Mark Morris work "L'Allegro, il Penseroso ed il Moderato," where, amid the crisscross of four horizontal lines of walking people, a stationary man and woman spot each other. At times the scene recalls the urban vortex of Busby Berkeley's "Lullaby of Broadway." And any Cunningham devotee will recall urban studies like his "CRWDSPCR," in which the movement of one human being is circumscribed by that of others.

By the evening rush, people are descending the Met Life escalators into the concourse, Macaulay wrote, but not just their direction was reversed.

Body language has altered plenty during the day: there's a much less economical variety of dynamics, speed and behavior. You now notice many different mixtures of legato, staccato and marcato in the way people walk, and a new liveliness in the way they stand; even those walking briskly now are able to multitask (looking to and fro, consulting phones, rubbing their faces).

All of them look less reserved, as if they'd gotten a load off their chests during the day, but also less touching and less polite; people now are more volatile, funny, sexy and open. (Downstairs the spectrum is ever larger: people run for trains, talk helter-skelter while waiting for them, eat meals.) They aren't more beautiful or characterful than before, but they're more animated and communicative. Only on the down escalators do people merge into one single current now. The early morning showed just one facet of city life, but by late afternoon the station reflects the diversity of the city as a whole.

In more than a century, Peter Lake was among the few characters whose given name was so closely associated with Grand Central, although others could claim that their affinity for the terminal was more than skin-deep. Take Jay Hogan, for example, a railroad enthusiast from Durham, Connecticut. In 2004, after winning a $50 gift certificate from a tattoo parlor, he had the Roman deities atop the terminal's façade replicated on his back.

Over the years, others have enjoyed more tangential connections to the terminal, among them Gregory Pantazi, a West Side restaurateur who in 1921 became the latest, but undoubtedly not the last, sucker to fulfill Peter Lake's credo. Pantazi paid $1,200 to two con men to "buy" Grand Central, which has probably been "sold" almost as many times as the Brooklyn Bridge. In 1929, according to urban legend, a debonair gentleman who introduced himself as T. Remington Grenfell, the vice president of the Grand Central Holding Corporation, offered two fruit sellers, Tony and Nick Fortunato, a lease that would allow them to transform the information booth into a branch of their greengrocery. The Fortunatos delivered a check to the imposters ($10,000 by some accounts, $100,000 by others), but when they showed up to renovate the booth—on April 1—they discovered they had been duped.

Passengers arrived with dreams, some dashed with a sudden dose of reality, and others fulfilled, with a little help from the railroad. In 1928, 15-year-old Leonard Lucarello of Union City, New Jersey, whose father was an iceman, ventured into the terminal with $350 he claimed to have borrowed from his father's business and tried to buy a ticket to Hollywood, where he figured he would be the next Rudolph Valentino. The Travelers Aid Society returned him home. There is no record that the young man ever made it into the movies.

In 1984, Tom Byrne, the assistant stationmaster, let Peter Getz make an announcement that reverberated over the public address system in the cavernous concourse: "Attention Helen Swiggett. Please go to the information booth. There's a boy there who wants to ask you to marry him." They were wed a year later.

SELLING HAS ALWAYS BEEN ASSOCIATED with Grand Central, whether some huckster was unloading the terminal itself on an unsuspecting sucker, promoting his own prospects to potential employers in the Big City, or pitching retail to passengers and passersby. Grand Central's oldest tenant is the Oyster Bar, which opened below sea level off 42nd Street even before the terminal did. Viktor Yesenky was hired by Union News to run the Oyster Bar on opening day and didn't retire until 1946. (Abe Mendel, who had a restaurant in the old station, passed up the space because it seemed too remote.) Distinguished by Rafael Guastavino's vaulting tile arch ceilings, the restaurant exemplified faded elegance by the time Jerome Brody, who transformed the Four Seasons, the Rainbow Room, and other glittering eateries, was approached to run it, in 1974. "Its oyster stew had become famous, but the rest of the menu could best be described as 'continental,'"

Brody later wrote. The place had been closed for two years. "With the decline of the long-haul passenger train system," he recalled, "came the decline of the restaurant." People no longer came to Grand Central to dine (they now do again). The marble columns had been wall-papered and painted aquamarine and the 500-seat restaurant had gone bankrupt. Brody took a chance and turned it into a destination and, aw shucks, the Oyster Bar says it sells 5 million bivalves a year. (The Oyster Bar is now employee owned; Marlene Brody, Jerome's widow, is the franchiser.)

Speaking of selling, Steve Kivel is the third generation running Central Watch, off the 45th Street passageway. His grandfather founded the business in 1952, and Kivel is now the terminal's second-longest tenant. "I've been here my whole life," said Kivel, who is in his early 40s and commutes daily from Westchester on the Hudson line. "I have literally grown up in Grand Central. The terminal has changed from somewhere you pass through by necessity to an actual destination. Our store is tiny, but we manage to make the most out of every square inch. I always compare it to working in a submarine. The rent has certainly changed over the last 60 years, but so has the price of everything else."

AS MENTIONED EARLIER, one reason the terminal closed at night was to keep the homeless from congregating there. Herding everyone out obviated the need for special treatment, for better or for worse, of people who sort of reverse-commuted in the 1980s from panhandling and other pursuits. They came home each night to Grand Central to sleep in overlooked crannies or squat in unused railway cars. Metro-North temporarily reopened the terminal at night when the temperatures fell into the teens but reversed the gesture after reported crime rose.

The homeless, like the commuters, were easy to stereotype, but each had his or her own story. There was Madeline, who became homeless when her grandmother died and who said she "saw the opportunity to be secure in Grand Central, to be secure for the rest of my life." She liked "the quality of people" there. Asked about Penn Station, she scoffed, "There's just no comparison."

Lee was a 55-year-old former car cleaner who apparently lost his job because he drank too much. He collected veterans' benefits when he could but was found most of the time near the shuttle entrance. There was Mama, a hunched panhandler who spoke little English and perched on a milk crate off Vanderbilt Avenue; she helped hand out clean clothes from the Salvation Army to young homeless women and rolls provided on the sly by a terminal bakery. She died of pneumonia on Christmas Day 1985; a volunteer named George

DURING THE 1970S AND 1980S, THE MAIN WAITING ROOM BECAME A HAVEN FOR THE HOMELESS.

McDonald saved her from potter's field. McDonald was inspired to create the Doe Fund, which emphasizes self-sufficiency for the homeless and fields a force of hundreds of Ready, Willing, and Able street cleaners.

Louis Napolitano was a transit police officer working the graveyard shift. His job was "get 'em up and keep 'em moving," but in his anti-loitering duty he also came to realize that "the longer you're here, you see it's just people trying to survive." He became a one-man outreach team, steering the homeless to permanent shelter and abiding by his own "don't ask, don't tell" policy ("After closing, don't come out where people can see you"). So did Bryan Henry, a Metro-North cop for 24 years until he retired in 2009 as a lieutenant. "From my perspective, it was simple," he said. "If you really care about a person, they sense it, and respect was the currency of the street."

Henry, who earned a degree in urban studies at Fordham while he was on the force, said he identified with the homeless because he left New York as a young boy to live in Jamaica in the Caribbean and then returned when he was 8. "I went through culture shock twice," he said. "That culture shock parallels people who are experiencing

"MOLE PEOPLE" SECRETED THEMSELVES IN THE TUNNELS BENEATH THE TERMINAL, EMERGING TO PANHANDLE.

homelessness and a disconnect from the mainstream." Henry said he was inspired by *Walking a Tightrope,* a book about Eastern philosophy. "In Buddhism, as one approaches enlightenment, one of the stages you go through is to be compassionate," he said. "It's my own personal philosophy to reach out to people that are less fortunate than I am." He added, "I'm constantly walking a tightrope. On the one hand, I'm trying to be compassionate. On the other hand, I'm trying to do my job as a police officer and make the terminal safe."

NOBODY IS SUPPOSED TO LIVE AT GRAND CENTRAL, but the terminal has been a second home to many employees, some of whom go unnoticed or just taken for granted. Others became legendary, celebrated as familiar beacons in a sea of anonymous faces—like Mathilda Taylor, manager of a newsstand, whose cat Mutzi was the terminal's favorite feline, and Lizzie Duryee, owner of a tiny shop that sold "every imaginable dress and accessory dear to the feminine heart and indispensable to the feminine peace of mind," but best known for the daily aphorisms she placed in her shop window.

In 1947, Fred Wright retired as a Pullman porter after 55 years of service, which started in 1892 when he was a water boy for the railroad at the age of 12. In the late 1940s, Rodney Cole, known to terminal employees as "Keys," was still working as a locksmith in Grand Central, as he had been for nearly two decades. In an era before coded security cards, his skill at defeating stubborn mechanisms or compensating for lost keys was legendary, earning him a reputation as a magician—a particularly appropriate distinction, since he had also assisted Harry Houdini in repairing the trick locks on his "escape-proof" trunks, which could be opened from the inside without a key.

In 1953, Jacob Bachtold, a Swiss émigré, retired at the age of 77 after 50 years of, well, clock watching. Known as "Jake the Clock Man," he had supervised the terminal's 1,000 or so clocks, a particularly onerous challenge twice a year because of daylight savings time. He had been hired by the Central in 1903 as an electrician and stable foreman for the six draft horses that spun the roundhouse turntable. Bachtold could have gotten a nice watch, but instead the railroad graciously presented him with a gold pass good for any run. And speaking of clocks, in 2009, Falt Watch Service and Repair closed its office on the third floor of the terminal, where it had operated since about 1930 and served as an official inspection site for railroad employees, who were required to present their watches for testing once a month.

In the 1950s, Ralston C. Young, a redcap, conducted noontime prayer meetings four days a week in a coach on Track 13. In 1956, Sigismundo Rienzi retired as a dining car steward after 40 years, during which, someone figured, he seated the equivalent of the entire population of Philadelphia. That same year, Raymond Oliva retired as a baggage handler. He served every president from Theodore Roosevelt to Dwight Eisenhower. An Italian immigrant, Pietro Ierardi, who arrived in New York penniless in 1880, was so diligent at polishing shoes at Grand Central that when he finally checked into a sanitarium in Stamford, Connecticut, in the late 1920s, a court accounting discovered he was worth $175,000.

Stephen T. Kelly, a retired manager of Grand Central, worked for the railroad for four decades. Once he allowed the Main Concourse to be transformed into a ballroom on New Year's Eve 1963 for a benefit. "Thirty-seven years a railroad man," he said. "And yesterday I had to go downtown to get fingerprinted for a cabaret license!"

For decades, Billy Keogh melodiously cried out the arrival times of trains and their tracks, as revealed by the Teletype at his fingertips. But while live announcements still are made periodically from the stationmaster's office—in addition to recorded warnings about unattended packages or watching the gap between the trains and the platform— train departures are not routinely announced with the proverbial "All aboard" (the way Daniel Simmons, the legendary train announcer at Penn Station, did). That's because

OFFICER PETER CHAMBERTIDES (LEFT) WITH BRYAN HENRY, WHO RETIRED AS A LIEUTENANT IN 2009 AND WAS KNOWN FOR HELPING THE HOMELESS.

most trains regularly leave on the same track, and, because they are not passing through as they would in a station, there is typically more time to board. (The "voice" of Grand Central belongs to Daniel Brucker, who joined Metro-North as a press secretary in 1987 and is now the terminal's irrepressible manager of tours. He described his dulcet tones as "sort of like the distant voice from the past—one that you'd hear coming from your Dumont television set, intoning about the marvels of power steering, awaiting you in your brand new 1952 DeSoto.")

In 1967, Lester Onderdonk of Hastings, who hailed from an old railroad family, was replaced by a 59-by-11-foot electric billboard installed over the ticket booths to display the arrival and departure of trains. He wasn't pleased with other people's notion of progress, which eliminated the jobs of three railroad employees who had wielded chalk to post the times on a blackboard in the waiting room under Vanderbilt Avenue. "I hope that when they plug in the new system, when it is finished in a week or two, the whole thing blows up," he told a reporter. It didn't, but the electromechanical board was eventually succeeded by rows of flipping panels for each letter and number (a version was immortalized at the Museum of Modern Art), and the flip board was replaced by another innovation from Solari Udine of Italy, liquid crystal display modules.

Progress, of sorts, also eliminated another job, Mary Lee Read's. She was the terminal's organist beginning in 1928 and presided from a console on the east end of the Philosophers' Gallery. Once, she was suddenly inspired to interrupt a Bach piece to play "What a Friend We Have in Jesus"—twice. Two years later, she told the *New Yorker* in 1947, she was informed that a man who had been walking through the station on his way to jump off the Brooklyn Bridge heard her performance. "It was his mother's favorite hymn, and he stopped and listened to it," she recalled. "It just broke his heart. Instead of jumping off the Brooklyn Bridge, he went to Cleveland and organized a mission." Read was touted as the only organist in America expressly forbidden to play the national anthem. The last time she did, during the evening rush on December 8, 1941, the day after the attack on Pearl Harbor, pedestrian traffic froze. Commuters missed their trains. She continued to play holiday favorites in the weeks preceding Thanksgiving, Christmas, and Easter through the mid-1950s. (Read's fan base rivaled that of Gladys Gooding, a fellow organist immortalized as the answer to a trivia stumper: Who was the only person who played in the same year for the Knicks, the Rangers, and the Brooklyn Dodgers?)

Five-foot-five Timothy P. Curley, a conductor, has regaled commuters on the 82-mile run north to Wassaic with local history and pop psychology as a former Transcendental Meditation instructor. One passenger recalled the time a bunch of rowdy prep school kids were acting out next to an elderly lady. "And he went up to the kids," the passenger remembered, "and he said, 'Is this lady bothering you?' And they immediately got quiet."

Harry Kelly, the stationmaster, grew up in the Bronx and has worked at Grand Central since 1973. He's responsible for 600 cleaners, custodians, ticket sellers, and craftsmen who work in the terminal. Also in 1973, when he was 21, Robert Leiblong, who commutes from Brewster, started working as a trackman to pay off his college loans. Later, he earned a master's degree in engineering and became Metro-North's senior vice president for operations, supervising a staff including 850 conductors and assistant conductors (165 of them women), 600 engineers who drive the trains (including 20 women), and 60 rail traffic controllers, among the more than 5,000 employees who maintain the trains and tracks.

Some alumni can't get enough of Grand Central. Edward G. Fischer joined the New York Central as a messenger in 1908, when he was 15, and rose to become the stationmaster known as "Mr. Courtesy." He kept a framed aphorism in his office that defined courtesy as "a little thing with a big meaning." Fischer retired as stationmaster in 1958 after a 49-year stint with the railroad but returned a year later as a part-time news dealer. "I love this place like a second home," he said. "I just couldn't stay away."

REDCAPS have been among Grand Central's most visible employees and, legend has it, they began there. James H. Williams, the son

A SMALL ARMY OF
REDCAPS SERVED
PASSENGERS.

of a slave, who began his career as a doorman at Thaley's Florist Shop on Fifth Avenue, was hired as a porter (their caps define them as "attendant") when the force included 25 whites and two blacks. He worked his way up to chief in 1909 and served 45 years, until his death in 1948 (when there was only one white redcap, Milton Newman, left). Along the way, Williams encouraged young black men to work their way through college as baggage handlers ("Do not tip the Red Caps," early timetables advised passengers). Some accounts say that he originated the redcaps when, as an enterprising teenager one Labor Day, he fastened a piece of red flannel to his hat as a signal that he was available to help with luggage, according to Eric Arnesen's *Brotherhoods of Color: Black Railroad Workers and the Struggle for Equality.*

Whatever the origins of the name, the distinctive cap caught on across the country. Williams, who always wore a white carnation in his lapel, "raised the dignity of carrying bags from something to do when there is no other job to that of public service, a job of self-respect requiring men of the best caliber," the playwright Abram Hill wrote in 1939, when redcaps were making about $2,000 a year, tips—typically a dime—included. "He has proved that the old superstition that Negroes would not work under a Negro is false." The Chief was well-known to generations of New Yorkers and visitors, including youngsters who needed to borrow money to get home after a costly weekend in the city. "'Jim will take care of you at the terminal' is a phrase many a young New Yorker has heard from his father and mother," one biographer wrote.

The civil rights leader Lester B. Granger worked as a redcap under the Chief, recalling what amounted to a postgraduate education at Grand Central as he "roamed the paved stretches of the station's labyrinths, chasing down travelers with bags as a beagle hound chases a rabbit." When Williams died, Granger wrote,

> remembering him with great affectionate sorrow will be 'Grand Central Alumni' from New York to California, and from Miami to Seattle. These former students of the Chief are, many of them, successful professional and businessmen, most of them with a tendency toward flat feet and ulcers. But one and all, they will acknowledge their terrific debt to Chief Williams, for he had the kindly wisdom to keep open at Grand Central a generous supply of jobs each year for Negro college students. He had the judgment to rule them with a rod of iron. But rule them as he might, he liked them and believed in them, and they today are grateful to him.

Williams commanded a small army of 500, of whom, he once estimated, 100 were attending college and another 25 were graduates. Samuel Battle, who became New York's first black police officer, was a redcap under Williams. In 1927, Williams's son Wesley was hired as the city's first black firefighter. Another son was a college president. When he died, Elizabeth Eckard, who supervised the Travelers Aid Society, said, "We can't run Grand Central without the Chief. He's as much a part of the place as the Twentieth Century."

COMMUTATION

I F ROMANTIC LONG-DISTANCE TRAINS defined the terminal in the first half of its 100 years, commuters have done so in the second half. Commuter trains never developed the cachet that their long-distance cousins acquired, but carrying passengers to and from New York's suburbs—giving the city its "tidal restlessness," E.B. White wrote—was becoming a larger share of Grand Central's traffic. (White himself bought his first copy of the *New Yorker* in the terminal in 1925 and later recalled, "I practically lived in Grand Central at one period—it has all the conveniences and I had no other place to stay.") In 1906, while the terminal was still being built, 10 million commuters rode the New York Central and the New Haven lines. By 1930, their ranks had more than tripled, to 36 million of the 47 million or so total passengers whom Grand Central Terminal accommodated that year.

METRO-NORTH, NOW THE NATION'S BUSIEST
COMMUTER RAILROAD, IS POISED TO HANDLE
100 MILLION PASSENGERS ANNUALLY, AS THE
TERMINAL'S BUILDERS PROJECTED.

For well over a century, suburban commuters have been caricatured and uncharitably denigrated as elitist tree-huggers rendered zombie-like by their daily ritual. The New York of the commuter, White acidly wrote, "is devoured by locusts each day and spat out each night," adding unapologetically, "The suburb he inhabits had no essential vitality of its own and is a mere roost where he comes at day's end to go to sleep. Except in rare cases, the man who lives in Mamaroneck or Little Neck or Teaneck, and works in New York, discovers nothing much about the city except the time of arrival and departure of trains and buses, and the path to a quick lunch…The commuter dies with tremendous mileage to his credit, but he is no rover."

Few profiles were as eviscerating as Gail Sheehy's in *New York* magazine in 1968, when New Yorkers were beginning to feel a little defensive about their town and wondering whether, in the middle of a transit strike two years earlier, the columnist Dick Schaap was engaging in bitter irony when, paraphrasing Mayor John V. Lindsay, he dubbed New York "Fun City." Sheehy's profile began: "They never stop moving. They come into Grand Central every morning off the 86-seat sit-up hearses. And every night the blank faces look out of Charlie Brown's bar at the Pan Am escalators and wait to go home at the same time on the same train in the same car with the same 'congenial group.'"

The daily tide of commuters might seem anonymous—even to their fellow passengers—but they fell into categories that Sheehy acerbically described. They included the congenial Mad Men going home to wives and families. "Avid agency and fashion geishas know they can learn from these men," she wrote. "Pick up the Avenue style, pick up a telephone recommendation from a bar car titillation. They are known as Belles of the Bar Car." The regulars included a less congenial character, she explained: "No one wants to become a Tunnel Inspector, a man who sits alone, speaks to no one and—when the morning train goes under at Park and 96th—races through to stand between the couplings of the two head cars." Regardless of which category the commuter belonged to, each shared the same fate, according to Sheehy: "There is one inexorable inevitability about his life: At both ends of his day, like margins, is another train to catch."

JOHN CHEEVER'S FICTIONAL SHADY HILL was populated by desperate commuters, and Gregory Peck's *Man in the Gray Flannel Suit* was one. But changing demography has challenged the stereotypes (nearly half the commuters today are women). And even when generalizations

NOW WHAT? PERPLEXED COMMUTERS CONVERGE ON THE INFORMATION BOOTH DURING A NEW YORK SUBWAY AND BUS WORKERS' STRIKE.

were more valid, each commuter had an individual story to tell, and the mass of commuters, like the earlier waves of long-distance passengers, came to Grand Central, at least when they first arrived, with dreams. Jim Link, an accountant from Greenwich, his grandfather, a psychiatrist, and his father, an artist, commuted in tandem from the suburbs for a century. "For over 100 years," he said in 2002, "one of us has been walking through Grand Central." Another commuter, Herbert Askwith of Larchmont, was responsible for single-handedly nudging the railroad to set its clocks and timetables to daylight time.

Commuting can foster a real camaraderie as fellow passengers celebrate passages into other life stages—people have been born and married in Grand Central and others have died there—or just enjoy a poker game or holiday cheer. By the middle of the 1930s, the impact of the Depression was beginning to fade, at least for well-heeled commuters from New Canaan, Connecticut. They petitioned the New York, New Haven & Hartford Railroad to restore the club car on the 5:12 from Grand Central with its white-coated attendant. "We're not rich men," said George H. Yuengling, an insurance broker. "We're all hard working fellows who like relaxation and are willing to pay a little extra to avoid the discomforts of ordinary commuting."

Bill Geist, the CBS television commentator, once recalled the Christmas party on Car No. 8657 on the New Haven's 5:20 from Grand Central to Westport. Regulars decorated the car and hired a six-piece band. Habitués of bar cars are no different from colleagues stopping at a saloon on the way home, except they are more likely to be excused for wobbling between stations.

A whole genre—stragglers who miss the last train before the terminal closes at 2 a.m.—has developed a culture of stranded "train wrecks," some of whom wash away their tears in a local bar or offer themselves up as "Cinderella fares" to lucky cabbies. (In cold weather, one door on 42nd Street is staffed by a police officer who lets stragglers and the homeless into a makeshift lobby.) In 1932, Norman L. Holmes of Danbury was so determined not to miss his train home that he stole an ambulance from St. Vincent's Hospital and drove it to Grand Central with its siren wailing (he crashed into a parked car on 44th Street and was arrested).

Other commuters managed happier endings. One man, a 65-year-old lawyer from Queens who had no choice but to stand on a crowded train from Grand Central to White Plains, won a jury verdict against the New York Central of $11.80—a refund of his $1.80 fare plus $10 in damages for "discomfort." That was in 1947, and his victory before a civil court judge was his second against the railroad. A decade earlier, he sued the New York Central because he was forced to stand on a train to Albany and won a precedent-setting verdict (a $2.80 refund and $45 for discomfort) that established the principle that passengers who purchased tickets for long-distance trains had to be guaranteed a seat.

Walter S. Titlar, an insurance man who had been commuting from Ossining to Manhattan for three months short of a half century, reaped his own reward after piling up 750,000 miles on the Hudson line. (When he started as a messenger for Metropolitan Life, his $7.20 monthly commutation fare was higher than his $5 weekly salary. When he retired at 65, he was making $300 a week and paying $30.95 for his monthly commute.) In 1961, Titlar donned a visored cap and fulfilled a 50-year boyhood dream, riding beside the engineer in the locomotive of the 5:22 from Grand Central.

SECRETS OF GRAND CENTRAL

S TAND IN THE MIDDLE of Grand Central's Main Concourse and you are surrounded by secrets: a hidden staircase a few feet away that, no matter how hard you look, you can't see; a 25,728-square-foot mistake; a lesser aberration that can barely be measured in inches; an underground room so vital during World War II that any unauthorized visitor might be shot; a hole in one corner of the ceiling and a small dark patch in another; special places to whisper and to kiss; why the departure times on the digital train boards are always wrong; a command post on a floor that, according to the elevator buttons, does not exist; and an existing but secluded railroad siding where even the chairman of Metro-North's parent, the Metropolitan Transportation Authority, was warned away by armed guards.

Let's begin with the easy ones, and some of the oddities you may have noticed before and always wondered about.

IN 1987, PHILIPPE PETIT MARKED GRAND CENTRAL'S
75TH ANNIVERSARY BY WALKING 80 FEET ABOVE
THE CONCOURSE, WITHOUT A NET.

WHY DOES SUCH AN ELEGANT BUILDING HAVE SO MANY BARE LIGHTBULBS?

When Grand Central opened in 1913, gaslight was still the norm in many places. The New York Central and the Vanderbilts were showing off. Not only had its trains been converted to electricity, but its entire new terminal was electric. What better way to dramatize modern technology, railroad officials figured, than to expose the bulbs themselves? And if you're wondering how many people it takes to change every lightbulb in Grand Central, the answer is six: about 4,000 bulbs in public areas were switched from incandescent to compact fluorescent bulbs in 2008.

AM I GETTING SQUIRRELLY, OR ARE THERE DECORATIVE ACORNS ALL OVER THE TERMINAL?

The Vanderbilts came from modest stock and, sorry to say, had no family crest. Commodore Vanderbilt adopted the acorn (from which mighty oaks grow) and oak leaves as a Vanderbilt emblem. They adorn some of the terminal's light fixtures and friezes (as well as semiprecious mosaics in the Billiard Room of The Breakers, the Vanderbilt family mansion in Newport, Rhode Island; the seal and various other artifacts at Vanderbilt University, which the Commodore endowed; and the crest of Silliman College at Yale, which was built with a gift from Frederick W. Vanderbilt). The terminal's acorns and oak leaves, the architect John Belle observed, are as discreet as "Ninas" in an Al Hirschfeld caricature.

Okay, so what's the big mistake in the concourse?

Put it this way: Cassius wasn't talking about Grand Central's cerulean ceiling when he said, "The fault, dear Brutus, is not in our stars, but in ourselves." Once the proposed office tower was scrubbed, architects considered enclosing the concourse with a skylight but settled on an artificial sky instead. On March 22, 1913, a little more than a month after the terminal opened, an amateur astronomer commuting from New Rochelle alerted railroad officials that the constellations were backward. That would not present a problem for linear locomotive engineers, but any mariner navigating by Grand Central's stars would wind up like another "Wrong Way" Corrigan.

So much for the artist Paul César Helleu's gleeful comment to the critic Frederick Mordaunt-Hall at the Ritz barbershop the morning after the ceiling was completed: "J'ai eu des ennuis, qui m'ont presque bouleversé, mais maintenant tout est bien—car les étoiles brillent au firmament" (I have been nearly bowled over with worries, but now all is well—for the stars shine in the firmament).

The alert commuter's discovery was doubly embarrassing because the railroad's recently published official guide boasted, "It is safe to say that many school children will go to the Grand Central Terminal to study this representation of the heavens, which places the celestial bodies within close range of vision. To insure astronomical accuracy and beauty of form, the highest authorities were consulted, among them Dr. Harold Jacoby of Columbia University, and the research was carried back to manuscripts and treatises of the Middle Ages."

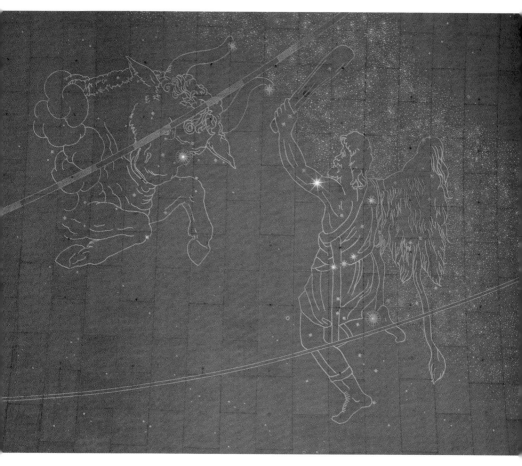

FOR SOME REASON, ORION THE HUNTER, BRANDISHING HIS CLUB, WAS REVERSED
TO FACE TAURUS THE BULL.

Red-faced railroad officials were caught short. Putting it
in the best light, they suggested that while no mortal had ever
seen the heavens from this perspective, the celestial mural represented God's view. It was designed by Helleu and executed

by him, J. Monroe Hewlett, Charles Guldbrandsen, and Charles Basing of Brooklyn on the basis of a chart provided by Professor Jacoby of Columbia, who was an expert on astronomy, but apparently not on how to wield a paintbrush in one hand while holding a diagram in the other.

Jacoby's chart was derived from Johann Bayer's famous Uranometria of 1603 (which, among other things, included a fly constellation that was merged into Aries by the International Astronomical Union in 1929. For some reason, Bayer reversed Orion—to face Taurus—so it is depicted correctly on the ceiling). Don't blame me, Jacoby insisted. "Apparently the diagram was placed on the floor and there copied to the ceiling," he explained blithely. "It might have been better if the artist had held the diagram over his head and transferred it, as it were, by looking through it."

Responding to suggestions that the backward sky was more decorative, Dorrit Hoffleit, a Harvard astronomer, wrote in 1945, "Which is more decorative, a map with New York on the Atlantic at the east side of the United States and San Francisco on the west, as we are accustomed to having it, or one 'inside out' with New York west and San Francisco east…? For some mysterious reason," Hoffleit concluded, "ostensibly 'decorative,' the constellations had been represented in reverse as if the artist had copied from the surface of a celestial globe, forgetting that the people in Grand Central would be looking up and out from the center of the vaulted heavens and not down from the outside."

Years later, Susan Jacoby, a memoirist, wrote that her great-uncle, the Columbia professor, "was a Jacoby man, and Jacoby men (all of whom possess a bent for mathematics) also have a tendency toward absent-mindedness and disorganization." She said it was easy to believe that he had not given instructions "on the critical detail of exactly where to place the chart while reproducing it on the ceiling," adding, too, that "Michelangelo may have lain on his back to paint the ceiling of the Sistine Chapel but no one ever noticed him holding a brush in one hand and a sketch in the other."

Deborah Fulton Rau, who studied the mural for the Beyer Blinder Belle architectural firm, agreed that the goal was allegorical rather than navigational. "The sky ceiling brought a map of the universe into Grand Central's orbit of travel, linking an ancient method of travel, that of using the positions of the stars for guidance, with a modern method of travel, the electrified train," she wrote. "The vivid and gilded presence of the zodiacal figures insured that their celestial message would impart to the daily commute, to the long journey not yet taken, a spirit that soared beyond the earthly realm of travel."

Beyer Blinder Belle's historic structure report concluded that the progression of constellations was not so much a mistake as a manifestation of artistic license for a last-minute substitution for a skylight through which, light pollution notwithstanding, the heavens would have been visible. "Their positions relative to one another and to the lines of the ecliptic and celestial equator were intentionally rearranged to create a decorative composition that was appropriate to the shape of the ceiling and the architecture of the space," the historians concluded.

AS LONG AS WE'RE LOOKING UP, WHAT ABOUT THAT OBVIOUS HOLE AND RECTANGLE IN THE CEILING?

THE CRAB EXTENDS ITS CLAW, AS IF TO REMOVE THE OFFENDING RECTANGLE (TOP), WHICH REMAINED AS A BEFORE-AND-AFTER REMINDER OF THE RESTORATION.

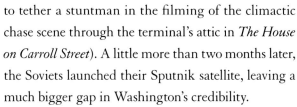
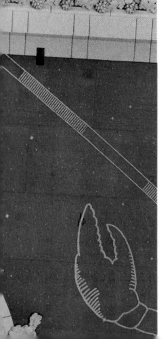

The five-inch-diameter hole dates to 1957 and can be blamed on the space race with the Soviet Union. Washington was seeking to reassure Americans that the country had not fallen behind and was trying to drum up support for more defense spending. A five-ton Redstone missile arrived on Track 16 by flatcar from Detroit (courtesy of Chrysler, which manufactured the missile). This explanation may sound fishy (the hole is just above the constellation Pisces) since the missile was only 63 feet long and the ceiling of the Main Concourse is much higher. Apparently, though, the hole was cut to accommodate a cable installed to keep the rocket from tipping over during the three weeks it was on display. Why the hole remained is unclear (it was also used to tether a stuntman in the filming of the climactic chase scene through the terminal's attic in *The House on Carroll Street*). A little more than two months later, the Soviets launched their Sputnik satellite, leaving a much bigger gap in Washington's credibility.

About that dark patch: It's in the northwest corner of the ceiling. It wasn't added there. Everything around it was removed. That symmetrical smudge is what the entire ceiling looked like until the late 1990s, when decades of tobacco and nicotine residue were washed away. According to Metro-North spokeswoman Marjorie Anders, MTA officials begrudgingly left the patch as a constant before-and-after reminder.

IF THE SKY CEILING IS THE BIG MISTAKE, WHAT'S THE LITTLE ONE?

Okay, it's not exactly a mistake, but the original blueprints for the Main Concourse called for matching east and west marble stairways modeled on the grand staircase of the Palais Garnier, the elegant Paris opera house. Only the west staircase was installed, however. Several theories survive as to why its counterpart was not. The most logical suggests that the shanties, tenements, and industrial buildings that dotted the East Side then offered little lure to pedestrians and that the East Balcony was supposed to have been the lobby for the unbuilt office tower. The staircase was belatedly completed in 1998, when the terminal was renovated, prompting a debate over whether a restored landmark should precisely mirror what existed before or what was originally proposed. The east stairway varies slightly from the original version as a subtle signal to architectural historians and to comply with the Americans with Disabilities Act, which requires 11-inch-wide treads and handrails that meet strict specifications.

WHAT THE WEST BALCONY LOOKED LIKE BEFORE THE 1990S RESTORATION.
MICHAEL JORDAN'S STEAK HOUSE OPENED AT RIGHT.

So where's the secret staircase?

Hint: It's a little like the kiosk that Graham Greene's Third Man disappears into in postwar Vienna. In the center of the circular marble and brass pagoda that serves as an information booth is a spiral staircase. It leads to the information booth on the terminal's Lower Level.

PASSENGERS AND PASSERSBY SURROUNDING THE INFORMATION BOOTH TYPICALLY SEEM TO BE IN PERPETUAL MOTION. INSIDE, CUSTOMER SERVICE REP VALERIE BRATHWAITE.

How can the train boards be wrong? They list the destination, track number, and departure time, same as in the official timetable.

All true, except for one vital fact that the railroad prefers not to tell passengers. In the old days, until 1985, when the departure time approached, conductors would activate a light to signal the gateman to close the gates at the entrance to the platform from the concourse. The railroad did away with those years ago, in part to save labor. Nowadays, tardy passengers can rush down the platform and still catch their train. Especially when, to accommodate stragglers, Grand Central's trains typically leave one minute later than the departure time listed on the train boards and in the timetable.

Speaking of time, how big is the clock on the south façade?

So big that when you're standing behind it, you can open up a window where the VI is and peer down Park Avenue. The clock is 13 feet in diameter. While it has been described as the largest display of Tiffany glass, Tiffany & Co. says it cannot confirm that claim.

DOES ANYONE LIVE AT GRAND CENTRAL AND LIST 89 EAST 42ND STREET AS THEIR ADDRESS?

No, unless you count any remaining "mole people" below it and train crews that occasionally sack out in bunk rooms. Nor did the financier John W. Campbell live there. He installed a corner office in 1923 that re-created a 13th-century Florentine palazzo. It was restored, after having been reincarnated in various lesser forms, including as a signalman's office and small jail for miscreants arrested by the Metro-North Police, since Campbell died in 1957.

Campbell was born in 1880, lived on Cumberland Avenue in a Brooklyn neighborhood now known as Fort Greene, and, without attending college, became senior executive and later president of his father's credit-reference firm, Credit Clearing

JOHN CAMPBELL MAY HAVE SLEPT THERE OCCASIONALLY, BUT HE DIDN'T LIVE THERE. HIS "APARTMENT" HAS BEEN TRANSFORMED INTO A TONY BAR.

THE FINANCIER JOHN W. CAMPBELL RE-CREATED A 13TH-CENTURY
FLORENTINE PALAZZO AS HIS OFFICE.

House, which specialized in garment industry finances and later merged with Dun & Bradstreet. In 1920, he was named to the board of the New York Central and later became chairman of the Hudson & Manhattan Railroad (now PATH). Among his other quirks, he hated to wear socks and he insisted that his pants never be wrinkled, so he hung them in his humidor while he worked at his desk in his underwear. He kept a steel safe in the fireplace.

While the 3,500-square-foot office was renovated in 1999 into a bar known as the Campbell Apartment (and included a pipe organ, a piano, a bathroom, and a kitchen), Campbell and his wife actually lived a few blocks away at 270 Park Avenue and later at the Westchester Country Club in Rye.

CAN YOU RENT THE TERMINAL FOR PRIVATE EVENTS?

Vanderbilt Hall, the former main waiting room just south of the Main Concourse on the terminal's south side, is available.

Five gold chandeliers hang from the 48-foot ceiling, and, Metro-North notes, their "light can be modified to create the ambience your event requires." The starting price for renting all 12,000 square feet for a one-time event: $25,000.

ARE THERE REALLY SPECIAL PLACES TO WHISPER AND TO KISS?

Technically, you can do either anywhere, but you might feel less self-conscious in the designated areas. The so-called Kissing Gallery (apparently so dubbed by a rewrite man for the *New York Herald*), near Tracks 39 to 42, is where arriving passengers on long-distance trains, including the 20th Century Limited, greeted friends and relatives. It is formally known as the Biltmore Room because it is under the old Biltmore Hotel, now the Bank of America Building. The 65-by-80-foot room will become the connection to the Main Concourse for Long Island Rail Road commuters.

AN ACOUSTICAL QUIRK SENDS EVEN A HUSHED WHISPER HURTLING ACROSS THE PARABOLIC CEILING NEAR THE OYSTER BAR.

Pssst. Can you keep a secret? Not if you reveal it in the Whispering Gallery, an acoustical quirk of architecture at the foot of the ramps leading to the Oyster Bar. The vaulted ceiling was designed by Rafael Guastavino, a Valencian architect who patented a design for interlocking terra-cotta tile to form self-supporting arches. Stand at the foot of one arch facing the wall and station someone diagonally at the other end. Even when you whisper, your voice travels along the parabolic curve of the ceiling and can be heard at the other end. Histories of Grand Central don't reveal whether Guastavino deliberately planned the reverberating effect or who discovered it.

Is it true that you can actually see sunspots in the terminal?

In midafternoon, when the sun shines straight up Park Avenue, place a white sheet of paper on the floor of the Main Concourse. The curlicued spaces in the semicircular grills on the terminal's southern façade can produce the same effect as a pinhole camera, reflecting an image of the sun that is 8 to 12 inches wide—complete with dark blemishes denoting sunspots.

Someone said Grand Central has the "safest" restroom in the world. C'mon.

Only if you define it as being safe from a speeding locomotive, then this is the place. The Lower Level restroom on the far western side of the terminal is buttressed by a crash wall several feet of concrete thick. It's adjacent to the lower loop tracks on which incoming trains could turn around and head outbound.

THE ELEVATOR BUTTONS IN THE FOUR CORNERS OF THE MAIN CONCOURSE ARE A MYSTERY. SOLVE IT.

After the trains, more people at Grand Central are transported on the escalators and 10 historic elevators than by any other means. Those four corners were intended as the lobby for the tower that Reed & Stem originally envisioned, just as the balconies were to serve as the tower's vestibules. For unexplained reasons, pushing E will get you to the balcony level (possibly referring to *entresol*, French for *esplanade*, or for *express*), U to the upper or Main Concourse level, L to the Lower Level or Dining Concourse, and P to the Lower Level platforms. The numbered buttons are reserved for Metro-North employees. The seventh floor, location of the situation room for emergencies and of the Fleet Department, which keeps track of all 1,300 engines and passenger cars, is unlisted.

THAT TAKES CARE OF GOING UP. WHAT ABOUT GOING DOWN? WHAT'S SO SECRET ABOUT THAT UNDERGROUND ROOM?

Don't mention it, even in the Whispering Gallery. Ninety feet below the Lower Level is a vast room known as M-42, which is accessible by a single elevator and a mazy staircase and was featured in a World War II navy training film as the safest place in New York in case of an atomic attack. Rows of transformers produce a one-note hum and convert alternating current to the direct current that powers Metro-North trains. At one end of the room are two ancient giant rotary converters, which the modern transformers replaced. The old converters were rumored to have been targeted during World War II by Nazi saboteurs seeking to cripple the terminal and disrupt American troop embarkations along the East Coast. (German saboteurs who landed by U-boat in Amagansett, Long Island, in 1942, and were seized soon after, did indeed visit Grand Central for a rendezvous at the information booth—"possibly New York's most popular meeting place," according to one account—and to visit a newsreel theater to catch up on current events and to watch recently released films of the previous December's attack on Pearl Harbor. While there was no direct evidence that M-42 was their objective, the FBI said that among their targets were "spots where railroads could be most effectively disabled.") Armed guards patrolled entrances to the room.

Blasted out of mica-peppered Manhattan schist, which forms the island's bedrock, this is the deepest basement in New York City—deeper than the cellar of the World Trade Center and the bullion vaults at the Federal Reserve Bank downtown. It's poised to lose that title, though. When the Long Island Rail Road access tunnels are completed around 2019, the lower commuter platform will be 140 feet below street level and more than 90 feet below the existing Lower Level Metro-North track. Forty-seven escalators and 22 elevators will carry passengers to street level, a journey that is expected to take about four minutes.

Now, what about that other underground secret, the rail siding?

It's known to Metro-North employees as Track 61, and myths abound as to its origin, history, and contemporary relevance. Some of the myths are actually true.

Originally, the spur ran beneath a railroad power plant, the railway branch of the YMCA, and a warehouse for the Adams Express Company. Those buildings, each less than two decades old, were razed to make room for the Waldorf-Astoria Hotel, which was built on the square block bounded by Park and Lexington Avenues and East 49th and 50th Streets (the F & M Schaeffer brewery was on the next block where St. Bartholomew's Church now stands). The two wide platforms used by the powerhouse and the express company remained.

If you're traveling on a track near the eastern perimeter of the train yards near 49th Street, you may see what looks like a rusted blue boxcar (parked on Track 63). Depending on the telling, the boxcar either carried the presidential automobile for FDR or is an otherwise nondescript maintenance car abandoned years ago. The storied spur is directly under the Waldorf and is accessible by a special freight elevator (which opens onto 49th Street, just east of the Waldorf garage, with another stairway on the 50th Street side), apparently placed there for the convenience and privacy of VIP guests to provide direct access to a train platform from the hotel.

How often it's been used for that purpose is debatable (although the platform was where the Santa Fe Railroad showed off its red, gold, and silver streamlined 6,000-horsepower locomotive in 1946, and where Filene's staged a fashion show in 1948 and Andy Warhol hosted an "underground party" in 1965).

In 1938, General John J. Pershing, the commander in chief of the American Expeditionary Forces in World War I, returned from convalescing in Arizona after a heart attack to attend his son's wedding and arrived at the hotel on the special spur. Pershing (for whom the square in front of the terminal is named) had a suite at the Waldorf. So did General Douglas MacArthur, whose special car and the observation car flying his five-star flag were parked on the "presidential siding."

President Franklin D. Roosevelt used the spur, in part to hide his disability from the public (the actual presidential rail car, a specially armored Pullman dubbed the Ferdinand Magellan, is on display at Miami's Gold Coast Railroad Museum). At least one Roosevelt visit to Track 61 is confirmed by Secret Service logs for October 21, 1944, when the president had a full day of campaigning in a 51-mile, four-borough motorcade in an open car despite a chilling rain, including rallies at Ebbets Field and the Garment Center. Officials conservatively estimated he had been seen by 1 million New Yorkers in a grueling tour aimed, in part, at dispelling rumors that he was unable to stand. His day was capped by a speech at the Waldorf to the Foreign Policy Association. At 10:05, according to the logs, he was to take the hotel's Lexington Avenue elevator "and then proceed via New York Central elevators to the New York Central Railway siding, located in the basement of the hotel, where his car will have been spotted." William D. Hassett, Roosevelt's correspondence secretary, later recalled:

> The speech over with, a Secret Service agent rescued Grace Tully and me from the throng of diners and we went down in the hotel elevator with the President and Mrs. Roosevelt to the spur track which was put in at the

construction of the new Waldorf-Astoria for the accommodation of the private cars of "economic royalists"—never, however, used but twice: once by General Pershing when he was ill, and now, of all persons, by the arch-foe of the privileged group for whose delectation this extravagant convenience was devised. Another irony of fate. The wheel has come full circle. We were soon out from under the Waldorf and on our way to Hyde Park.

The wheels are still turning, as Peter Kalikow, who was the chairman of the Metropolitan Transportation Authority, discovered to sobering effect in 2003. He was inspecting progress on the East Side Access project to connect the Long Island Rail Road to Grand Central when, he recalled, "someone said over there is a railroad car used by President Roosevelt and I said, 'let's go look at it.'" Before he and his party could proceed any farther, several well-dressed, polite, but persuasively armed men in suits emerged from the underground shadows and stopped them. "It's his railroad," an aide said, gesturing to Kalikow. To which a Secret Service agent replied, "Not today." Kalikow later learned that President George W. Bush was at the Waldorf for a United Nations General Assembly session and the Secret Service had secured the siding beneath the hotel as a potential escape route, accessible from inside the hotel and from a side-street door, in case the presidential motorcade was obstructed or threatened. That was neither the first nor the last time the siding was reserved for a modern commander in chief. When the president stays at the Waldorf, not only is the underground siding secured, but a special, fully manned diesel-powered train has been kept idling there in case he has to be whisked off Manhattan island.

GIVEN ALL THAT IT'S INVESTED, I GUESS METRO-NORTH NOW OWNS GRAND CENTRAL.

Good guess, but no cigar. As Bill Clinton might say, it depends on what your definition of *owns* is. The terminal was originally owned by the New York & Harlem Railroad, which in 1873 leased it to the New York Central for 400 years. In 1983, Metro-North became a sublessee of Conrail, which had assumed the Central's commuter service. Eleven years later, the lease, by then with American Premier Underwriters, a real estate holding company that bought the building from the bankrupt Penn Central, was amended, extending the term from 2031 to February 28, 2274, the date the original lease between the Central and New York & Harlem Railroad would have expired. (The Harlem, which hadn't run its own trains since 1869, still owned the terminal, while the railroad itself was owned by American Premier Underwriters.) The amendment barred construction above the terminal but preserved the air rights. In 2006, American Premier Underwriters sold the building and its air rights to Midtown Trackage Ventures, a limited liability corporation that includes Argent Ventures and Midtown TDR Ventures. (At that point, outstanding New York & Harlem Railroad 3.5 percent bonds due in 2043 were redeemed.)

The "owner" is Andrew Penson, a real estate investor in his early 50s who lives in Manhattan (no, he's not a commuter) with his family and occasionally plays tennis at the terminal (but never played with toy electric trains). In 2006, his Midtown Trackage Ventures bought the property, which includes 75 miles of track to Poughkeepsie and 82 miles to Wassaic, from American Premier Underwriters; its parent, American Financial Group (which acquired the bankrupt Penn Central's real estate); and the Owasco River Railway for about $80 million. The sale included 1 million square feet of air rights (the lease grants the MTA another 100,000, but they cannot be sold until Midtown TDR Ventures sells or uses their air rights). "We're basically a tenant, but it's effectively ours," said Robert Paley, the MTA's director of transit-oriented development, who has never met Penson.

Metro-North pays $2.24 million annually to its landlord under the extended lease that expires on February 28, 2274 (which, when the lease was made, was as far in the future as the mid-1700s was in the past). The $2.24 million, which is not so much rent as a mortgage payment, will remain the same until 2019, when the MTA has an option to buy the terminal and track right-of-way (and intends to, although the owner has an option to extend the date to 2032). The assessed valuation of the terminal alone is $300 million.

Penson, the son of a co-op converter, is a graduate of New York Law School and former lawyer at Jones Day. He plunged into real estate in earnest in the mid-1990s by buying the debt on distressed properties, especially mortgages that had been bought by Japanese banks. He is the managing member of a Delaware-based limited liability company, Midtown Trackage Ventures, which includes his partners in Argent Ventures and two outside institutional investors (Argent once owned an interest in the Chrysler Building and still has a stake in the Capitol Records Tower in Hollywood; in 1998 Penson made a bid for the Washington Redskins). Although he never played with model trains as a kid, the thought of owning Grand Central immediately appealed to him. "It was the right time when the opportunity presented itself," he recalled, "although I immediately thought of the old joke about buying the Brooklyn Bridge."

I GET THE GCT LOGO FOR THE TERMINAL, BUT WHAT DOES THE CENTENNIAL LOGO MEAN?

You may not know everything about the GCT logo. If you turn it upside down, it looks like an anchor, which evokes Commodore Vanderbilt's shipping empire. The centennial logo, designed by a Westchester commuter, Michael Beirut, and his team at Pentagram (and drawn by Joe Marianek), features the concourse's iconic brass, four-faced clock. The original self-winding mechanism was designed by two Brooklynites, Charles Pratt (who founded Pratt Institute) and Henry Chester Pond. Built by the Seth Thomas Company, the clock is aligned to true North. On the centennial logo, the clock is set at 7:13. In 24-hour time, that is 19:13, which is the year Grand Central opened.

HOW IT WORKS

E D KOCH WAS STILL THE MAYOR IN 1988. Attempts to enforce a curfew in Tompkins Square Park on the Lower East Side resulted in a "police riot" that sparked scores of complaints about brutality. *Phantom of the Opera* opened on Broadway. Cher won an Oscar for *Moonstruck*. Smoking was banned on short-hop domestic flights. The White House acknowledged that Nancy Reagan relied on astrological advice to arrange the president's schedule. The Supreme Court upheld a New York City law barring private clubs from generally excluding women and minorities. And on April 6, at Control Point No. 212 on Track 4, a mile west of the Mount Vernon station, an eight-car New Haven train traveling from Grand Central to Connecticut to pick up morning rush-hour passengers slammed into another deadhead, a five-car train that was stopped while overhead catenary power lines were being repaired. Railroad officials blamed human error for the crash, in which the 42-year-old engineer, who

JOHN TRAVERSO AND JAMES FAHEY (RIGHT)
IN THE COMMAND CENTER, WHICH CONTROLS
795 MILES OF METRO-NORTH TRACK.

had received no previous moving violations, was killed. It was the first and last fatal crash in a nearly three-decade history of Metro-North.

The system's 795 miles of track (covering routes stretching 385 miles) are controlled from a secure command center on the sixth floor of Grand Central (in case of any damage or threat to the terminal, a duplicate operations center can be up and running at an undisclosed location). A nondescript door at the back of the center opens onto a narrow, dank shaft, which provides access to the rose-colored stained-glass clock that fronts on 42nd Street. The juxtaposition of the two rooms makes for a stark contrast. The clock ticks in a grimy, rough-hewn chamber illuminated by bare bulbs and accessible only by several rickety ladders. On the other side of the door, two 9-by-30-foot video screens, each two stories tall, can display the location of every train on every track or zoom in to pinpoint problem areas. A dozen railroad traffic controllers staff two banks of computer terminals, each monitoring a specific geographic area.

Until 1983, when the system was modernized and automated (it was consolidated at Grand Central in 1998 and renovated again in 2010), it took 108 workers per shift to perform the same function. John Kroll is the chief of operations, overseeing a system that dispatches one train every 30 seconds on each of four tracks during the three-hour "rush hours" and as many as 700 on a single day.

As long ago as 1922, transit officials proposed a new suburban station at Park Avenue and 32nd Street to relieve Grand Central and Pennsylvania Station, but the decline of long-distance traffic eased pressure on the 66 Upper Level tracks 15 feet below street level and the 57 tracks on the Lower Level, 26 feet farther down. The operations center also handles Amtrak trains from Spuyten Duyvil to

A DOZEN CONTROLLERS PLUS SUPERVISORS STAFF TWO BANKS OF COMPUTER TERMINALS, EACH MONITORING A DISTINCT GEOGRAPHIC AREA.

Poughkeepsie and from New Rochelle to New Haven, CSX freight trains that use the Metro-North tracks (some actually terminate in Grand Central), and work trains (including the garbage train that leaves from Track 14).

General Railway Signal Company built the system, which tracks trains by a low-voltage current that completes a circuit as the wheels of the train pass over. Platforms at the railroad's 121 stations appear on the screens as yellow rectangles—lots of them on the left side of the double screen, which depicts the Grand Central train yards, where the "ladder" of tracks funnel into the four north of 59th Street (the Harlem and New Haven lines split off in the Bronx at Woodlawn, and the

Hudson at Mott Haven). An occupied track appears in red. A three- or four-digit number identifies the direction of the train and its station of origin. Control points are where trains can switch from one track to another, and a column headed by a red bar lists trains that are running late, so that their routes can be rejiggered around detours or other trains to get them on time again (one reason that Metro-North boasts a 98 percent on-time record, defined by the industry standard as within 5 minutes and 59 seconds of the timetable). Visual and audible indicators in locomotive cabs signal engineers when to slow down or stop. If they fail to respond to a red signal, the air brakes automatically stop the train. The maximum speed limit is 79 mph.

"There is no possible way to override the system, and there has been no crash since this system was put in place," Kroll said, in one of those knock-wood conversations. "There is always the possibility of human error, but it would take a calamity of errors by a lot of humans for it to happen to this system. It's foolproof. A crash is impossible."

ROBERT P. SARACENI, a civil engineer with a master's in business who retired in 2011 as general superintendent of the terminal, oversaw the mail room, maintenance people and other services, including the information booth (which used to be staffed 24 hours a day to answer "all that the stranger may ask about New York"; one man who demanded "What time does the last train leave?" was stunned by the reply: "You should live so long"). The superintendent sees to it that the temperature hovers around a constant 75 degrees (although the mercury can approach 120 degrees in the summer on some train platforms).

R.L. SMITH OF QUEENS RETIRED IN 2011 AS A STATION-MASTER. HE HAD WORKED AT GRAND CENTRAL FOR 62 YEARS.

ISAAC BLAIR, A CARPENTER, BUILT A NEW SOLID OAK DOOR FOR THE TERMINAL THAT HE HUNG ON THE ORIGINAL BRASS HINGES.

ABOUT 600 METRO-NORTH EMPLOYEES WORK AT THE TERMINAL, INCLUDING TICKET SELLERS, USHERS, AND CLEANERS, LIKE CORDALEE ALLEN.

GIUSEPPE D'AMBROSIO, A MASON, DISPLAYS A SLAB OF THE SPECIALLY QUARRIED TENNESSEE MARBLE TO FIX THE CONCOURSE FLOOR AND WALLS.

GRAND CENTRAL'S FULL-TIME CRAFTSMEN INCLUDE FRANK SPITALERI, A MACHINIST. THE LATHE IS A TERMINAL ORIGINAL.

DANNY SANT HELPED
MAINTAIN THE TERMINAL'S
MASSIVE ARRAY OF STEAM
LINES AND OTHER UTILITIES.

THEY DELIVER:
ERIC HARRIS, VALERIE
GRAND, FARIDA SULTANA,
AND WAYNE DABBS
HANDLE THE LOADING DOCK
AT DEPEW PLACE.

NICK GIAMONNA (RIGHT)
IS THE CHIEF ENGINEER OF
THE TERMINAL'S SERVICE
PLANT, ASSISTED HERE
BY MANNY OJEDA.

About 20 members of Grand Central's volunteer fire brigade—otherwise ordinary people who work in the terminal (seven others are paid)—respond to hundreds of emergencies a year by foot or in four suped-up golf carts equipped with flashing red lights. Among the volunteers is Jade Hargraves, who works in the information booth on the Main Concourse. She originally signed up for the brigade's first aid course to respond to emergencies in her own family. "I have one child," she said. "He's the reason I started C.P.R. in the first place. He thinks it's real cool that his mom is a firefighter/E.M.T."

SAL OLIVA (RIGHT) IS CHIEF OF THE FIRE BRIGADE. EMERGENCY MEDICAL VOLUNTEERS AND FULL-TIME EMPLOYEES INCLUDE JONATHAN LEE, SANDRA NIXON, DUNG HOAI DINH, AND ANTHONY LAMANNA.

OFFICERS JAMES NICASTIO AND DOMINGO OJEDA, SERGEANT WILLIAM SCHADE, AND OFFICERS PARTI STARKS, ANTHONY FAZIO, AND DAVID STEIBLE, WITH DOOLEY OF THE K-9 UNIT.

The police force at Grand Central is 80 strong. Under Conrail, it was headed by a woman, Captain Dorothy Schulz, for the first time, in 1979. From the days of "Grand Central Pete" on, the terminal's law enforcement team has been deployed against hucksters, swindlers, pickpockets, and more serious threats and circumstances. George P. Metesky, the 53-year-old former Con Edison worker from Waterbury, Connecticut, who began a terror streak in 1940 as the "Mad Bomber," targeted Grand Central five times until he was captured in 1957.

On September 11, 1976, Croatian nationalists who planted a bomb in a coin locker provided instructions for disarming it, but the operation went awry, wounding 30 people and killing a New York City Police Department bomb squad expert. In 1983, a bank robbery by a hatchet-wielding man was foiled, but a bank guard's gun accidentally discharged, causing a panic. Gunfire erupted again in 1990 when police wounded a burglary suspect as he got off a train. The last reported murder in greater Grand Central was in the subway, in 1988, when a 38-year-old man was charged with shooting his former companion.

Michael R. Coan, chief of the MTA Police (which absorbed the Metro-North force in 1998), says most of the incidents handled by District 5—his Grand Central cops—are "aided cases," when passengers or passersby get sick. His force arrests about 100 people a year, mostly for shoplifting or petty theft.

MICHAEL R. COAN IS CHIEF OF THE MTA POLICE, WHICH INCLUDES DISTRICT 5—GRAND CENTRAL.

IN 2011, railroad employees and passengers turned in 24,691 items to Grand Central's Lost and Found office. By the end of the year, 13,126—more than half—were reunited with their owners. In any given year, the items typically lost by passengers and found by fellow riders or railroad workers include 3,000 coats and jackets (they're

stored on a mechanized rack, the kind found in dry-cleaning stores), 2,500 cell phones, 2,000 sets of keys, 1,500 wallets or purses, 1,100 umbrellas, countless eyeglasses, and enough books to stock a small library.

SOME 25,000 ITEMS ARE TURNED IN ANNUALLY TO GRAND CENTRAL'S LOST AND FOUND OFFICE, WHERE REPOSITORIES INCLUDE A BIN LUGGED BY VALERIE BLANCHARD AND OVERFLOWING WITH EYEGLASSES.

The list of atypical items is considerably shorter but borders on the bizarre: a pet beagle who wandered off and boarded a southbound train at Crestwood, artificial limbs (usually from patients at the veterans' hospital in Montrose), $9,999 in cash stuffed into a pair of socks, a neck brace, a hockey stick, dentures, and a living will, lost by a mother whose daughter was about to have open-heart surgery (a frantic search found the document before the operation began).

A silver vase found on a seat wins the prize for weirdest abandoned item, hands down. Terminal officials say that it turned out to have been left deliberately by a widow whose husband claimed a few too many times that he came home late because he had been stuck on a train. The vase contained his ashes, and his wife figured leaving them on a train indefinitely was just retribution. She finally retrieved the vase a few weeks later.

Mike Nolan supervises a staff that tries mightily to reunite lost items with their owners. Meticulous cataloging guarantees that as many as 80 percent of lost items are eventually returned, particularly laptop computers, which contain tantalizing hints. Identifying the elusive owner by examining his desktop files, said Nolan's predecessor, Frederick Chidester, a former police lieutenant, "I can see that he's a lawyer, he's got a big pharmaceutical company involved in a lawsuit against him, and he's got a case pending in Superior Court in Westchester. We can track it down by going through the court docket to find out what cases are pending against that company, and then we might find a name that matches with the lawyer on the defendant's side."

Precise descriptions of items deposited in collection bins at local stations or in the Lost and Found office on the Lower Level of Grand Central are typically entered into an inventory database, including the date, time, train number, and even seat number where the item was discovered. If an item is not retrieved after 90 days, it is likely to be donated to charity or sold. Expensive items are placed in a safe and are kept longer, sometimes for years.

"There are a lot of people who lose things that shouldn't be lost," Chidester said, including drug couriers, some of whom return for their missing bags only to be arrested. "It's not a case of trickery," Chidester said. "It's a case of stupidity." Pretty much the same can be said for another type of customer, who's hoping to find something that someone else lost. "We can recognize a 'shopper' because they are not sure when they lost something, where they lost it, or what, exactly, it was they lost."

Audrey Johnson, a 55-year-old commuter from Stamford who collects teddy bears (she had 1,033 at last count), has worked for the railroad since 1979, first as a Conrail police officer (she majored in criminology) and since 1989 cheerfully fielding questions in the information booth and the stationmaster's office as a customer service representative. She defines customer service broadly, once even following a passenger's directions to inject him with insulin as he suffered diabetic shock.

The question people ask most, she said, is "How do I get out of the building?" The second, predictably, is "Where is the bathroom?"

ALWAYS SERVING CUSTOMERS:
AUDREY JOHNSON.

SINCE 2001:
A SPACE ODYSSEY

FOR A HALF CENTURY Grand Central's peak traffic day had been reported as July 3, 1947, when 252,288 passengers arrived or departed for the Fourth of July weekend and the start of summer vacations. September 11, 2001, probably broke that record, but everybody was too busy to count.

Harry Kelly, the stationmaster, was on his way to work that morning from Tarrytown. After hearing the news, he ordered a Grand Central–bound through train to pick him up. "When it stopped at 125th Street," he recalled, "I'll never forget the look of people escaping the city and caked with dust and soot." Fearful of further attacks, transit officials evacuated the terminal. Trains headed to Grand Central were halted north of 125th Street, reversed direction, and disgorged their passengers at outlying stations.

THE CLOCK, FLANKED BY DIGITAL VERSIONS
OF THE CENTENNIAL LOGO.

In front of the terminal, scores of travelers formed a semicircle around Millie Martinez, a New York City Transit employee, as she tried to direct straphangers to commuter trains because full service had not resumed on most subway lines. "If you are going to the Bronx, Queens or Brooklyn," she said through a megaphone, "take the Metro-North train to Fordham Road. Then take the 12 bus to Pelham Bay. Then take the 14 bus to Parkchester. From Parkchester, you can take the Q-44 to Flushing, Queens. From Flushing, take the bus to where you're going in Queens. And from Flushing you can also take the bus that you have to take to Brooklyn."

Eventually, a single entrance to Grand Central, on Lexington Avenue, was reopened. Commuters were admitted one by one after being searched. Within a few hours, the terminal was teeming again. The first train left at 12:30 and, in a Dunkirk-like evacuation, one train after another departed for points north as soon as they were loaded. "People asked, 'How far can I get?' and bought tickets to the end of the line," Kelly recalled.

Kelly, whose younger sister worked for a brokerage firm on the 22nd floor of One World Trade Center (she survived), remained at the terminal's operation control center after a brief evacuation. He directed an assistant to the alternate command headquarters in Westchester in case it needed to be activated. "We had to wing it then," he said. "Now we have a Code Black terror system." Today, from the stationmaster's office, surveillance cameras can scan and zoom in on virtually any cranny of the terminal, direct firefighters and personnel to the precise site of an emergency, and disable exhaust fans to stop the spread of smoke or other contaminants.

In New York City, the first decade of the 21st century—the 10th decade in the life of Grand Central Terminal—began with a tragedy of biblical proportions. Grand Central responded by serving as the city's "ark." Since then, the terminal has more than lived up to its name, aging with the grace and elegance of a dowager empress and the resourcefulness and resiliency of a nimble adolescent making the most of his capacity to grow.

THE EAGLE HAS LANDED—TWO OF THEM, IN FACT. THE RELICS OF THE OLD DEPOT NOW PERCH ABOVE THE TERMINAL'S ENTRANCES.

WHILE WILLIAM WILGUS'S ORIGINAL VISION for a glorious Terminal City flanking Park Avenue was never realized, the Grand Central Zone is ripe for redevelopment again. Plans call for more space for rent in the terminal itself and in new skyscrapers along the avenue.

In 1982, the City Planning Commission created a special Midtown zoning district to encourage development west of Sixth Avenue. The incentives worked. Spurred by the Renaissance of Times Square and the vast potential for the Hudson Yards west of Penn Station, Midtown West has boomed. Still on Mayor Michael R. Bloomberg's agenda before he leaves office at the end of 2013 are zoning changes to revitalize Midtown East, where more than 80 percent of the office buildings are more than 50 years old. With tenants demanding floor space with higher ceilings and fewer columns, the existing zoning would allow only smaller buildings than those that now exist between Third and Fifth Avenues and from East 39th Street to East 59th.

So far, only two buildings, the former Philip Morris headquarters on 42nd Street and the 47-story 383 Madison between 46th and 47th Streets (originally the Bear Stearns Building, later owned by JPMorgan Chase), which opened in 2001, have been built with the air rights from Grand Central.

A NEW WAITING ROOM DECORATED WITH MURALS COMMISSIONED BY ARTS FOR TRANSIT AND ORIGINAL BENCHES.

The planning commission was expected to approve rules that would ease the transfer of more than a million square feet of remaining air rights from Grand Central and provide other incentives to develop as much as 4.4 million more square feet in the corridor, including the MTA's own headquarters building at 347 Madison, and 237 Park, which also owns Depew Place, the tiny street astride the terminal between Lexington and Park. Depew Place also borders the Grand Central Post Office, which is the oldest survivor—opened in 1909 and older even than Grand Central itself—of the original Terminal City built atop the railroad's marshaling yards. In 1992, a 38-story skyscraper, 450 Lexington Avenue, was completed above the post office, whose first floor of red granite and upper stories of limestone are separated by a limestone band decorated with—what else?—acorns.

MORE DEVELOPMENT AND MORE PASSENGERS also mean more pedestrians. They finally caught a break after decades of terrifying attempts to cross the Fourth Avenue train tracks during the 19th century and almost as perilously dodging motor vehicles in the 20th on the half-mile between 46th and 56th Streets mysteriously devoid of "Walk/Don't Walk" signs.

The reason the signs were missing was not aesthetic. Rather, they posed an engineering challenge. Park Avenue is really the "roof" of the Grand Central train yards; the side streets are bridges that span the avenue. The deck is only 18 to 24 inches thick—not thick enough to support the foundation ordinarily required for traffic signal poles without piercing the rail-tunnel roof.

For decades, recalcitrant railroad executives accustomed to getting their way rebuffed city officials, who didn't want the blame for disrupting train service. "In dealing with the railroads in those days, it was like dealing with an alien from another planet," said Sam Schwartz, who was the city's traffic commissioner in the 1980s. "The bureaucracies spoke completely different languages. The railroads thought they received some kind of right to do whatever they wanted to do when Adam left Eden, that it was somehow divinely given to them." Finally, in 2007, city transportation commissioner Janette Sadik-Khan and Eliot G. Sandler, then the executive director of the MTA (and Sadik-Khan's predecessor), agreed to install 12 "Walk/Don't Walk" signs and 8 traffic signals at 11 intersections after figuring out a way to anchor them in the roadway without causing leaks in the rail-yard roof.

In the last decade, pedestrians have also benefited from the opening of entrances to the terminal from as far north as 48th Street through a 1,000-foot-long Northwest Passage and a 1,200-foot-long Northeast Passage that run parallel to the Upper Level tracks.

• • •

WHEN METRO-NORTH acquired Conrail's commuter operations in New York and Connecticut in 1983, regular commuters accounted for 65 percent of the railroad's passengers on the three lines east of the Hudson River. By 2005, their share had fallen to 49.4 percent. (Reverse commuters, while still a distinct minority, grew to 6 percent of Metro-North riders from 2 percent during the same period.) Since 1984, the number of New York City–bound commuters has climbed 17 percent, while the number of other riders rose 126 percent. Regular commuters to Manhattan still fill about two-thirds of the seats sold on weekdays, but the railroad has aggressively courted other categories of off-peak riders (a strategy that William Wilgus had suggested as early as 1918: "An increase from 10 percent of the railroad's 24-hour capacity to 20 percent would cut the fixed charges per passenger in half and reduce the total cost by some 25 percent"). Since 1985, Metro-North has increased the number of weekday trains from 471 to more than 600. In mid-2012, MTA Chairman Joseph Lhota announced that the railroad would add 230 more trains, mostly in off-peak hours and on weekends, in what he described as the largest service expansion since Metro-North's inception.

On-time performance has reached a record high (for 2011, 97.4 percent on the Hudson, 97.1 percent on the Harlem, and 93.7 percent on the New Haven for the morning rush; and 98.5 percent, 97.8 percent, and 95.1 percent, respectively, in the afternoon). So has annual passenger traffic. Since 1983, when Metro-North was created, ridership has doubled. It topped 82 million in 2011, when, for the first time, the number of Metro-North commuters surpassed their Long Island Rail Road counterparts (even before the East Side Access project, now scheduled for completion by 2020, delivers another 40,000 a day to Grand Central) and was projected to grow between 2 and 4 percent in 2012.

METRO-NORTH ESTIMATES that 10,000 people come to Grand Central every weekday just to eat (among the 150,000 or so daily walk-ins, plus 60,000 tourists, 130,000 subway riders and 400,000 Metro-North passengers—for a total of nearly 275 million annually). Revenue from more than 70 tenants occupying 134,000 square feet of retail space has soared from $7 million in 1994, before the terminal was renovated, to $27 million gross in 2011 (compared to operating expenses for retail operations of less than $10 million and for the entire terminal, including electricity, sanitation, other employees, and materials of about $50 million). Revenue per square foot, said Paul Kastner, a vice president of Jones Lang LaSalle, which manages commercial rentals for the MTA, surpasses that of many successful shopping malls. Renting out Vanderbilt Hall and the taxi stand generated nearly $3 million in 2010. With Michael Jordan's steak house and the Oyster Bar already calling Grand Central home, leases were signed for another Danny Meyer Shake Shack and an Eli's bread and vegetable venue, and the MTA said it was soliciting bids for two more restaurants, a 12,300-square-foot space that includes the west side of Vanderbilt Hall, and a 4,700-square-foot location above Grand Central Market.

EMPLOYEE LOCKERS AND LOUNGES BEING BUILT ABOVE THE OLD WAITING ROOM IN 2010. THE SPACE HAS HOUSED A GALLERY, STUDIOS, AND TENNIS COURTS.

(In addition to generating revenue, the influx of diners also produced long lines for women's restrooms, a consequence Metro-North resolved by reserving the restrooms in the waiting room near the stationmaster's office for women only.)

Some older tenants complained that Grand Central was being transformed into a trendy, but faceless, suburban mall. In 2009, Alfred Catalanotto's Central Market Grill was replaced by a takeout version of the Napa Valley steakhouse Tri Tip Grill. (Catalanotto, whose family has operated food shops in the terminal for more than three decades, opened a hot-dog stand called Frankies Dogs on the Go on the Lower Level.)

Scott Stein, whose family opened Grand Central Jewelers in the terminal in 1923, said a few years ago that his 500-square-foot Grand Central Optical in the Lexington Passage was more successful than a second 1,100-square-foot store he opened on Madison Avenue when the terminal was being renovated. "My return is 70 percent higher in Grand Central," he said, where people are now more likely to linger and spend money than when the terminal was a decrepit hulk (or when it first opened and the Central boasted that "every facility is progressively arranged so that no step need be retraced, no time lost").

Jeanne Giordano, who was hired by Metro-North in 1988 to help remake the station, couldn't believe the contrast between then and today—when most of the 300 applicants for 74 booths at the December holiday fair in 2011 had to be rejected and long-time tenants have to compete with hungry newcomers when their leases expire. Some became victims of their own success. "Twelve years ago, I didn't want to come there, there was nothing there," said Sushil Malhotra, who was courted to open Café Spice and Feng Shui and who will have to

APPLE INC. TASTEFULLY JOINED THE TERMINAL'S OTHER TENANTS IN 2011, ON THE EAST BALCONY ATOP THE NEW STAIRCASE.

compete in the public renewal process when his leases expire in 2015. "But now, because I'm successful there, anybody can outbid me." One measure of the competition is the lengths to which Apple computer went in its bid to open its largest store in the nation on the terminal's East Balcony in 2011, where the baggage check used to be. Apple paid $5 million just to buy out the prior tenant's lease. Its bid (Apple's rent starts at $1.1 million annually, but the lease does not include a share of sales) was formally submitted in linen-lined boxes, like a "wedding gift," to Metropolitan Transportation Authority officials.

EXTENDING COMMUTER SERVICE farther north on the Hudson line has met with mixed reviews, from residents who fear overdevelopment versus developers and would-be commuters. In 2001, the Harlem line was extended from Dover Plains to Wassaic. Further expansion beyond Dutchess County into Columbia County would require an amendment to the Metropolitan Transportation Authority's charter and would also subject residents of Columbia County to MTA taxes. In 2009, Metro-North opened a new station, Yankees–East 153rd

Street, which provides access to the new Yankee Stadium from the Harlem, Hudson, and New Haven lines. The Harlem and New Haven now have access to the Hudson line station through Mott Haven in the Bronx, the first time that regular service has operated on that section of the junction. On the New Haven, a new station was being built in West Haven, the overhead catenary system was being upgraded, and sections of track were being straightened to accommodate the 150 mph maximum of Amtrak's Acela.

The LIRR's East Side Access project was projected in 1978 to cost $332 million and take less than seven years to complete. By 2004, it was supposed to cost $4.4 billion and be completed in 2012. The cost estimate has skyrocketed to nearly twice that amount and the debut of the new service is now scheduled for 2019 at the earliest. (If that seems like a long wait, consider that a proposed link was first reported by the *Times* in 1885.) A 350,000-square-foot concourse will eliminate 15 tracks in the Madison Avenue train yard, which has a storage capacity of 165 rail cars, and the terminal's lower loop for turnarounds—leaving 14 platform tracks on the Lower Level, plus one reserved for freight, and 29 on the Upper Level, plus one for trash removal. To complete the project, Amtrak has to tunnel under the Harold Interlocking in Sunnyside, Queens (named for Harold Avenue, which became 39th Avenue), where 14 tracks converge and the daily complement of 600 commuter trains and 48 Amtrak trains make it the busiest rail intersection in the country. Many Metro-North officials privately consider the access project a boondoggle, forced on them by Senator Alfonse M. D'Amato as what amounted to a going-away present to his Long Island constituent base.

Even when the East Side Access is complete, don't hold your breath for a direct connection between Grand Central and Penn Station—even though the Long Island Rail Road's new bilevel eight-track tunnel into Grand Central from Queens via the lower level of the 63rd Street subway tunnel actually extends as far south as the East 30s to provide a storage area for idle trains (so burrowing less than a half mile more west might not seem so daunting). Also, the long-delayed transformation of the Farley post office building on Eighth Avenue into a spiffy Moynihan Station, named for the senator who championed public transportation, might help bring to the forefront a connection that has been on the back burner for decades. To access the West Side station and provide intermediate service in the Bronx and Manhattan, southbound New Haven trains could switch to the Hell Gate line in New Rochelle and Hudson trains could switch at Spuyten Duyvil and proceed under Riverside Park on Amtrak's Empire Connection.

THE METROPOLITAN TRANSPORTATION AUTHORITY barred smoking on all commuter trains back in 1988, but bar cars—"lurching lounges," one writer called them—have survived several attempts to phase them out. Grand Central itself got greener during its 10th decade. The terminal claims to have the largest newspaper-recycling program under one roof in the entire country. About four tons of newsprint are collected for recycling daily and taken by rail to the Bronx. Every two or three days, 13 tons of discarded newspapers are removed, for a total of 352 tons in 2010.

Incandescent bulbs were replaced everywhere and even the stars in the zodiac burned more brightly. Decades of 10-watt incandescent bulbs and then fiber-optic tubes that dimmed since they were installed in 1997 were replaced in 2010 by light-emitting diodes, not only producing a more accurate intensity of the stars but also saving manpower and electricity. A chemical heat-absorption system that uses steam to cool the terminal with 3,000 tons of chilled salt water daily is being converted from steam to electric.

While the sky ceiling attracts most of the attention, about a quarter of the 45,000 square feet of pink marble floor was being replaced as the terminal entered its second century. The quarry where the marble originated closed in the 1980s but was reopened to accommodate the project. A two-year, $21 million exterior restoration was begun in 2003 to remove the soot from auto exhaust that had clung to the terminal's 21,000 limestone blocks since they were last bathed three decades before. The famous clock, tongues of solar flares radiating from its center, was regilded with 23.75-karat Italian gold, and the four-ton statue of Commodore Vanderbilt got new steel supports and was gently blasted clean with walnut shells.

THAT GRAND CENTRAL SURVIVED because it was landmarked has been greeted ambivalently whenever custodians of the terminal have sought to renovate. Deciding whether to belatedly install the east staircase that was originally proposed created a hubbub in the 1990s. Preservation watchdogs approved the conversion from incandescent lights to fluorescent (although Metro-North had to search for round bulbs because the common spiral versions didn't conform to the terminal's landmark status), but a proposal to add moving images to the digital advertising signs at the entrance to train platforms was rejected. It was okay to use exterior doorframes with gray-green Benjamin Moore

No. 214040 and to install the eagle on the Park Avenue viaduct, but nine oak columns topped by light fixtures at a restaurant on the southwest balcony were deemed three too many. Watchdogs objected when the Oyster Bar installed a 12-foot-long sign, a re-creation of one that had been destroyed in a fire in 1997. The old sign could have remained indefinitely, but the restaurant required permission from the landmarks commission to re-create it.

IN PART FOR PIONEERING THE CONCEPT OF AIR RIGHTS, in 2012 the American Society of Civil Engineers designated Grand Central as a National Historic Civil Engineering Landmark, an honor it shares with the Erie Canal and the Hoover Dam. Andrew W. Herrmann, president of the society, said that in addition to its architectural bona fides, the terminal "also represents a triumph in civil engineering, a fact that goes unnoticed because much of the engineering work that went into the design and construction of the terminal is largely hidden from view." Moreover, the society said, "The system still works, as the terminal accommodates 750,000 visitors daily and more than 750 incoming and departing trains." In 2011, Metro-North also became the first American railroad to win the international Brunel Award for design excellence from the Watford Group and the Center for Industrial Design in Transportation. "Metro-North carries the most passengers every year on the American continent," the award citation said, "and has undergone both extraordinary changes of company culture as well as the shift to incorporation of design as a strategic business tool." Metro-North president Howard Permut said the award recognized "Metro-North's 30-year-long sea change from an unreliable and decrepit railroad into the premier passenger railroad in North America."

EPILOGUE:
THE SECOND CENTURY

THROUGH THE OLD GRAND CENTRAL, 21 million passengers passed to and fro last year," the *Times* gushed just before the new terminal opened in 1913. "Owing to the perfection of the new arrangement, five times as many, or more than the whole population of the United States, can be handled just as easily in 12 months." Initially, the terminal was criticized as being too big for any traffic demand that could ever be made upon it. Now, a century later, Grand Central is finally nearing the 100 million passengers annually projected when it opened—instead of falling victim to its own success as what the *Times'* Herbert Muschamp called "a flawed symbol of civic pride." During the 1990s renovation, he wrote, the terminal seemed to be "in effect, a double agent," because "while undeniably a great urban landmark, it is also a monument to the centrifugal forces—first trains, then cars, now modems—that since the 1920s have hastened the suburban exodus of the middle class."

THIS CLASSIC VIEW WAS ECLIPSED BY THE
PHILLIP MORRIS BUILDING ACROSS 42ND STREET.

The flow was never one-way, though. Rather, it epitomized E.B. White's "tidal restlessness," which he believed defined metropolitan New York. If Grand Central began almost by accident—triggered by the fatal 1902 collision in the Park Avenue Tunnel—its rebirth has been the result of deliberate and enlightened leadership. It is no accident that the railroads served by the terminal did not suffer another fatal crash in more than 24 years. The graceful reincarnation of an inspired Gilded Age monument to private enterprise as a model of sound public investment has been no accident either.

HAD GRAND CENTRAL BEEN DEMOLISHED, the impact would have been humongous and global. "Hurting Grand Central inflicts millions of private pains as well as one big civic one," the *New Yorker* wrote in 1975, when that threat was very real. "Suburban ladies who put on white gloves and a hat to meet at the Biltmore, commuters, children who go away to school—it is impossible for them not to realize that when they come to (or come back to) New York they are greeted not by any small or neutral experience but by a marvelously accessible grandeur, thoroughly democratic but vast enough to encompass the most outlandish aspiration."

Instead of succumbing to the Penn Central's desperately shortsighted survival strategy, the terminal was reconstituted in the original architects' vision as a grand public space. If, as architect Robert A.M. Stern wrote, Reed & Stem and Warren & Wetmore created "a convincing expression of the belief that the goals of capitalism are not inimical to the enhancement of the public realm," then the Metropolitan Transportation Authority has squared the circle in demonstrating that the public realm and capitalism can not only coexist, but thrive together.

"To educate and raise taste seems like an unimaginably difficult task," Nathan P. Glazer of Harvard observed,

> and yet it has happened. Consider the example of the preservation movement. Would it be possible to tear down Pennsylvania Station in New York today? Hardly. We have financial benefits for remodeling historic landmarks that we did not have in 1963, which has permitted the restoration and reuse of huge 19th- and 20th-century railroad stations; we have more effective means of legal intervention, as was demonstrated in the successful suit to prevent a tower from being placed on top of Grand Central Station; and supporting both we have a public that appreciates architecture more, even if it can be bamboozled and confused by publicity and false authority.

Even Frank Lloyd Wright, not a great fan of New York City, expressed a begrudging admiration for Grand Central. In the mid-1950s, Andy Rooney was a writer for a morning television show hosted by Will Rogers Jr. at the terminal's CBS studios. Rooney was assigned to chaperone Wright, who was staying at the Plaza and was a guest on the show. "Wright grumbled about everything during the drive from the Plaza to the Vanderbilt Avenue side of Grand Central; he detested New York," Rooney recalled.

> There was access by elevator from the west side to our studio but I decided to force a tour on him. I took him down the marble steps off Vanderbilt and walked down kittycorner, past the clock, to the elevators in a little cubicle on the north side near the stairway that goes to the lower level. Those elevators went when they tore down the terminal buildings.

I recall clearly that he stopped and looked back across the grand room before we got on the elevator. The sun's rays were slanting down toward the information booth from the windows above where the Kodak picture is now. "It is a grand building, isn't it?" he said, almost apologetically, and I accepted this as a retraction for all the terrible things he'd been saying about everything else. We went to the third floor on the elevator and started across the catwalk. It's one of the great sights in New York for me. Thousands of purposeful people going their own directions and with doors and stairs and levels enough for all of them in Grand Central.

Midway across, Wright stopped and neither of us said anything. He must have stood there for more than five minutes, and I didn't speak because I knew nothing I had to say could match what he was thinking.

One measure of Grand Central's success is the cachet the name now carries. In 1930, an imposing 53-story skyscraper across the street at 60 East 42nd Street was christened the Lincoln Building (after the Lincoln Storage Company and the Lincoln National Bank, which had occupied the site). In 2009, the owners, W&H Properties, moved the lobby's bronze plaques, on which the Gettysburg Address and the Second Inaugural Address were immortalized, and evicted Daniel Chester French's sculpture of the "seated Lincoln," the model for the Lincoln Memorial in Washington, from the lobby. The building was renamed One Grand Central Place, confirming, said Fred C. Posniak, senior vice president of W&H, "the building's reputation as the premier prewar trophy property within the Grand Central District, as well as its unsurpassed location directly across from Grand Central

Terminal." Just a decade earlier, any such association with Grand Central would have been considered toxic. Not anymore.

IN 1932, THOMAS WOLFE and his accommodating editor, Maxwell Perkins, boarded a train at Grand Central for Perkins's weekend home in New Canaan, Connecticut. Trains figured prominently in Wolfe's fiction, and in his life too. He and Perkins had been drinking a good deal that Thursday night (Wolfe "enjoys eating and drinking, and all of what is known of the good things in life," Perkins later wrote).

For whatever reason, at the last minute Wolfe changed his weekend plans and precipitately jumped from the moving train. The six-foot-six author splayed onto the platform, breaking his arm and severing a vein. Eight years later, Wolfe's *You Can't Go Home Again* was published posthumously. His novel was about George Webber, a fledgling author, who tries to do just that—to go home again—this time from Penn Station, which, Wolfe wrote, was, like Grand Central, "murmurous with the immense and distant sound of time."

> Great, slant beams of moted light fell ponderously athwart the station's floor, and the calm voice of time hovered along the walls and ceiling of that mighty room, distilled out of the voices and movements of the people who swarmed beneath. It had the murmur of a distant sea, the languorous lapse and flow of waters on a beach. It was elemental, detached, indifferent to the lives of men. They contributed to it as drops of rain contribute to a river that draws its flood and movement majestically from the great depths, out of purple hills at evening.

Few buildings are vast enough to hold the sound of time, and now it seemed to George that there was a superb fitness in the fact that the one which held it better than all others should be a railroad station. For here, as nowhere else on earth, men were brought together for a moment at the beginning or end of their innumerable journeys, here one saw their greetings and farewells, here, in a single instant, one got the entire picture of the human destiny. Men came and went, they passed and vanished, and all were moving through the moments of their lives to death, and all made small tickings in the sounds of time—but the voice of time remained aloof and unperturbed, a drowsy and eternal murmur below the immense and distant roof.

Wolfe's evocation of Penn Station reverberates in the imaginary "silent bubble of space" that propelled Tony Hiss through Grand Central and in David Marshall's "accidental music" of the Main Concourse. Referring to Penn Station *and* Grand Central, Lewis Mumford wrote that "the major quality of each station, one that too few buildings in the city today possess, is space—space generously even nobly handled."

As for the Penn Station that Mumford rhapsodized, though, you can't go *there* again. And, for all its glory, for all the nostalgia that Penn Station still generates and richly deserves, of the two mega-stations, arguably Grand Central transformed the nation's norms and Manhattan's cultural geography to a much greater extent. By serving as the underpinning for Park Avenue, the railroad provided a haven for New York's super-rich, who, Mike Wallace, the coauthor of *Gotham*, observes, had been on the run for a century from Washington Square, Union Square, and even from their doubtful redoubts on Fifth Avenue.

"The vast Park Avenue structures, dense with others of their own kind, provided a stability the rich had never known," Wallace says. "And the establishment of the Upper East Side as a wealthy enclave helped to draw hotels, department stores and luxury shops uptown." If Penn Station was a catchment for commuters from the east, Grand Central channeled commuting managers and professionals from the northern suburbs to Midtown (an incentive for corporate headquarters to roost there). The flow of commercial travelers and tourists transformed "a second-string business district to full-fledged rival of Wall Street" and generated demand for hotels and office buildings. "Finally," Wallace argues, "the terminal itself was a powerful Midtown magnet, with its great soaring concourse, its barrel-vaulted Roman bath, its staircase as grand as the Paris Opera's, its ceiling that was vaster than St. Peter's nave, and in the opinion of some equally sublime. The romance of its 20th Century Limited service, the beauty and boldness of the enterprise itself—all were crucial factors in shifting the city's cultural and commercial center of gravity to its doorstep."

Grand Central, Paul Goldberger wrote, was never "as overpowering or as grandiose as the late Pennsylvania Station," and its very integrality—the way "it wove its way into the fabric of New York City so subtly and so tightly that it couldn't be ripped out"— may have been the overriding virtue that demanded it survive into a second century. Today, "the sound of time" still reverberates every day at Grand Central, which, more than any other place, embodies the voice of the city and the rhythms of urban America.

ACKNOWLEDGMENTS

THANKS, first, to my gracious *New York Times* colleagues, especially Jeff Roth and David Dunlap, and to my other fellow correspondents on whose reporting I relied. Thanks, too, to my *Times* editors, Carolyn Ryan, Wendell Jamieson, and Diego Ribadeneira, for their indulgence and encouragement, and to the *Times'* Phyllis Collazo.

Frank English, the former Metropolitan Transportation Authority photographer, contributed his passion for Grand Central and was a rich source of visual and figurative images. Beginning with Joseph Lhota, the chairman, everyone at the MTA and Metro-North was enormously gracious and magnanimous, especially Dan Brucker, Paul Flueranges, Robert Paley, Jim Fahey, William Goldstein, Susan Fine, Michael Coan, Mike Vitiello, Harry Kelly, John Kroll, Audrey Johnson, Robert Leiblong, Adam Lisberg, and Robert Saraceni and many of Metro-North's other 5,800 employees. Marjorie Anders patiently and diligently fielded hundreds of questions and generously vetted details.

Among my favorite sources are archivists and librarians. They actually delight in providing information.

Thanks are due to Tom Lannon of the New York Public Library; Louise Mirrer and her knowledgeable staff at the New-York Historical Society; Susan Henshaw Jones and Sarah Henry at the Museum of the City of New York; Vin Cippola of the Municipal Art Society; Peg Breen of the New York Landmarks Conservancy; Gabrielle Shubert and her team at the Transit Museum; Amanda Burden and her staff, especially Rachaele Raynoff, at the Department of City Planning; and Bob Tierney and his crew at the Landmarks Preservation Commission. Thanks, too, to John Belle, Frank Prial Jr., and Maxinne Leighton of Beyer Blinder Belle.

Grand Central Publishing embraced this book from the beginning. I am enormously grateful to my editor, Rick Wolff, and his team, including Meredith Haggerty, Jimmy Franco, Bob Castillo, Dorothea Halliday, Beth Tondreau, Peggy Holm, and Thomas Whatley.

My agent, Andrew Blauner, deserves a medal for perseverance. This book was his idea and he conscientiously saw it through.

Special thanks to Shelby White, Arthur Browne, Meredith Kane, Paul Neuthaler, Dixie and Barry Josephson, Karen Salerno, and Tom McDonald—you each know how much you helped.

AND, OF COURSE, AN ETERNAL THANK YOU TO MARIE, MIKE, SOPHIE, WILLIAM, AND JESSICA.

ART CREDITS

A NOTE ON SOURCES

QUOTATIONS from contemporary sources come mostly from interviews or correspondence by the author with, among others, Peter Stangl, Richard Ravitch, Peter Kalikow, Joseph Lhota, Kent Barwick, Laurie Beckelman, John Belle, Ben Cheever, Nina Gershon, Judah Gribetz, Ashton Hawkins, Tony Hiss, Karl Katz, Harry Kelly, Caroline Kennedy, Maxinne Leighton, Fred Papert, Andrew Penson, Frank Prial Jr., James Sanders, John Zuccotti, and Metro-North officials and employees.

Other citations include contemporary news accounts, among them, articles by my *Times* colleagues; fiction and nonfiction books, magazines, screenplays, and other publications cited in the text, the bibliography, or both; primary sources, including letters and other documents from the New York Central Railroad and William J. Wilgus and others in the collections of the New York Public Library, the New-York Historical Society, the New York Railroad Enthusiasts and its Williamson Library, the New York Transit Museum, and the New York Central System Historical Society website, http://nycshs.org/; and documents from the New York City Landmarks Preservation Commission, the Metropolitan Transportation Authority, and other city, state, and federal agencies.

BIBLIOGRAPHY

Anderson, Jervis. *A. Philip Randolph: A Biographical Portrait.* Berkeley: University of California Press, 1972.

Belle, John, and Maxinne R. Leighton. *Grand Central: Gateway to a Million Lives.* New York: W.W. Norton, 2000.

Brody, Jerome. *The Grand Central Oyster Bar & Restaurant Seafood Cookbook.* New York: Crown Publishers, 1977.

Burns, Ric, and James Sanders, with Lisa Ades. *New York: An Illustrated History.* New York: Alfred A. Knopf, 1999.

Daughen, Joseph R., and Peter Binzen. *The Wreck of the Penn Central.* Washington, DC: Beard Books, 1999.

Diehl, Lorraine B. *The Late Great Pennsylvania Station.* New York: Four Walls Eight Windows, 1985.

Dobbs, Michael. *Saboteurs: The Nazi Raid on America.* New York: Vintage Books, 2005.

Dolkart, Andrew, and Matthew A. Postal. *Guide to New York City Landmarks.* Hoboken, NJ: John Wiley & Sons, 2009.

Fitch, James M., and Diana S. Waite. *Grand Central Terminal.* New York State Parks and Recreation, Division of Historic Preservation, 1974.

Gratz, Roberta Brandes. *The Battle for Gotham: New York in the Shadow of Robert Moses and Jane Jacobs.* New York: Nation Books, 2010.

Grogan, Louis V. *The Coming of the New York and Harlem Railroad.* Pawling, NY: Louis V. Grogan, 1989.

Grow, Lawrence. *Waiting for the 5:05: Terminal, Station and Depot in America.* New York: Main Street/Universe Books, 1977.

Hanley, Sally. *A. Philip Randolph: Labor Leader.* New York: Chelsea House Publishers, 1989.

BIBLIOGRAPHY

Harlow, Alvin. *The Road of the Century: The Story of the New York Central*. New York: Creative Age Press, 1947.

Helprin, Mark. *Winter's Tale*. San Diego: Harcourt Brace Jovanovich, 1983.

Hiss, Tony. *The Experience of Place: A New Way of Looking at and Dealing with Our Radically Changing Cities and Countryside*. New York: Alfred A. Knopf, 1990.

Hiss, Tony. *In Motion: The Experience of Travel*. New York: Alfred A. Knopf, 2010.

Horn, Cathy. "1902 Park Avenue Tunnel Collision: A New Rochelle Tragedy." http://www.rootsweb.ancestry.com/~nywestch/NewRoc1902/index.htm.

Hungerford, Edward. *Men and Iron: The History of the New York Central*. New York: Thomas Y. Crowell, 1938.

Ingber, Sandy. *The Grand Central Oyster Bar & Restaurant Complete Seafood Cookbook*. New York: Stewart, Tabori & Chang, 1997.

Jackson, Kenneth T. *Crabgrass Frontier: The Suburbanization of the United States*. New York: Oxford University Press, 1985.

Johnston, Bob, and Joe Welsh, with Mike Schafer. *The Art of the Streamliner*. New York: Metro Books, 2001.

Marqusee, Mike, and Bill Harris, editors. *New York: An Anthology*. Boston: Little, Brown, 1985.

Marshall, David. *Grand Central*. New York: Whittlesey House, 1946.

Meeks, Carroll L.V. *The Railroad Station: An Architectural History*. New Haven, CT: Yale University Press, 1956.

National Geographic. *Inside Grand Central*. DVD. National Geographic Channel, 2005.

New York Central. *The Greatest Highway in the World: Historical, Industrial and Descriptive Information of the Towns, Cities and Country Passed Through Between New York and Chicago Via the New York Central Lines*. New York: N.p., 1921.

Okrent, Daniel. *Great Fortune: The Epic of Rockefeller Center*. New York: Penguin, 2003.

"100 Years of Dust and Glory." *Popular Mechanics*, September 2001, 70–75.

Potter, Janet Greenstein. *Great American Railroad Stations*. New York: Preservation Press, 1996.

Powell, Kenneth. *Grand Central Terminal: Warren and Wetmore*. London: Phaidon Press, 1996.

Reed, Henry Hope. *The Golden City: A Pictorial Argument in the Controversy Over Classical vs. Modern Fashion in American Architecture and Other Arts*. New York: W.W. Norton, 1971.

Sanders, James. *Celluloid Skyline: New York and the Movies*. New York: Alfred A. Knopf, 2001.

Schlichting, Kurt C. *Grand Central's Engineer: William J. Wilgus and the Planning of Modern Manhattan*. Baltimore: Johns Hopkins University Press, 2012.

Schlichting, Kurt C. *Grand Central Terminal: Railroads, Engineering and Architecture in New York City*. Baltimore: Johns Hopkins University Press, 2001.

Stanley, Ed. *Grand Central Terminal: Gateway to New York City*. New York: Mondo Publishing, 2003.

Stephens, Carlene E. *On Time: How America Has Learned to Live by the Clock*. Boston: Bullfinch Press, 2002.

Stern, Robert A.M., Gregory Gilmartin, and John Massengale. *New York 1900: Metropolitan Architecture and Urbanism 1890–1915*. New York: Rizzoli, 1983.

Stern, Robert A.M., Gregory Gilmartin, and Thomas Mellins. *New York 1930: Metropolitan Architecture and Urbanism Between the Two World Wars*. New York: Rizzoli, 1987.

Stern, Robert A.M., David Fishman, and Thomas Mellins. *New York 1960: Architecture and Urbanism Between the Second World War and the Bicentennial*. New York: Monacelli Press, 1995.

Stern, Robert A.M., David Fishman, and Jacob Tilove. *New York 2000: Architecture and Urbanism Between the Bicentennial and the Millennium*. New York: Monacelli Press, 2006.

Stiles, T.J. *The First Tycoon: The Epic Life of Cornelius Vanderbilt*. New York: Vintage Books, 2010.

BIBLIOGRAPHY

Toth, Jennifer. *The Mole People: Life in the Tunnels Beneath New York City.* Chicago: Chicago Review Press, 1993.

Vestner, Eliot N., Jr. *Meet Me Under the Clock at Grand Central: A Family History and Memoir.* N.p.: Eliot N. Vestner Jr., 2010.

Wallace, Mike, and Edwin G. Burrows. *Gotham: A History of New York City to 1898.* New York: Oxford University Press, 1999.

Warren, John. *Before I Even Got to Grand Central Station I Sat Down and Wept.* London: Scorpion Publications, 1979.

WGBH Educational Foundation. "Grand Central," written and produced by Michael Epstein, *American Experience*, DVD. Public Broadcasting Service, 2008.

Whyte, William H. *City: Rediscovering the Center.* New York: Doubleday, 1988.

Wood, Anthony C. *Preserving New York: Winning the Right to Protect a City's Landmarks.* New York: Routledge, 2008.

Zeisloft, E. Idell. *The New Metropolis: 1899.* SharingHistory.com.

Zimmermann, Karl R. *20th Century Limited.* St. Paul: MBI Publishing, 2002.

ONE OF THE MOST POPULAR ATTRACTIONS THAT ALL VISITORS SHOULD CONSIDER IS THE WORLD-FAMOUS WALKING/AUDIO TOUR OF GRAND CENTRAL TERMINAL. FOR MORE INFORMATION, YOU CAN VISIT WWW.GRANDCENTRALTERMINAL.COM/INFO/AUDIOTOUR.CFM.

INDEX

Page numbers in italics indicate illustrations.

INDEX

ABOUT THE AUTHOR

SAM ROBERTS has been the *New York Times'* urban affairs correspondent since 2005. Before that, he was deputy editor of the *Times'* Week in Review section, urban affairs columnist, and deputy metropolitan editor. Prior to joining the *Times*, he worked at the *New York Daily News* as a reporter, city editor, and political editor.

He is the coauthor of a biography of Nelson Rockefeller, published in 1977; and the author of *Who We Are: A Portrait of America Based on the Latest U.S. Census,* published in 1994; *Who We Are Now: The Changing Face of America in the 21st Century*, published in 2004; *The Brother: The Untold Story of Atomic Spy David Greenglass and How He Sent His Sister, Ethel Rosenberg, to the Electric Chair*, published in 2001, which was a finalist for the National Book Critics Circle Award; and *A Kind of Genius: Herb Sturz and Society's Toughest Problems,* published in 2009. An anthology of his podcasts, titled *Only in New York: An Exploration of the World's Most Fascinating, Frustrating and Irrepressible City*, was also published in 2009. He is the editor of *America's Mayor: John V. Lindsay and the Reinvention of New York*, published in 2010.

He is the host of *The New York Times Close Up*, an hour-long weekly news and interview program on New York 1 (the all-news cable channel), produced in association with the *New York Times* and which he inaugurated in 1992.

A graduate of Cornell University in 1968, he lives in New York.

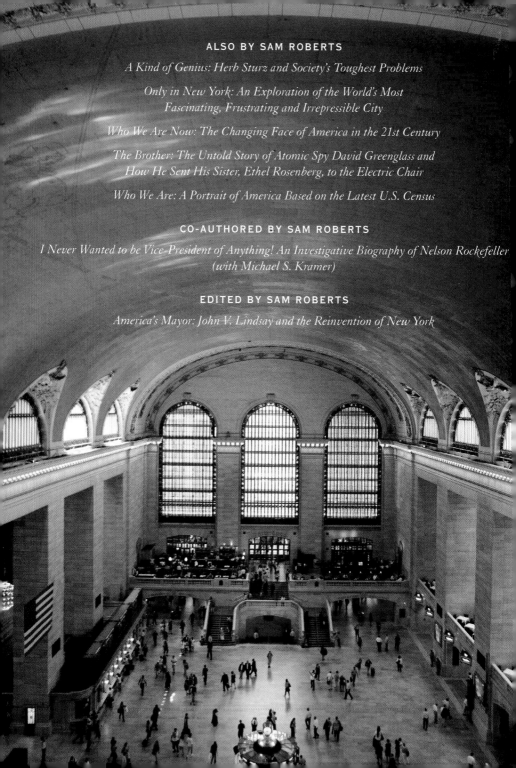